USDA United States
Department
of Agriculture

Forest Service

Rocky Mountain
Research Station

Resource Bulletin
RMRS-RB-10

December 2010

Utah's Forest Resources, 2000–2005

Larry T. DeBlander, John D. Shaw, Chris Witt,
Jim Menlove, Michael T. Thompson, Todd A. Morgan,
R. Justin DeRose, and Michael C. Amacher

Abstract

FIA is responsible for periodic assessments of the status and trends of the renewable resources of America's forests. Fundamental to the accomplishment of these assessments are the State-by-State resource inventories, which are now conducted on an annual basis. This report summarizes the results, interpretations, and future significance of Utah's annual inventory. The organization and layout of this report begins with a short introduction of FIA's annual inventory system and then a detailed description of its inventory methods. After an overview of the report tables, the bulk of the report is contained in the "Forest Resources" and "Current Issues" and "FIA Indicators" sections, and finishes with a discussion of Utah's Timber Products. The "Forest Resources" section is outlined similar to past periodic reports for ease of comparisons. The "Current Issues" and "FIA Indicators" sections cover topics considered pertinent to Utah's forests relative to the information FIA collects, and points to other related or more in-depth studies and research.

The Authors

Larry T. DeBlander is a Forester and a member of the Analysis Team with the Interior West Inventory and Analysis Program at the Rocky Mountain Research Station in Ogden, UT. He holds a B.S. degree in Forest Science from Pennsylvania State University.

John D. Shaw is a Forester and Analysis Team Leader with the Interior West Inventory and Analysis Program at the Rocky Mountain Research Station in Ogden, UT. He holds B.S. and M.S. degrees in Natural Resources Management from the University of Alaska, Fairbanks and a Ph.D. in Forest Ecology from Utah State University.

Chris Witt is an Ecologist and a member of the Analysis Team with the Interior West Inventory and Analysis Program at the Rocky Mountain Research Station in Ogden, UT.
He holds B.S. and M.S. degrees in Ecology from Idaho State University.

Jim Menlove is an Ecologist and a member of the Analysis Team with the Interior West Inventory and Analysis Program at the Rocky Mountain Research Station in Ogden, UT. He holds a B.S. degree in Biology from the University of Utah and an M.S. degree in Zoology and Physiology from the University of Wyoming, both with an emphasis in ecology.

Michael T. Thompson is a Forester and a member of the Analysis Team with the Interior West Inventory and Analysis Program at the Rocky Mountain Research Station in Ogden, UT. He holds a B.S. degree in Forestry from North Carolina State University.

Todd A. Morgan is the director of the Forest Industry Research Program at The University of Montana's Bureau of Business and Economic Research in Missoula, MT. He received a B.A. degree in Philosophy and a B.S. degree in Forest Science from Pennsylvania State University and an M.S. degree in Forestry from The University of Montana.

R. Justin DeRose is a Ph.D. candidate in the Department of Wildland Resources and Ecology Center at Utah State University, Logan, UT. He has B.S. and M.S. degrees in Forestry (from Utah State University and University of Maine, respectively) and is currently working toward his Ph.D. in Forest Ecology. His research broadly covers production ecology and silviculture of spruce-fir forests in the eastern United States and disturbance ecology of spruce-fir forests of the Rocky Mountains.

Michael C. Amacher is a Research Soil Scientist in the Forest and Woodland Ecosystems Research Program at the Rocky Mountain Research Station in Logan, UT. He also serves as the western soils Indicator Advisor in the Indicators of Forest Health program. He has B.S. and M.S. degrees in chemistry and a Ph.D. in soil chemistry, all from Pennsylvania State University.

Contact author: Larry T. DeBlander, ldeblander@fs.fed.us, (801) 625-5204

Acknowledgments

The Rocky Mountain Research Station gratefully acknowledges the cooperation and assistance of the Intermountain Region, Forest Service, U.S. Department of Agriculture; the Utah State Forester and other Utah State Land Department personnel; the Bureaus of Land Management and Indian Affairs; the Utah State University Forestry Extension; and the National Park Service, U.S. Department of the Interior. The authors extend a special note of thanks to private landowners who provided information and access to field sample plots, and to the field staff who collected the inventory data.

Contents

Preface

The Forest Inventory and Analysis (FIA) program is managed by the Research and Development organization within the USDA Forest Service in cooperation with State and Private Forestry and National Forest Systems. Since the McSweeny-McNary act of 1928, FIA has been operating for some 80 years under various names (Forest Survey, Forest Inventory and Analysis) as the Nation's continuous forest census. FIA is responsible for periodic assessments of the status and trends of the renewable resources of America's forests. Fundamental to the accomplishment of these assessments are the State-by-State resource inventories, which are now conducted on an annual basis. This report summarizes the results, interpretations, and future significance of Utah's annual inventory.

Early FIA inventories stressed information on the country's commercial timber situation; forest land was covered in a broader sense mainly for its water, recreation, and forage values, and problems related to multiple-use management. Today the Forest Service has significantly enhanced the FIA program by increasing our capacity to analyze and publish data, and by expanding the scope of our data collection to include soil, understory vegetation, tree crowns and damage conditions, down woody debris, and lichen community composition.

The organization and layout of this report begins with a short introduction of FIA's annual inventory system and then a detailed description of its inventory methods. After an overview of the report tables, the bulk of the report is contained in the "Forest Resources," "Current Issues," and "FIA Indicators" sections, and finishes with a discussion of Utah's timber products. The "Forest Resources" section is outlined similar to past periodic reports for ease of comparisons. The "Current Issues" and "FIA Indicators" sections cover topics considered pertinent to Utah's forests relative to the information FIA collects, and points to other related or more in-depth studies and research.

The "Forest Resources," "Current Issues," and "FIA Indicators" topics are organized into three sub-sections: (1) a "Background" section that discusses, in general, the importance of the topic; (2) an "Inventory results" section that presents data and results—often with figures and tables; and (3) a "Discussion" section that conveys the meaning or significance of the results. In addition, throughout the report reference is made to Appendix A, which covers much of Interior West FIA's past inventory history as it is relevant to today's annual inventories.

I. Introduction

This report contains highlights of the status of Utah's forest resources, with discussions of pertinent issues based on the first 6 years of inventory under the new Forest Inventory and Analysis (FIA) annual system (Gillespie 1999). In 1998, the Agricultural Research Extension and Education Reform Act (also known as the Farm Bill) mandated that inventories would be conducted throughout United States forests on an annual basis. This annual system integrates FIA and Forest Health Monitoring (FHM) sampling designs resulting in the mapped-plot design, which includes a nationally consistent plot configuration with four fixed-radius subplots; a systematic national sampling design consisting of one plot in each approximately 6,000-acre hexagon; annual measurement of a proportion of permanent plots; data or data summaries within 6 months after yearly sampling is completed; and a State summary report after 5 years.

Interior West Forest Inventory and Analysis (IWFIA) implemented the new annual inventory strategy starting in Utah in 2000. The strategy for the western United States involves measurement of 10 systematic samples (or subpanels) each of which represents approximately 10 percent of all plots in the State. The 6 inventory years covered in this report are 2000 through 2005. Although the Farm Bill requires reports after 5 years, the Utah report was delayed to give the IWFIA program time to work through national inconsistencies with past and current forest land definitions.

In this report, some of the factors affecting definitional differences, such as stocking or crown cover, have been reconciled with the past through a process called "plot-filtering," which re-classified forest land with 5 to 9 percent cover as a potentially new land class called "other wooded land." This process is discussed in more detail in Appendix A, along with changes in other definitional factors such as tree-form, species, and forest type algorithms, which could not be reconciled due to various reasons. In summary, Appendix A discusses the potential effects each factor has on past versus current forest land definitions. Field data for the previous periodic report for Utah (O'Brien 1999) was inventoried in 1993. To the extent possible, comparisons will be made to the 1999 report both in terms of the changes in definitions and protocols listed above, and real change in forest conditions.

Although Utah is the second driest State in the United States, 36 percent (19.5 million acres) of the State's total area is considered forest or other wooded land. A large portion of Utah's timber types occurs in the Uinta and Wasatch Mountain ranges of the Southern Rockies, the Utah Mountains of the Great Basin, and the higher elevations of the Colorado Plateau. The Uinta Mountains, in northeastern Utah, are a sub-range of the Rocky Mountains and are unusual for being the highest range in the contiguous United States running east to west. The Wasatch Range, which stretches over 200 miles from the Utah-Idaho border south through central Utah, is generally considered the western edge of the greater Rocky Mountains, and the eastern edge of the Great Basin region. The Colorado Plateau is roughly centered on the four corners region of the southwestern United States and occupies southeastern Utah. Utah's woodland types are scattered throughout these mountain ranges at lower elevations, and throughout much of southern Utah on the Colorado Plateau. The distribution and composition of forests are determined by many factors such as elevation, aspect, soils, climate, and past fire history, and their influences are discussed in this report.

Annual inventory summaries are updated each spring to include the most recent subpanels of data available to the public. Data may be downloaded in table form or queried using a variety of online tools (http://fia.fs.fed.us/tools-data/default.asp). After 2010, a full assessment of ten subpanels of data will be included in the upcoming 10-year (full cycle) report. In 2010, the re-measurement phase of the inventory will begin by re-measuring the first subpanel of plot data collected in 2000.

USDA Forest Service Resour. Bull. RMRS-RB-10. 2010

1

2

USDA Forest Service Resour. Bull. RMRS-RB-10. 2010

II. Inventory Methods

Plot Configuration

The national FIA plot design consists of four 24-foot radius subplots configured as a central subplot and three peripheral subplots. Centers of the peripheral subplots are located at distances of 120 feet and at azimuths of 360 degrees, 120 degrees, and 240 degrees from the center of the central subplot (USDA Forest Service 2000-2005a). Each standing tree with a diameter at breast height (d.b.h.) for timber trees, or a diameter at root collar (d.r.c.) for woodland trees, 5-inches or larger is measured on these subplots. Each subplot contains a 6.8-foot radius microplot with its center located 12 feet east of the subplot center on which each tree with a d.b.h./d.r.c. from 1.0-inch to 4.9-inches is measured.

In addition to the trees measured on FIA plots, data are also gathered about the stand or area in which the trees are located. Area classifications are useful for partitioning the forest into meaningful categories for analysis. Some of these area attributes are measured (e.g., percent slope), some are assigned by definition (e.g., ownership group), and some are computed from tree data (e.g., percent stocking).

To enable division of the forest into various domains of interest for analysis, it is important that the tree data recorded on these plots are properly associated with the area classifications. To accomplish this, plots are mapped by condition class. Field crews assign a number to the first condition class encountered on a plot. This condition is then defined by a series of discrete variables attached to it (i.e., land use, stand size, regeneration status, tree density, stand origin, ownership group, and disturbance history). Additional conditions are identified if there is a distinct change in any of the condition-class variables on the plot.

Sample Design

Based on historic national standards, a sampling intensity of approximately one plot per 6,000 acres is necessary to satisfy national FIA precision guidelines for area and volume. Therefore, FIA divided the area of the United States into non-overlapping, 5,937-acre hexagons and established a plot in each hexagon using procedures designed to preserve existing plot locations from previous inventories. This base sample, designated as the Federal base sample, was systematically divided into a number of non-overlapping panels, each of which provides systematic coverage of the State. Each year the plots in a single subpanel are measured, and subpanels are selected on either a 5-year (eastern regions) or 10-year (western regions) rotating basis (Gillespie 1999). For estimation purposes, the measurement of each subpanel of plots can be considered an independent, equal probability sample of all lands in a State, or all plots can be combined to represent the State.

Three-Phase Inventory

FIA conducts inventories in three phases. Phase 1 uses remotely sensed data to obtain initial plot land cover observations (prefield) and to stratify land area in the population of interest to increase the precision of estimates. In Phase 2, field crews visit the physical locations of permanent field plots to measure traditional inventory variables such as tree species, diameter, and height. In Phase 3, field crews visit a subset of Phase 2 plots to obtain measurements for an additional suite of variables associated with forest and ecosystem health. The three phases of the enhanced FIA program are discussed in the following sections.

Phase 1—Remotely sensed data in the form of aerial photographs, digital orthoquads, and satellite imagery are used for initial plot establishment. Each plot is assigned a digitized geographic location, and a human interpreter determines whether a plot has the potential to sample forest or other wooded land. Plot locations that are accessible to field crews and have the potential to sample forest or other wooded land are selected for further measurement via field crew visits in Phase 2.

The only remote sensing medium used for stratification in Utah was 2004 MODIS satellite imagery. The spatial resolution of the MODIS imagery used was 250 meters. Three strata were recognized: forest/other wooded land, nonforest land, and census water. Depending on geography and sampling intensity, geographic divisions are identified within a State for area computation and are referred to as estimation units. In Utah, individual counties served as the estimation units. The area of each estimation unit is divided into strata of known size using the satellite imagery and computer-aided classification. The classified imagery divides the total area of the estimation unit into pixels of equal size and assigns each pixel to one of H strata. Each stratum, h, then contains n_h ground plots where the Phase 2 attributes of interest are observed.

To illustrate, the area estimator for forest land for an estimation unit in Utah is defined as:

$$\hat{A}_g = A_{Tg} \sum_{h=1}^{H} \frac{n'_{hg}}{n'_g} \frac{\sum_{i=1}^{n_{hg}} y_{ihg}}{n_{hg}}$$

where:

$\hat{A}_g$ = total forest area (acres) for estimation unit g

A_{Tg} = total land area (acres) in estimation unit g

H = number of strata (3)

n'_{hg} = number of Phase 1 points in stratum h in estimation unit g

n'_g = total number of Phase 1 points in estimation unit g

y_{ihg} = forest land condition proportion on Phase 2 plot i in stratum h in estimation unit g

n_{hg} = number of Phase 2 plots in stratum h in estimation unit g

Phase 2—In Phase 2, field crews record a variety of data for plot locations sent to the field by Phase 1 (USDA Forest Service 2000-2005a). Before visiting privately-owned plot locations, field crews consult county land records to determine the ownership of plots and then seek permission from private landowners to measure plots on their lands. The field crews determine the location of the geographic center of the center subplot using geographic positioning system (GPS) receivers. They record condition-level variables that include land use, forest type, stand origin, stand-size class, site productivity class, forest disturbance history, slope, aspect, and physiographic class. For each tree, field crews record a variety of variables including species, live/dead status, diameter, height, crown ratio, crown class, damage, and decay status. Office staff personnel apply statistical models using field crew measurements to calculate values for additional variables such as individual tree volume and per unit area estimates of number of trees, volume, biomass, growth, and mortality.

Phase 3—The third phase of the enhanced FIA program focuses on forest health. Phase 3 is administered cooperatively by the FIA program, other Forest Service programs, other federal agencies, state natural resource agencies, universities, and the Forest Health Monitoring (FHM) program. Phase 3 is the ground survey portion of the Forest Health Monitoring (FHM) program and was integrated into the FIA program in 1999. The Phase 3 sample consists of a $^1/_{16}$ subset of the Phase 2 plots, which equates to one Phase 3 plot for approximately every 95,000 acres. Phase 3 measurements are obtained by field crews during the growing season and include an extended suite of ecological data (USDA Forest Service 2000-2005b). Because each Phase 3 plot is also a Phase 2 plot, the entire suite of Phase 2 measurements is collected on each Phase 3 plot at the same time as the Phase 3 measurements.

Sources of Error

Sampling Error—The process of sampling (selecting a random subset of a population and calculating estimates from this subset) causes estimates to contain errors they would not have if every member of the population had been observed and included in the estimate. The 2000-2005 FIA inventory of Utah is based on a sample of 5,382 plots systematically located across the State (a total area of 54.3 million acres); a sampling rate of approximately one plot for every 10,096 acres.

The statistical estimation procedures used to provide the estimates of the population totals presented in this report are described in detail in Bechtold and Patterson (2005). Along with every estimate is an associated sampling error that is typically expressed as a percentage of the estimated value but that can also be expressed in the same units as the estimate or as a confidence interval (the estimated value plus or minus the sampling error). This sampling error is the primary measure of the reliability of an estimate. An approximate 67 percent confidence interval constructed from the sampling error can be interpreted to mean that under hypothetically repeated sampling, approximately 67 percent of the confidence intervals calculated from the individual repeat samples would include the true population parameter if it were computed from a 100-percent inventory. The sampling errors for State-level estimates are presented in Appendix E (table 37).

Users may compute statistical confidence for subdivisions of the reported data using the formula below. Because sampling error increases as the area or volume considered decreases, users should aggregate data categories as much as possible. Sampling errors obtained from this method are only approximations of reliability because homogeneity of variances is assumed. The formula is:

$$SE_s = SE_t \frac{\sqrt{X_t}}{\sqrt{X_s}}$$

SE_s = sampling error for subdivision of State total
SE_t = sampling error for State total
X_s = sum of values for the variable of interest (area, volume, biomass, etc.) for subdivision of State total
X_t = sum of values (area, volume, biomass, etc) for State total

Measurement Error—Errors associated with the methods and instruments used to observe and record the sample attributes are called measurement errors. On FIA plots, attributes such as the diameter and height of a tree are measured with different instruments, and other attributes such as species and crown class are observed without the aid of an instrument. On a typical FIA plot, 30 to 70 trees are observed with 15 to 20 attributes recorded on each tree. In addition, many attributes that describe the plot and conditions on the plot are observed. Errors in any of these observations affect the quality of the estimates. If a measurement is biased—such as tree diameter consistently taken at an incorrect place on the tree—then the estimates that use this observation (e.g. calculated volume) will reflect this bias. Even if measurements are unbiased, high levels of random error in the measurements will add to the total random error of the estimation process. A Quality Assurance Program is an integral part of all FIA data collection efforts to ensure that all FIA observations are made to the highest standards possible (see "Quality Assurance Analysis" in Section IV for more details).

Prediction Error—Errors associated with using mathematical models (such as volume models) to provide information about attributes of interest based on sample attributes are referred to as prediction errors. Area, number of trees, volume, biomass, growth, removals, and mortality are the primary attributes of interest presented in this report. Area and number of trees estimates are based on direct observation and do not involve the use of prediction models; however, FIA estimates of volume, biomass, growth, and mortality used model-based predictions in the estimation process.

III. Overview of Tables

FIA is currently working on a revised National Core Table set that will expand the suite of tabled information to incorporate more of the core FIA Program, using both Phase 2 and 3 data. Appendix E contains an interim set of tables supporting this report, using Utah annual data (cycle 2) for the years 2000 through 2005. There are a total of 37 tables with statistics for land area, number of trees, wood volume, biomass (weight), growth, mortality, and sampling errors. Table 1 is the only table that includes all land types or land status; the rest are for accessible forest land or timberland. Table 37 shows sampling errors for area, volume, net growth, and mortality at the 67 percent confidence level. Additional tables in the text of this report that supplement specific sections are numbered consecutively as they appear, starting with table 1.

To avoid confusion with tables found in the body of this report and tables found in the appendices, Appendix E and Appendix F tables will be referred to beginning with "Appendix E" or "Appendix F" followed by the table number. Appendix E also contains a list of all report tables with table headings.

USDA Forest Service Resour. Bull. RMRS-RB-10. 2010

7

IV. Overview of Forest Resources

The following sections discuss the status and possible trends of Utah's forest land resources in terms of area, volume, number of trees, biomass, growth/mortality, and stand density index (SDI) using annual data collected from 2000 through 2005; another section discusses quality assurance (QA) of inventory data using data collected from 2001 through 2005. "Area" is the only section under "Overview of Forest Resources" that will include separate summaries of forest land, other wooded, and nonforest lands; the remaining "Overview of Forest Resources" sections will focus only on the forest land base. Exclusion of other wooded land from forest land summaries of volume, biomass, etc., facilitates compatibility with similar Resource Planning Act (RPA) statistics, and is consistent with FIA's current definition of forest land. Other wooded lands (see Appendix A), by definition, contain few trees and thus little volume and biomass, but are important as an ecotone, at least from an area perspective.

Area

Background—Area by different land classifications (e.g., land class, ownership, forest type, etc.) provides the overall perspective and context for the "Overview of Forest Resources," "Current Issues and FIA Indicators," and "Timber Products" sections of this report. Although area estimates are somewhat confounded by past definitional changes, primarily in woodland forest types, Utah's total forest land base appears to be on the increase (table 1). In addition, the partitioning of the new land class (other wooded land) provides further context, especially in many of Utah's arid, sparsely vegetated forest types like juniper woodland.

Table 1--Total area (acres) by ownership class and land class, Utah, cycle 2, 2000-2005.

Owner group	Ownership class	Forest land	Other wooded	Nonforest and water	Grand Total
Forest Service	National Forest	6,251,534	217,622	1,703,495	8,172,651
	Other National Forest	7,432	--	52,024	59,457
Forest Service Total		**6,258,966**	**217,622**	**1,755,519**	**8,232,107**
Other Federal	Bureau of Land Management	6,799,821	926,492	15,165,602	22,891,915
	National Park Service	345,183	71,716	1,488,911	1,905,810
	Department of Defense or Energy	9,951	--	1,717,340	1,727,291
	Fish and Wildlife Service	10,886	--	61,274	72,160
Other Federal Total		**7,165,840**	**998,209**	**18,433,127**	**26,597,176**
State and local government	State	1,513,682	95,993	4,433,359	6,043,033
	Local (county, municipal, etc.)	11,266		18,979	30,245
State and local government Total		**1,524,947**	**95,993**	**4,452,337**	**6,073,278**
Private	Undifferentiated private	3,012,701	238,830	10,180,657	13,432,189
Private Total		**3,012,701**	**238,830**	**10,180,657**	**13,432,189**
Grand Total		**17,962,455**	**1,550,654**	**34,821,641**	**54,334,750**

All table cells without observations in the inventory sample are indicated by --.

Inventory Results: Land Class—The State of Utah covers over 54 million acres (table 1). Thirty-three percent (almost 18 million acres) of the area meets the definition of forest land, and about 3 percent (1.6 million acres) meets the definition of other wooded lands. The remaining 64 percent (35 million acres) is classified as nonforest or water. Figure 1 displays the distribution of FIA field plots by two land classes (forest land and other wooded) and ownership in Utah.

USDA Forest Service Resour. Bull. RMRS-RB-10. 2010

9

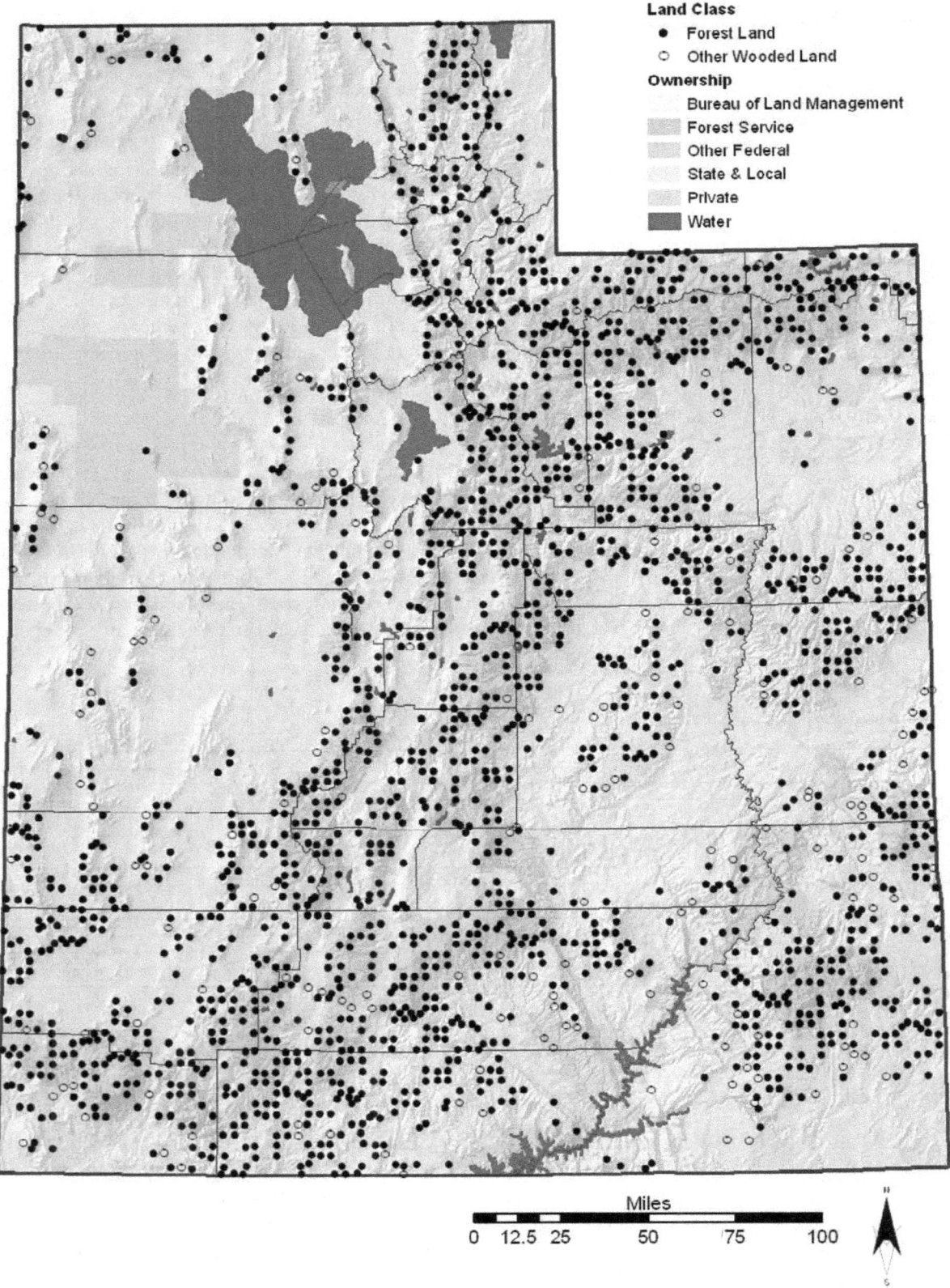

Land Class
- ● Forest Land
- ○ Other Wooded Land

Ownership
- Bureau of Land Management
- Forest Service
- Other Federal
- State & Local
- Private
- Water

Miles

0   12.5 25   50   75   100

Figure 1—Distribution of inventory plots by land class and ownership, Utah, cycle 2, 2000-2005. Note: plot locations are approximate and some on private land are randomly swapped.

USDA Forest Service Resour. Bull. RMRS-RB-10. 2010

Inventory Results: Owner Class—Table 1 shows that over 75 percent of Utah's total land area is in the public domain, which also includes over 83 percent of the total forest land area. The Bureau of Land Management (BLM) contains the largest proportion of Utah's nonforest lands (44 percent), followed by private lands (29 percent), and State lands (13 percent). The BLM also contains the majority of forest land, at 38 percent, followed by National Forest Systems (NFS) at 35 percent; however, a larger proportion (76 percent) of NFS lands is forested compared to BLM lands (30 percent). The major breakdown of ownership for other wooded lands is BLM at 60 percent, private at 15 percent, and NFS at 14 percent.

The BLM and IWFIA worked jointly, under the administration of the BLM, on a report specific to forest lands that used the 5 percent cover definition for forest land (Bottomley and Menlove 2006). In this BLM report, estimates of forest land for the same reporting period in Utah was greater due to differences in forest land definitions.

Inventory Results: Forest Type—Forest type refers to the predominant species in a stand, based on plurality of tree stocking. Table 2 presents area by forest type for both forest and other wooded land classes. At 44 percent (7.9 million acres), pinyon-juniper woodland is by far the most common forest type on forest land in Utah, followed by juniper woodland and deciduous oak woodland at 11 percent each, and aspen at 9 percent. In contrast to forest land, the most common forest type on other wooded lands is juniper woodland (34 percent), followed by pinyon-juniper woodland (32 percent), and nonstocked (29 percent).

Table 2--Area (acres) of timber/woodland forest types by forest type and land class, Utah, cycle 2, 2000-2005.

Timber/woodland type	Forest type	Forest land	Other wooded	Grand Total
Timber type	Aspen	1,640,330	10,620	1,650,950
	Blue spruce	6,988	--	6,988
	Cottonwood	31,564	--	31,564
	Douglas-fir	650,453	22,718	673,171
	Engelmann spruce	491,425	--	491,425
	Foxtail pine-bristlecone pine	24,501	--	24,501
	Limber pine	22,685	--	22,685
	Lodgepole pine	393,175	--	393,175
	Ponderosa pine	388,385	6,915	395,300
	Engelmann Spruce-subalpine fir	172,942	--	172,942
	Subalpine fir	397,054	--	397,054
	White fir	355,031	--	355,031
Timber types Total		**4,574,535**	**40,252**	**4,614,787**
Woodland type	Cercocarpus woodland	412,356	5,070	417,426
	Deciduous oak woodland	1,986,909	11,692	1,998,601
	Juniper woodland	1,994,831	534,787	2,529,618
	Intermountain maple woodland	242,480	--	242,480
	Pinyon-juniper woodland	7,904,926	491,271	8,396,197
	Rocky Mountain juniper	310,720	25,265	335,985
Woodland types Total		**12,852,222**	**1,068,085**	**13,920,307**
Nonstocked	Nonstocked	535,699	442,317	978,016
Nonstocked Total		**535,699**	**442,317**	**978,016**
Grand Total		**17,962,455**	**1,550,654**	**19,513,109**

All table cells without observa ions in the inventory sample are indicated by --.

In past reports, forest types have often been separated into timber and woodland types (Appendix C). Timber types are characterized by stands where the plurality of stocking is from species where diameter is measured at breast height, as opposed to root collar (woodland types). In this report, both forest and other wooded land classes may contain timber or woodland forest types. Table 2 shows the general dominance of woodland forest types in Utah. Seventy-two percent (12.9 million acres) of all forest land comprises woodland types, while 25 percent (4.6 million acres) comprises timber types. Considering only other wooded land, 69 percent (1.1 million acres) comprises woodland types, and only 3 percent (40 thousand acres) comprises timber types. Not surprisingly, 45 percent (0.4 million acres) of all Utah's nonstocked land (forest and other wooded), occurs on other wooded land. (See "Other Wooded Land" in Section V for further discussions on nonstocked issues.)

The distribution of forest types in Utah is influenced by many factors such as elevation, moisture, aspect, soils, climate, and past fire history. Due to Utah's arid nature, moisture, which is heavily influenced by elevation, is a major factor. The ecoregions of the United States are classified in descending order by domains, divisions, provinces, and sections. The entire State of Utah lies within the Dry Domain of Bailey's ecoregions (Bailey 1978) containing six distinct provinces. Ranging from under 4,000 to over 13,000 feet in elevation, all six provinces in Utah (four desert and two mountain) contain forest and other wooded lands. Figure 2 displays the distribution of FIA field plots by forest type, ecoregion province, and elevation for forest and other wooded lands. Some forest types have been combined for ease of display: aspen and cottonwood; Engelmann spruce-subalpine fir, blue spruce, and subalpine fir; limber and foxtail pine-bristlecone pine; deciduous oak woodland and intermountain maple woodland; and juniper woodland and Rocky Mountain juniper.

Inventory Results: Reserved Status and Productivity—Reserved lands are lands withdrawn from management for production of wood products. For context on the importance of wood products to Utah's local and regional economies, and for comparisons between the often widely differing stand characteristics of nonreserved versus reserved lands, table 3 presents the area of forest and other wooded lands by reserved status, owner class, and productivity. Eighty-nine percent (17.4 million acres) of Utah's forest and other wooded lands are in nonreserved status, leaving 11 percent (2.1 million acres) as reserved. Seventy-five percent of all Utah's forest land is unproductive, which means it is not capable of producing wood volumes of at least 20 cubic feet per acre per year. Most of these lands are woodland forest types, which are unproductive by definition.

Timberland, defined in this report as nonreserved productive forest land, is an important classification describing the potential availability of timber products. Twenty-two percent (about 4.0 million acres) of all forest land in Utah meets the definition of timberland.

Discussion—The use of crown cover to separate and exclude other wooded land from forest land helped reconcile much of Utah's apparent increases in forest land compared to past inventories (see "Plot-filtering and the definition of forest and other wooded lands" in Appendix A). Nevertheless, Utah's current annual inventory still shows about a 14-percent (2.3-million acre) positive difference from the total forest land area (15.7 million) inventoried in 1993 (O'Brien 1999, table 1). In addition to the effects of crown cover, Appendix A discusses some of the expected definitional impacts between the inventories in terms of tree-form, species, plot imagery, and changing forest type algorithms. These remaining factors would collectively favor further perceived increases in forest land, and more likely in woodland types than in timber types, which is where the majority of the forest land increase occurred. This could potentially explain much of the 14 percent difference. However, the lack of similar plot-filtering field variables for determining why past periodic plots where called nonforest precludes the plot-to-plot

12

USDA Forest Service Resour. Bull. RMRS-RB-10. 2010

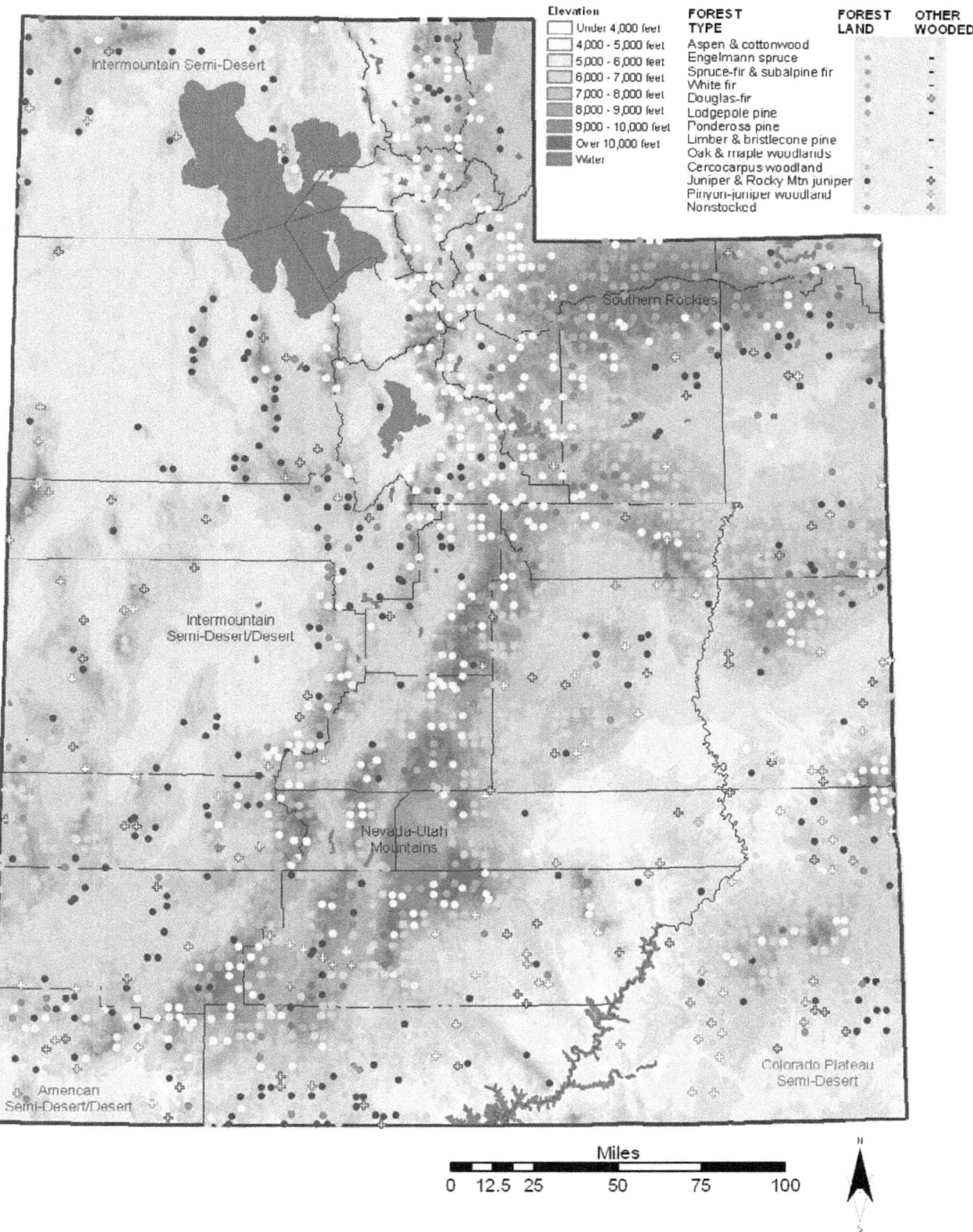

Figure 2—Distribution of inventory plots by forest type, ecoregion province, land class, and elevation, Utah, cycle 2, 2000-2005. Note: plot locations are approximate and some on private land are randomly swapped.

Table 3--Area (acres) of forest land and other-wooded by reserved status, ownership class, and productivity, Utah, cycle 2, 2000-2005.

Reserved status	Ownership class	Forest land		Forest land Total	Other wooded		Other wooded Total	Grand Total
		Productive	Unproductive		Productive	Unproductive		
Not reserved	National Forest	2,995,232	2,736,563	5,731,795	61,110	145,714	206,824	5,938,619
	Bureau of Land Management	140,612	5,739,981	5,880,593	5,031	821,761	826,792	6,707,385
	Department of Defense or Energy	--	9,951	9,951	--	--	--	9,951
	State	154,172	1,261,015	1,415,187	2,457	85,438	87,895	1,503,082
	Local (county, municipal, etc.)	11,266	--	11,266	--	--	--	11,266
	Private	690,510	2,319,048	3,009,558	17,929	220,901	238,830	3,248,389
Not reserved Total		3,991,791	12,066,558	16,058,350	86,528	1,273,814	1,360,342	17,418,691
Reserved	National Forest	398,826	120,914	519,739	--	10,798	10,798	530,537
	Other National Forest	--	7,432	7,432	--	--	--	7,432
	Bureau of Land Management	10,211	909,017	919,228	--	99,700	99,700	1,018,928
	National Park Service	64,864	280,319	345,183	--	71,716	71,716	416,899
	Fish and Wildlife Service	--	10,886	10,886	--	--	--	10,886
	State	--	98,495	98,495	--	8,098	8,098	106,592
	Private	--	3,143	3,143	--	--	--	3,143
Reserved Total		473,900	1,430,206	1,904,106	--	190,312	190,312	2,094,418
Grand Total		4,465,691	13,496,764	17,962,455	86,528	1,464,126	1,550,654	19,513,109

All table cells without observations in the inventory sample are indicated by --.

14

USDA Forest Service Resour. Bull. RMRS-RB-10. 2010

analysis needed to break down the definitive causes of real "on-the-ground" changes. As a result, the following comparisons between inventories remain tempered by these definitional differences.

In terms of ownership, 82 percent of Utah's apparent forest land increase occurred on BLM, NFS, and State lands (table 1). A comparison of figures 1 and 2 shows that most of the higher elevation NFS lands contain the majority of the timber types, and the lower elevation BLM lands contain the majority of the woodland types and other wooded lands.

Two woodland forest types accounted for most of the net increase in Utah's forest area: an increase of about 1.2 million acres in deciduous oak woodland, and over 900 thousand acres in juniper woodland (table 2). Increases in deciduous oak woodland are related to the tree-form issue discussed in Appendix A. In addition, three timber forest types changed substantially from previous estimates. Although the combined annual Engelmann spruce-subalpine fir and subalpine fir types changed little compared to periodic spruce-fir, the apparent decrease in Engelmann spruce-subalpine fir is due to a partial shifting of area to subalpine fir, which is a new forest type not present in past periodic inventories. Since Gambel oak is a common component of Douglas-fir and ponderosa pine types, there was a substantial shift in Douglas-fir and ponderosa pine types to deciduous oak woodland, which is related to changes in the forest type algorithm issue discussed in Appendix A. The remaining forest types have stayed fairly stable with the exception of aspen, which has increased by about 15 percent (212 thousand acres).

Although the total reserved land in Utah has changed little since 1993, the amount of timberland has decreased by 15 percent (712 thousand acres). Of the definitional factors discussed in Appendix A, cover and changing forest type algorithms have the largest influence on the decrease in timberland area. This is due to the previous threshold of only 5 percent cover to qualify as timberland on sites mixed with larger amounts of woodland species, rather than the species with plurality of stocking as in annual inventories. As a result, at least some of these stands would switch to woodland types under annual inventory standards.

Number of Trees

Background—Estimates of numbers of trees are expanded from trees per acre to the population level. The composition of forests by different species is an indicator of forest diversity. In addition, dead trees, or snags, are an important component of forested landscapes, playing crucial roles in wildlife habitat, nutrient cycles (including carbon), fire fuel loading, and soil formation.

Inventory Results—Nearly 8.4 billion live trees 1.0-inch diameter and larger are estimated to occur on Utah forest land (Appendix E, table 10). Gambel oak is by far the most abundant species in the State, with 41 percent of the live trees on forest land (fig. 3). The second most abundant species is Utah juniper, with 11 percent of the live trees, followed by common or twoneedle pinyon and aspen, each with about 9 percent of live trees. The most abundant timber conifer species on forest land is subalpine fir with over 5 percent of the live trees.

On timberland (nonreserved and productive) in Utah, there are 650 million live growing-stock trees 5.0-inches diameter and greater, of which aspen is the most common with nearly 36 percent (Appendix E, table 11). The next most abundant growing-stock species on timberland are lodgepole pine with over 16 percent, subalpine fir with 15 percent, Douglas-fir with 12 percent, Engelmann spruce with 10 percent, white fir with 7 percent (combined with subalpine fir in Appendix E, table 11 as true fir), and ponderosa pine with nearly 4 percent.

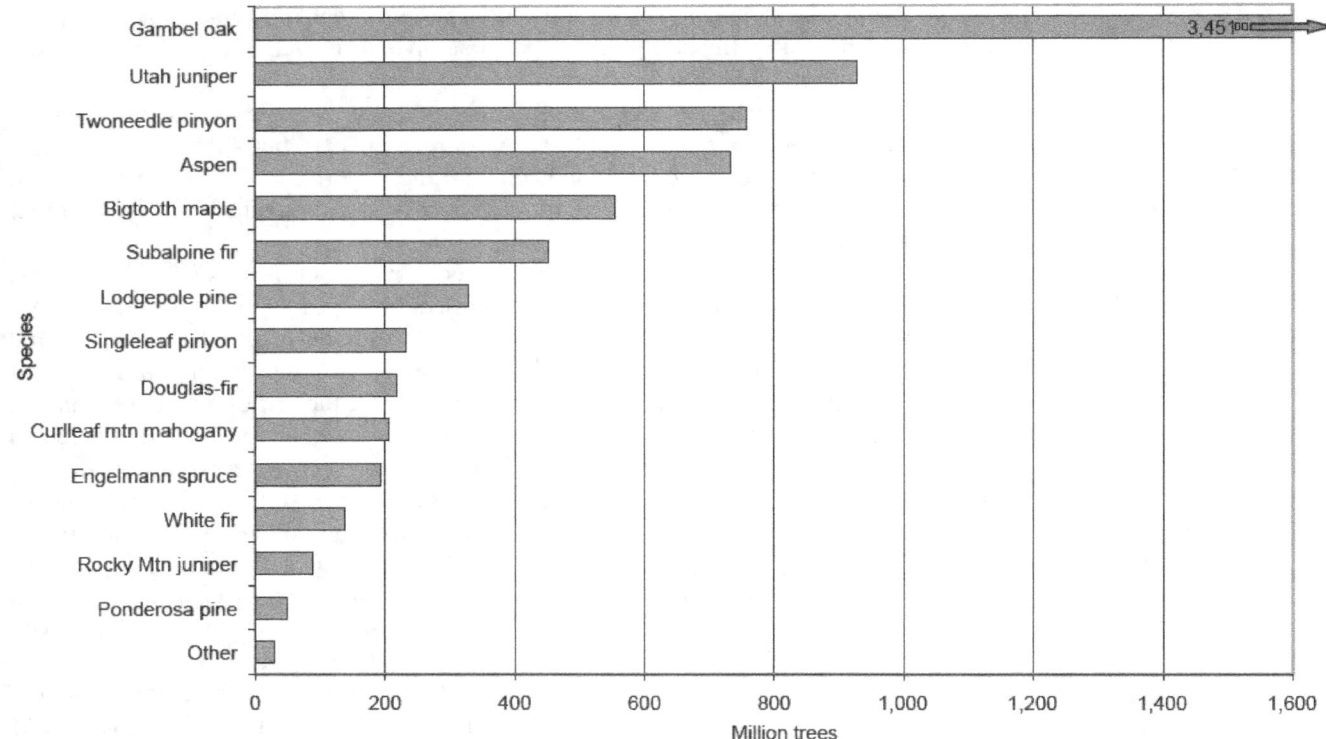

Figure 3—Number of live trees 1.0 inch diameter and greater by species on forest land, Utah, cycle 2, 2000-2005.

Figure 4 shows numbers of live trees by diameter class (whether measured at breast height or root collar), and shows the expected distribution of many smaller trees compared to larger trees. Overall, trees less than 5.0-inches diameter make up 75 percent of all live trees. Over half (54 percent) of the trees smaller than 5.0-inches diameter are Gambel oaks. Conversely, the second most common live tree, Utah juniper—a larger and longer-lived species—makes up 60 percent of live trees 15.0-inches diameter and larger.

There are an estimated 347 million standing dead trees at least 5.0-inches diameter on forest land in Utah (table 4), or an average of 19.3 snags per acre. As with live trees, larger snags are less common than smaller snags, and often contribute more significantly to the landscape components mentioned above. The average density for snags 11.0-inches diameter and larger is 5.6 per acre. Very large snags, 19.0-inches diameter and larger, occur on Utah forests at about 0.8 per acre. In all size classes, the most common species for snags is Utah juniper. In both larger snag classes (11.0-inches and over and 19.0-inches and over), the most abundant timber species for snags is Engelmann spruce. Snag densities are calculated over all forest land in the State, and do not take into account irregular distributions of dead trees caused by localized mortality events like fires, insect outbreaks, and diseases. Densities may vary considerably when looked at by sub-levels of forest land, such as ownerships, counties, or forest types.

Discussion—Our annual inventory results show an increase of 34 percent of live trees on forest land in Utah since 1993, from 6.3 billion (O'Brien 1999, table 14) to 8.4 billion trees (Appendix E, table 10). The primary reason for the increase is related to

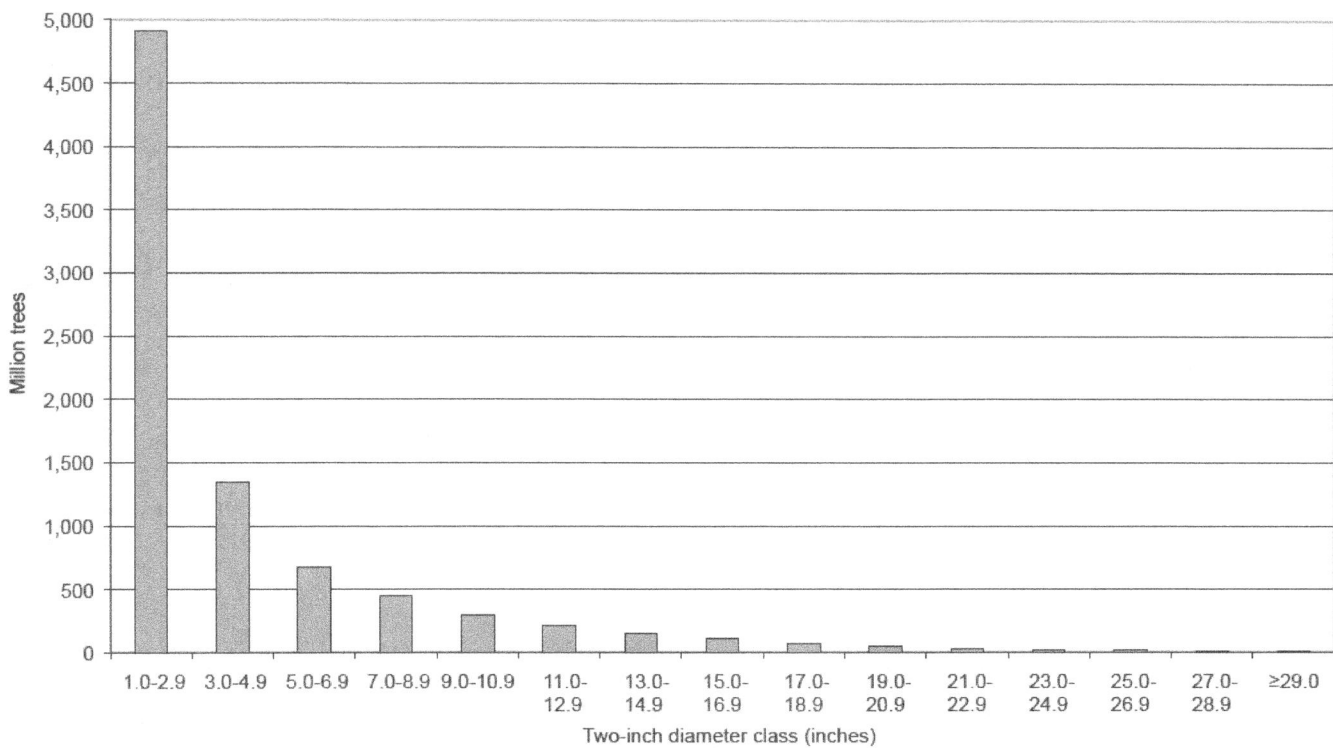

Figure 4—Number of live trees 1.0 inch diameter and greater by diameter class on forest land, Utah, cycle 2, 2000-2005.

Table 4--Number of snags by diameter class and snags per acre (number of snags at least the minimum diameter ÷ 17,962,455 acres) on forest land, Utah, cycle 2, 2000-2005.

Species	Number of snags Diameter class (inches)				Snags per acre Minimum diameter		
	5.0 - 10.9	11.0 - 18.9	≥ 19.0	All classes	5.0	11.0	19.0
Blue spruce	55,486	--	--	55,486	0.0	--	--
Common or twoneedle pinyon	23,437,181	11,790,332	739,599	35,967,113	2.0	0.7	0.0
Douglas-fir	8,313,713	5,004,678	1,689,913	15,008,304	0.8	0.4	0.1
Engelmann spruce	8,613,500	8,034,354	2,363,279	19,011,134	1.1	0.6	0.1
Great Basin bristlecone pine	56,996	56,996	56,996	170,989	0.0	0.0	0.0
Limber pine	390,399	273,639	120,355	784,392	0.0	0.0	0.0
Lodgepole pine	19,078,145	3,613,786	503,367	23,195,299	1.3	0.2	0.0
Ponderosa pine	518,665	1,497,846	799,671	2,816,182	0.2	0.1	0.0
Rocky Mountain juniper	2,302,557	1,181,687	153,328	3,637,572	0.2	0.1	0.0
Singleleaf pinyon	5,031,414	1,594,365	168,058	6,793,837	0.4	0.1	0.0
Subalpine fir	35,110,046	8,347,075	648,464	44,105,585	2.5	0.5	0.0
Utah juniper	46,110,249	31,227,999	6,444,209	83,782,457	4.7	2.1	0.4
White fir	8,176,786	3,927,797	869,370	12,973,953	0.7	0.3	0.0
Softwoods Total	**157,195,137**	**76,550,555**	**14,556,611**	**248,302,303**	**13.8**	**5.1**	**0.8**
Aspen	58,557,341	6,034,573	181,247	64,773,160	3.6	0.3	0.0
Bigtooth maple	1,701,897	--	--	1,701,897	0.1	--	--
Curlleaf mountain-mahogany	11,874,334	2,343,251	122,076	14,339,661	0.8	0.1	0.0
Fremont cottonwood,Rio Grande cottonwood	75,643	--	--	75,643	0.0	--	--
Gambel oak	16,637,340	227,562	--	16,864,903	0.9	--	--
Narrowleaf cottonwood	317,551	327,581	60,333	705,465	0.0	0.0	0.0
Hardwoods Total	**89,164,105**	**8,932,967**	**363,656**	**98,460,728**	**5.5**	**0.5**	**0.0**
All species	**246,359,243**	**85,483,522**	**14,920,267**	**346,763,031**	**19.3**	**5.6**	**0.8**

All table cells without observations in the inventory sample are indicated by --.

a few species that were most influenced by the tree form requirements (see Appendix A), particularly Gambel oak, along with bigtooth maple and curlleaf mountain-mahogany. The increases in the numbers of live trees of these three species (nearly 2.3 billion trees) add up to more than the increase for all forest land (2.1 billion trees). Gambel oak often occurs in dense thickets of small trees; indeed, 97 percent of all of the Gambel oaks measured were less than 5 inches diameter. Although Gambel oak was the most common species reported in the previous Utah report, the current estimate is more than double the previous estimate.

The species showing the largest decrease in number of live trees since 1993 was aspen (0.2 billion fewer trees). This may appear contradictory, considering the increases in both the area of the aspen forest type and net volume in aspen (see "Growth and Mortality" in this section for more aspen context). However, the decrease in live aspens occurred almost exclusively in trees less than 9.0 inches diameter, while trees over 11.0 inches diameter increased by 20 percent. This would indicate that some young, dense aspen stands are maturing into stands of larger trees, accompanied by self-thinning mortality of smaller trees. This trend is not currently being off-set by the establishment of more young and dense aspen stands (see additional discussion in "Aspen Mortality" in Section V).

Volume and Biomass

Background—Estimates of gross and net volume include only the merchantable portion or saw-log portion (e.g., cubic-foot, board-foot) of trees, while biomass describes aboveground tree weight by various components (merchantable bole and bark, tops and limbs, saplings). Net volumes are computed by deducting rotten, missing, or form defect from gross volume. Biomass estimates for this report are based on gross volumes and exclude foliage. Volume and biomass equation sources are documented in Appendix D.

Inventory Results—Tables 12 through 16 in Appendix E show net volume of live trees 5.0 inches diameter and greater on Utah forest land by various categories. The total net volume of wood in live and standing dead trees 5.0 inches diameter and greater on Utah forest land is 15.7 and 2.3 billion cubic-feet, respectively (fig. 5). The predominant species are Utah juniper, which comprises over 25 percent of the total live net cubic-foot volume, followed by aspen and common pinyon at 12 percent each, Engelmann spruce at 10 percent, and Douglas-fir at 9 percent. Engelmann spruce comprises 18 percent of the total standing dead volume, followed by 16 percent for subalpine fir, 13 percent for aspen, 12 percent for Utah juniper, and 10 percent for lodgepole pine. The total weight of oven-dry biomass in live (1.0 inch diameter and greater) and standing dead trees (5.0 inches diameter and greater) on Utah forest land is 309 and 49 million tons, respectively (fig. 6).

Another way to look at volume and biomass is by forest type, for which net volume and biomass per acre can be computed (table 5). These estimates include the different species that occur within each forest type. Engelmann spruce-subalpine fir has the highest net volume of live trees, 5.0 inches diameter and greater, at 2,918 cubic feet per acre, and the highest biomass of live trees, 1.0 inch diameter and greater, at 48.1 tons per acre. In contrast, pinyon-juniper woodland, the most common forest type in Utah, has about 675 cubic feet per acre of volume and 12.4 tons per acre of biomass. Estimates for foxtail/bristlecone pine, limber pine, and blue spruce may not be representative due to small samples.

The net volume of growing-stock trees on nonreserved productive timberland in Utah is over 7 billion cubic feet (Appendix E, table 17). Aspen makes up 25 percent of the total growing-stock volume, followed by Engelmann spruce at 18 percent, Douglas-fir at 16 percent, subalpine fir at 14 percent, and lodgepole pine at 11 percent. Table 19 (Appendix E) shows the volume of sawtimber trees (International ¼-inch rule) on

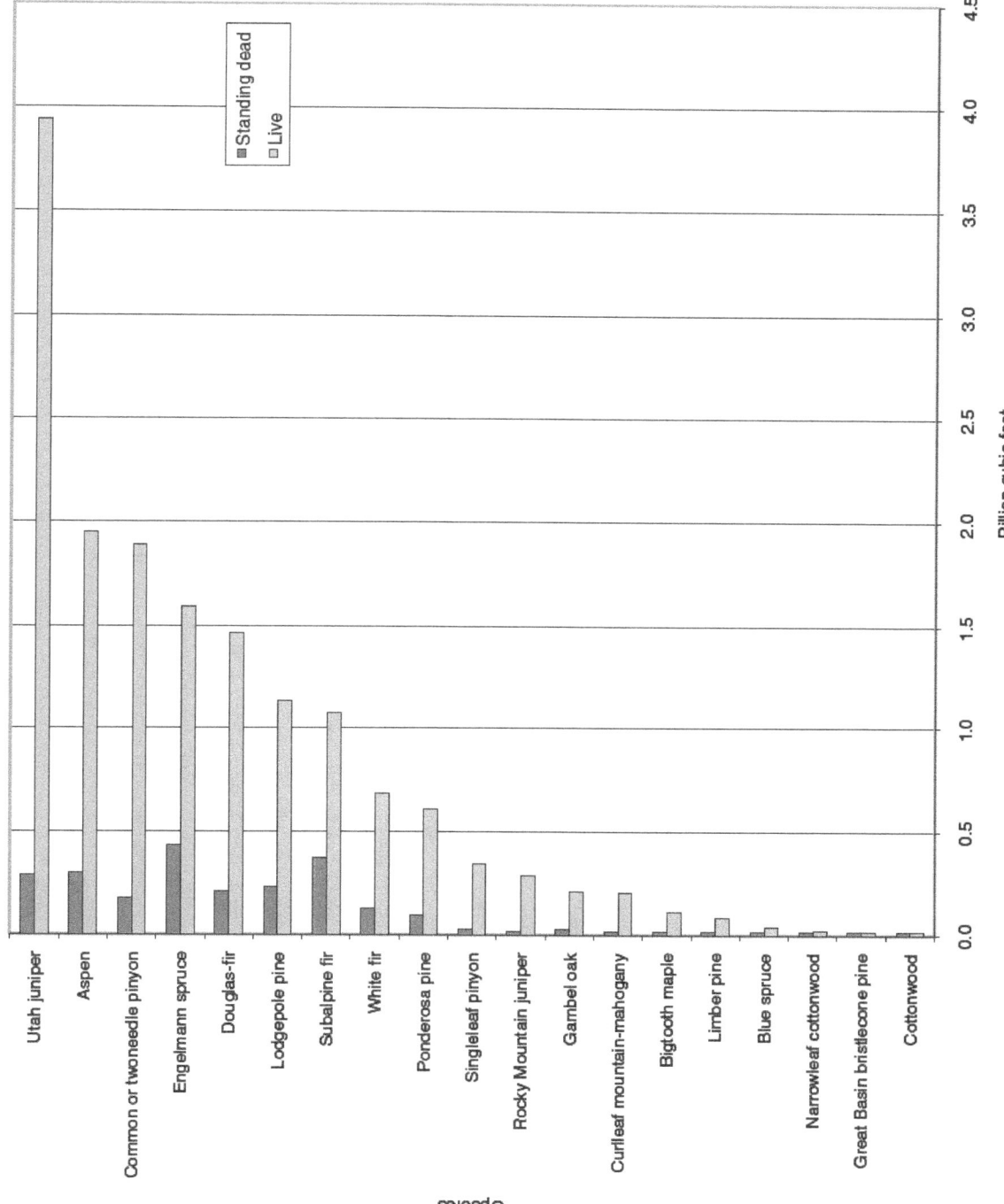

Figure 5—Net cubic-foot volume of live and standing dead trees 5.0 inches diameter and greater by species on forest land, Utah, cycle 2, 2000-2005.

USDA Forest Service Resour. Bull. RMRS-RB-10. 2010

19

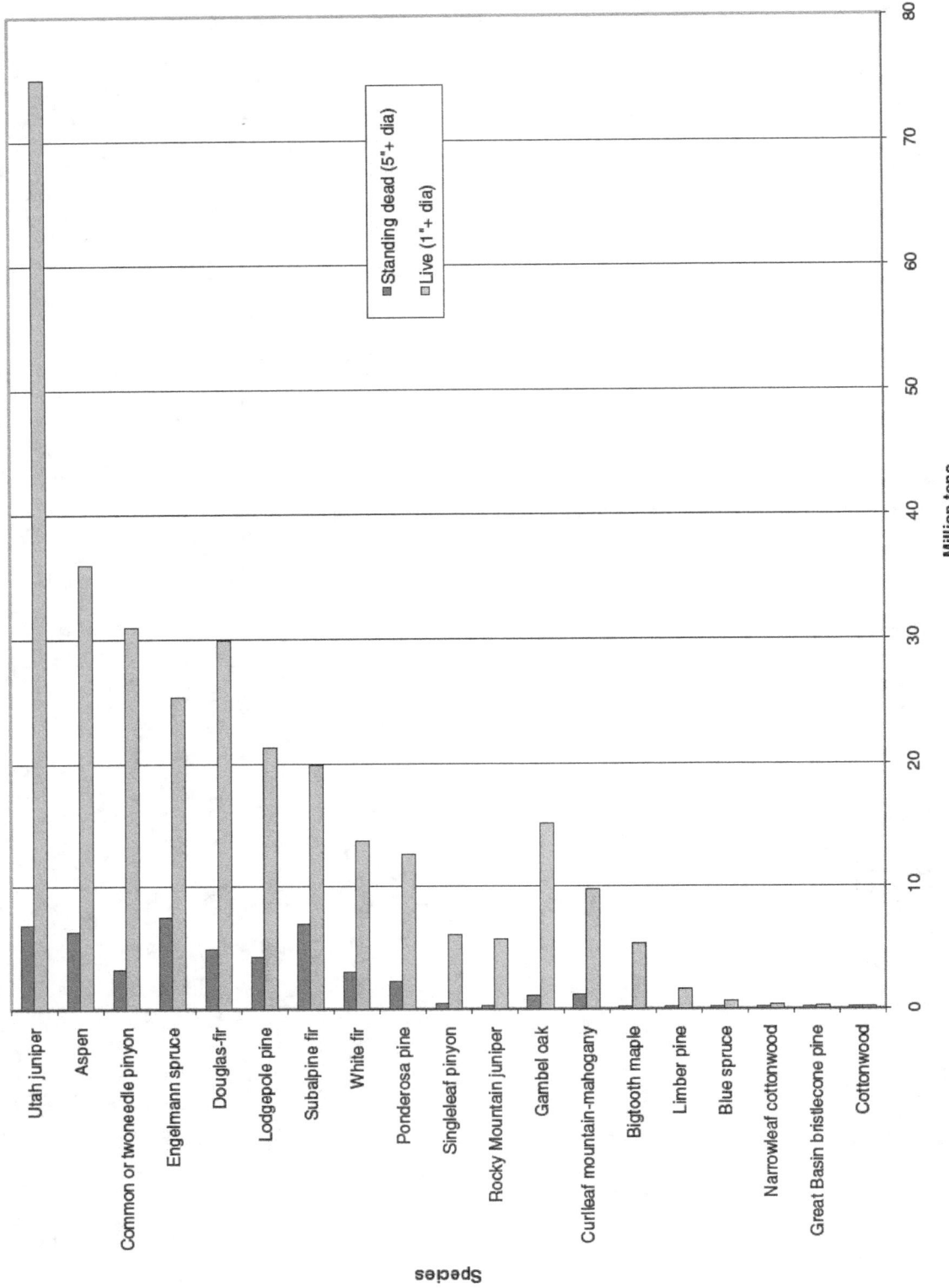

Figure 6—Oven-dry weight biomass of live and standing dead trees by species on forest land, Utah, cycle 2, 2000-2005.

Table 5--Net volume (cubic-feet) and biomass (tons) per acre of live trees by forest type on forest land, Utah, cycle 2, 2000-2005.

Forest type	Net volume	Biomass
Engelmann spruce-subalpine-fir	2,918	48.1
Engelmann spruce	2,632	43.1
Lodgepole pine	2,295	44.2
White fir	1,937	38.4
Douglas-fir	1,847	36.9
Blue spruce	1,824	26.7
Limber pine	1,756	33.4
Subalpine fir	1,635	30.0
Aspen	1,571	29.2
Ponderosa pine	1,415	29.5
Foxtail pine-bristlecone pine	973	21.4
Rocky Mountain juniper	959	19.7
Pinyon-juniper woodland	675	12.4
Cottonwood	674	11.5
Intermountain maple woodland	497	18.9
Cercocarpus woodland	492	19.6
Juniper woodland	451	8.8
Deciduous oak woodland	172	8.4
Nonstocked	36	0.7
Grand Total	**873**	**17.2**

nonreserved productive timberland at about 26.6 billion board feet (22.2 billion board-feet Scribner rule). Engelmann spruce accounts for the majority of sawtimber at 23 percent, followed by Douglas-fir at 19 percent, aspen at 16 percent, and subalpine fir at 15 percent. The total weight of oven-dry biomass in live trees 1.0-inch diameter and greater on nonreserved productive timberland land is over 135 million tons (Appendix E, table 29).

Discussion—There was a 14 percent increase in forest land in Utah since 1993, mostly associated with increases in the deciduous oak woodland and juniper types (see "Area" discussion in Section IV). In conjunction with this, total live volume of trees 5.0 inches diameter and greater showed a small increase of 3.5 percent over the 1993 data (O'Brien 1999, table19). This shows that compared to area, the definitional impacts are minor in terms of changes in volume. Species contributing to most of the live volume increase were aspen, Utah juniper, lodgepole pine, and Rocky Mountain juniper; species with the largest decreases in volume were Douglas-fir and Engelmann spruce. Direct comparisons to past biomass are not plausible because different biomass definitions and computations were used in the previous inventory. In general, the current volume and biomass estimates are more correlated with each other.

Although there was a 15 percent decrease in area of nonreserved productive timberland, net volume of growing-stock trees on these lands decreased only 6 percent, down from 7.4 billion cubic feet in 1993. Also, as in 1993, aspen continues to comprise the greatest percentage of growing-stock volume, as does Engelmann spruce and Douglas-fir for sawtimber volume.

Growth and Mortality

Background—Forest vigor and sustainability can be assessed using change components: growth, mortality, and removals. Growth, as reported here, is the average annual growth volume calculated from a sample of tree increment core measurements

USDA Forest Service Resour. Bull. RMRS-RB-10. 2010

21

based on the previous 10 years of growth. Mortality is the average annual net volume of trees that have died in the 5 years prior to the year of measurement, and removals, in general, are the annual net volume of trees that were removed from the inventory as the result of harvesting activity. The estimate of Utah's removal volume was obtained from a separate study discussed in "Section VII — Timber Products."

As State annual inventory cycles are completed, future reports will assess change components through remeasurement of the permanent annual field plots rather than tree core samples or identification of 5-year mortality trees; however, alternate methods are being investigated for woodland species growth (see "Quality Assurance Analysis" in this section).

Inventory Results—Gross annual growth of all live trees 5.0 inches diameter and greater on Utah forest land totaled about 253 million cubic feet while mortality reduced gross growth by about 175 million cubic feet for a net growth of about 78 million cubic feet (Appendix E, table 21, 23). Figure 7 shows a comparison of gross growth and mortality by species. Aspen has the highest gross growth with almost 20 percent of the total, followed by subalpine fir with 12 percent, Douglas-fir with 11 percent, lodgepole pine and Engelmann spruce with 10 percent each, and Utah juniper with 9 percent. Engelmann spruce has the highest mortality at 23 percent of the total, followed by subalpine fir at 20 percent, common pinyon and Douglas-fir at 10 percent each, and white fir and aspen at 8 percent each. Engelmann spruce at 15.1 million cubic feet, followed by subalpine fir at 3.9 million, and white fir at 0.4 million, are the only species with negative net growth (gross growth minus mortality). Spruce mortality is discussed in more detail in Section V "Current Issues." Aspen by far has the highest net growth at 35.3 million cubic feet, which is 46 percent of Utah's total net growth on forest land.

Mortality events are usually infrequent and localized and thus often difficult to accurately detect; however, annual inventories can provide unique opportunities to assess yearly trends in mortality, especially during medium to large scale events like the drought-related pinyon-juniper die off of the early 2000's (Shaw 2006; Shaw and others 2005). Also see Section V for further discussions of pinyon-juniper and spruce mortality. Figure 8 shows the average annual mortality by measurement year and cause of death. Utah's peak mortality occurred in 2003 at 28 percent of total mortality, followed by 26 percent in 2005, and was at its lowest in 2000 at 8 percent. Insects were the greatest cause of tree mortality at 42 percent of total mortality, followed by fire at 25 percent, and disease at 16 percent.

The average annual net growth and mortality of growing-stock trees on nonreserved productive timberland in Utah is 47.2 and 108.9 million cubic feet, respectively (Appendix E, table 24, 28). Although only 25 percent of Utah's forest land is productive timberland, it contains 61 percent of the State's annual net growth and 62 percent of the annual mortality.

Discussion—Is aspen declining in Utah (Bartos and Campbell 1998; O'Brien 1999)? Current annual inventory comparisons of aspen area and volume to the 1993 report suggest not, although the distribution of volume and numbers of aspen trees appears to be moving from fewer small-diameter to more large-diameter trees. In addition, net growth for aspen in 1992 was 31.7 million cubic feet, compared to 35.3 million cubic feet from the annual inventory, which had positive net growth for all diameter classes (see Section V for further discussions of aspen decline). As in 1992, insects continue to be the greatest cause of death for all species combined, and subalpine fir is the only species with negative growth in both inventories.

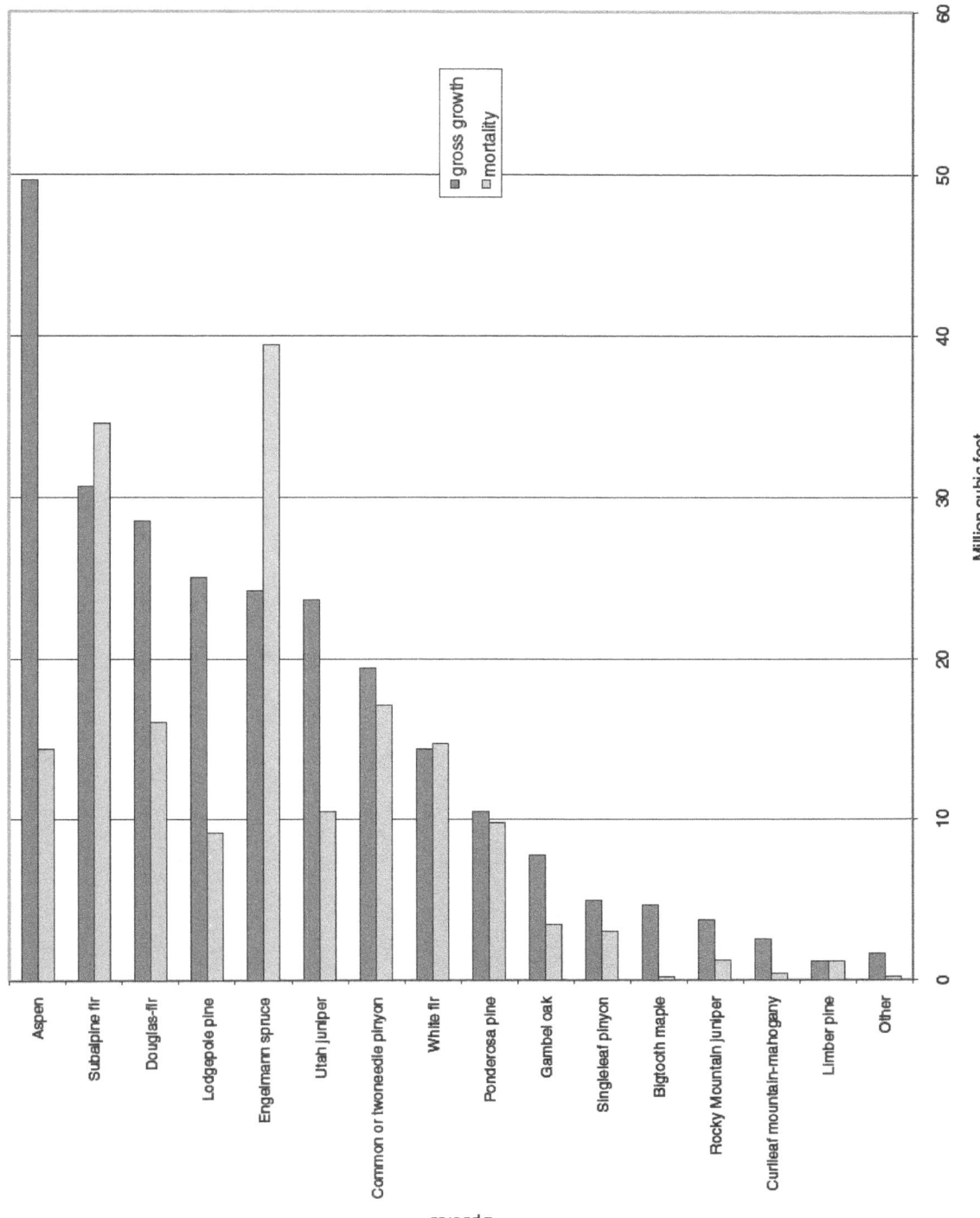

Figure 7—Gross growth (253 million cubic feet) and mortality of live trees 5.0 inches diameter and greater by species on forest land, Utah, cycle 2, 2000-2005.

USDA Forest Service Resour. Bull. RMRS-RB-10. 2010

23

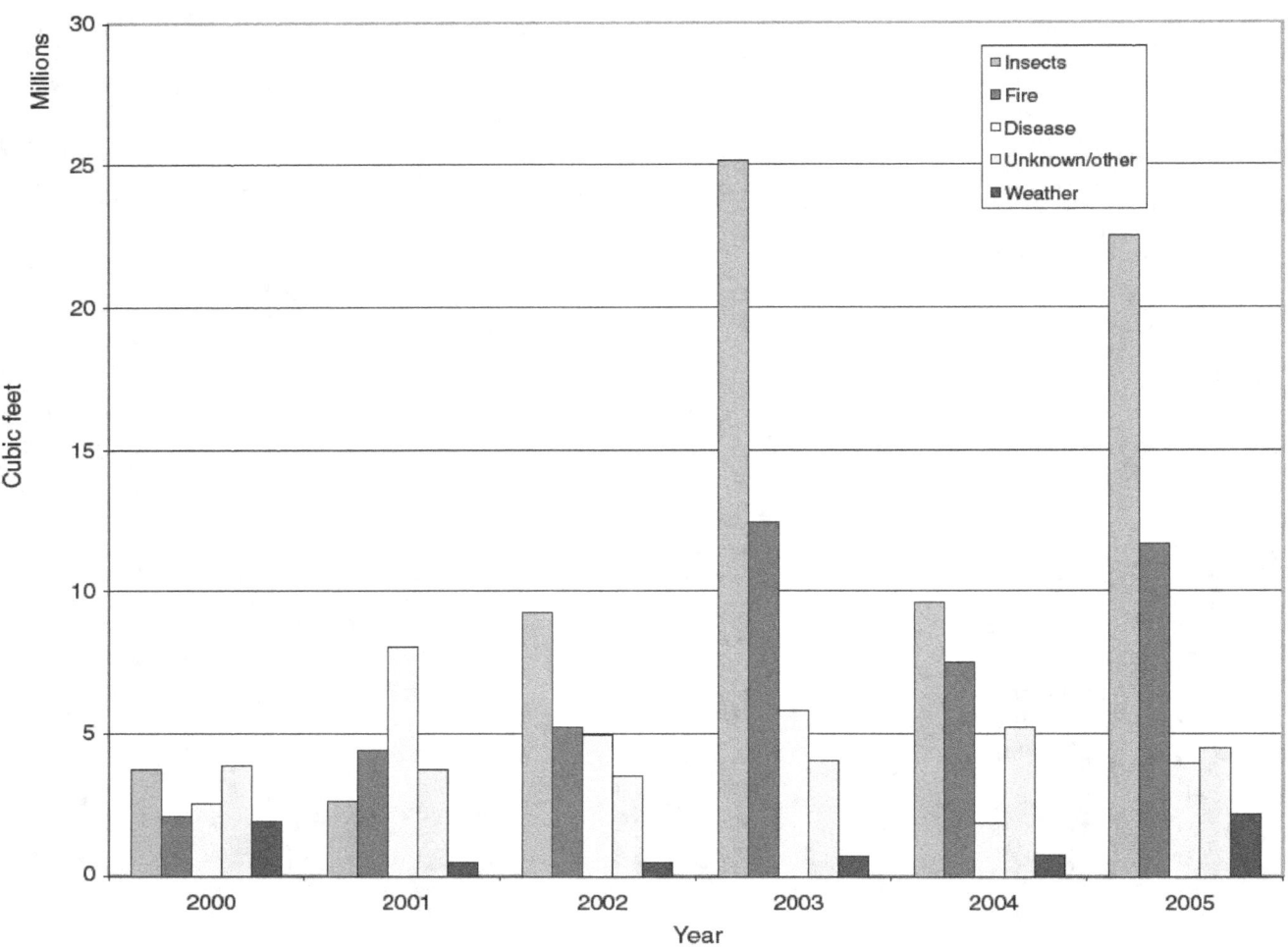

Figure 8—Average annual mortality of live trees by cause of death and year (subcycle), Utah, cycle 2, 2000-2005.

Stand Density Index (SDI)

Background—Stand density index (SDI) (Reineke 1933) is a relative measure of stand density, based on quadratic mean diameter of the stand and the number of live trees per acre. In the western United States, silviculturists often use SDI as one measure of stand structure to meet diverse objectives such as ecological restoration and wildlife habitat (e.g., Lilieholm and others 1994; Long and Shaw 2005; Smith and Long 1987).

SDI is usually presented as a percentage of a maximum SDI for each forest type. Maximum SDI is rarely, if ever, observed in nature at the stand scale because the onset of competition-induced (self-thinning) mortality begins to occur at about 60 percent of the maximum SDI. Average maximum density, which is used in normal yield tables, and is equivalent to the A-line in Gingrich-type stocking diagrams (Gingrich 1967), is equal to approximately 80 percent of maximum SDI. There are several reasons why stands may have low SDI. Stands typically have low SDI following major disturbances, such as fire, insect attack, or harvesting. These stands remain in a low-density condition until regeneration fills available growing space. Stands that are over-mature can also have low SDI, because growing space may not be re-occupied as fast as it is released by the mortality of large, old trees. Finally, stands that occur on very thin soils or rocky sites may remain at low density indefinitely, because limitations on physical growing space do not permit full site occupancy. A site is considered to be fully occupied at 35 percent of maximum SDI. At lower densities, individual tree growth is maximized but stand growth is below potential, while at higher densities, individual tree growth is below potential, but stand growth is maximized (Long 1985).

Originally developed for even-aged stands, SDI can also be applied to uneven-aged stands (Long and Daniel 1990; Shaw 2000). Stand structure can influence the computation of SDI, so the definition of maximum SDI must be compatible with the computation method. Because FIA data include stands covering the full range of structure, the maximum SDIs are currently being revised for FIA forest types (Shaw and Long, in preparation). The provisional revised maximum SDIs, which are compatible with FIA computation methods, are shown in table 6. SDI was computed for each condition that sampled forest land using the summation method (Shaw 2000), and the SDI percentage was calculated using the maximum SDI for the forest type found on the condition.

Table 6--Maximum SDI by forest type, Utah, cycle 2, 2001-2005.

Forest Type	Maximum SDI
182 Rocky Mountain juniper	425
184 Juniper woodland	385
185 Pinyon-juniper woodland	370
201 Douglas-fir	485
221 Ponderosa pine	375
261 White fir	500
265 Engelmann spruce	500
266 Engelmann spruce-subalpine fir	485
268 Subalpine fir	470
269 Blue spruce	500
281 Lodgepole pine	530
365 Foxtail pine-bristlecone pine	470
366 Limber pine	410
703 Cottonwood	360
901 Aspen	490
925 Deciduous oak woodland	475
953 Cercocarpus woodland	415
954 Intermountain maple woodland	540
999 Unknown / nonstocked	475

Inventory Results—The distribution of SDI values in Utah is relatively balanced. Figure 9 shows that stands appear to be well-stocked, with over 51 percent of forest acres at least fully occupied (SDI equal to 35 percent or greater). This distribution is unexpected considering that many forest acres were affected by insects and fire during the period covered by this inventory.

Discussion—There was considerable drought-related mortality of common pinyon starting in 2003, although Utah forests were generally less affected than those in other southwestern States (Shaw and others 2005). In some parts of Utah, Engelmann spruce and aspen were affected by drought and insects as well (see Section V on aspen, spruce, and pinyon mortality). With time, low-density stands should increase in relative density due to growth of the surviving trees. Whether or not there will be additional in-filling by regeneration will depend on a number of factors, including the timing of seed crops and favorable climatic conditions. These trends should be captured by future plot measurements.

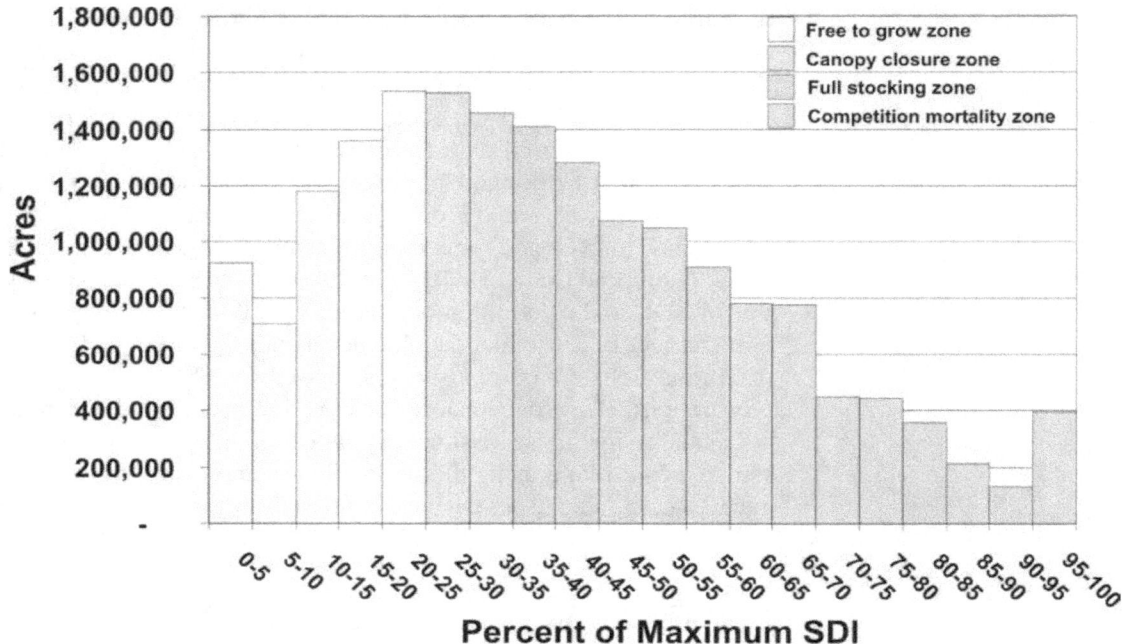

Figure 9—Distribution of stand density on Utah forest land, cycle 2, 2000-2005.

Quality Assurance Analysis

Background—FIA employs a Quality Assurance (QA) Program to ensure the quality of all collected data. The goal of the QA program is to provide a framework to assure the production of complete, accurate, and unbiased forest information of known quality. Specific Measurement Quality Objectives (MQO) for precision are designed to provide a performance objective that FIA strives to achieve for every field measurement. These data quality objectives were developed from knowledge of measurement processes in forestry and forest ecology, as well as the program needs of FIA.

The practicality of these MQOs, as well as the measurement uncertainty associated with a given field measurement can be tested by comparing data from blind check plots. Blind check data are paired observations where, in addition to the field measurements of the standard FIA crew, a second QA measurement of the plot is taken by a crew without knowledge of the first crew's results (Pollard and others 2006). The QA data for this analysis were collected between 2001 and 2005 and then compared for measurement precision between two independent FIA crews' observations. Therefore, for many FIA variables, the data quality is measured by the repeatability of two independent measurements.

Inventory Results—The results of the QA analysis for this reporting period are presented in tables 7 and 8. Table 7 describes tolerances for condition-level variables, and table 8 describes tree-level variables. Tolerances are the "accepted" range of variability between two independent observations, for checking or comparison purposes. Each variable and its associated tolerance are followed by the percentage of total paired records that fall within one, two, three, and four times the tolerance. The last four columns show the number of times out of the total records the data fell outside the tolerance.

Table 7—QA results for condition-level variables from 84 conditions in Utah, cycle 1, 2001-2005.

National core variables	Tolerance	Percentage of data within tolerance				Number of times data exceeded tolerance				Records
		@1x	@2x	@3x	@4x	@1x	@2x	@3x	@4x	
Condition status	No tolerance	96.4%				3				84
Reserve status	No tolerance	97.6%				2				84
Owner group	No tolerance	94.0%				5				84
Forest type (Type)	No tolerance	89.6%				7				67
Forest type (Group)	No tolerance									
Stand size	No tolerance	88.1%				8				67
Regeneration status	No tolerance	98.5%				1				67
Tree density	No tolerance	100.0%				0				67
Condition nonsampled reason	No tolerance									
Owner class	No tolerance	92.9%				6				84
Owner status	No tolerance	87.5%				1				8
Regeneration species	No tolerance									
Stand age	±10 %	95.5%	95.5%	95.5%	95.5%	3	3	3	3	67
Disturbance 1	No tolerance	83.6%				11				67
Disturbance year 1	±1 yr	83.3%	100.0%			1	0			6
Disturbance 2	No tolerance	92.3%				1				13
Disturbance year 2	±1 yr									
Disturbance 3	No tolerance	100.0%				0				1
Disturbance year 3	±1 yr									
Treatment 1	No tolerance	100.0%				0				67
Treatment year 1	±1 yr									
Treatment 2	No tolerance									
Treatment year 2	±1 yr									
Treatment 3	No tolerance									
Treatment year 3	±1 yr									
Physiographic class	No tolerance	67.2%				22				67
Present nonforest use	No tolerance									

Regional variables	Tolerance	@1x	@2x	@3x	@4x	@1x	@2x	@3x	@4x	Records
Percent crown cover	±10 %	91.0%	97.0%	100.0%		6	2	0		67
Percent bare ground	±10	82.1%	94.0%	98.5%	98.5%	12	4	1	1	67
Habitat type 1	No tolerance	65.7%				23				67
Habitat type 2	No tolerance	56.7%				29				67
Condition class number	No tolerance	100.0%				0				84

USDA Forest Service Resour. Bull. RMRS-RB-10. 2010

27

Table 8—QA results for tree variables from 1,301 trees in Utah, cycle 1, 2001-2005.

National core variables	Tolerance	Percentage of data within tolerance				Number of times data exceeded tolerance				Records
		@1x	@2x	@3x	@4x	@1x	@2x	@3x	@4x	
DBH	±0.1/20 in.	90.6%	96.3%	98.0%	98.0%	38	15	8	8	406
DRC	±0.1/20 in.	66.4%	79.2%	85.0%	88.8%	301	186	134	100	895
Azimuth	±10°	97.5%	98.8%	98.9%	99.1%	32	16	14	12	1301
Horizontal distance	±0.2/1.0 ft	75.2%	89.0%	94.3%	96.4%	322	143	74	47	1301
Species	No tolerance	98.8%				15				1301
Tree genus										
Tree status	No Tolerance	99.9%				1				1301
Rotten/Missing cull	±10 %	92.2%	96.4%	98.0%	98.9%	83	39	21	12	1069
Total length	±10 %	79.1%	93.9%	98.1%	99.0%	223	65	20	11	1069
Actual length	±10 %	55.8%	76.7%	86.0%	90.7%	19	10	6	4	43
Compacted crown ratio	±10 %	69.2%	91.8%	97.7%	99.2%	350	93	26	9	1135
Uncompacted crown ratio (P3)	±10 %	96.7%	98.8%	99.3%	99.8%	31	11	7	2	946
Crown class	No tolerance	81.0%				216				1135
Decay class	±1 class	90.9%	96.4%	100.0%		15	6	0		165
Cause of dea h	No tolerance	73.1%				18				67
Mortality year	±1 yr	97.0%	100.0%			2	0			67
Condition class	No tolerance	100.0%				0				1301
New tree										
Regional variables										
Mistletoe	±1 class	99.5%	99.7%	99.7%	99.9%	6	3	3	1	1135
Number of stems	No tolerance	88.5%				103				895
Percent missing top	±10 %	98.8%	99.0%	99.2%	99.4%	13	11	9	6	1069
Sound dead	±10 %	81.2%	88.4%	91.5%	93.4%	201	124	91	71	1069
Form defect	±10 %	64.3%	77.0%	85.0%	91.0%	107	69	45	27	300
Current tree class	No tolerance	98.4%				21				1301
Radial growth	±1/20 inch	61.2%	74.7%	85.3%	89.8%	95	62	36	25	245
Breast height tree age	±10 %	70.1%	85.1%	94.3%	98.9%	26	13	5	1	87
Root collar tree age	±10 %	39.9%	69.9%	80.4%	85.6%	92	46	30	22	153
Seed/Sap timberland tree age	±10 %	33.3%	58.3%	75.0%	83.3%	8	5	3	2	12
DRC using IW MQO	±0.2 in/stem	80.7%	90.2%	93.3%	94.5%	173	88	60	49	895
DRC single stem	±0.2 in/stem	85.7%	92.9%	95.4%	95.9%	83	41	27	24	581
DRC multi stem	±0.2 in/stem	71.3%	85.0%	89.5%	92.0%	90	47	33	25	314
Horiz dist-timberland	±0.2/1.0 ft	96.3%	99.3%	99.5%	99.8%	15	3	2	1	406
Horiz dist-woodland	±0.2/1.0 ft	65.7%	84.4%	92.0%	94.9%	307	140	72	46	895
Total length: saplings	±10 %	72.8%	93.1%	97.4%	98.7%	63	16	6	3	232
Actual length: saplings	±10 %	100.0%				0				1

For example, table 8 shows that there were 406 paired records for the variable "d.b.h." (diameter at breast height). At the 1X tolerance level, almost 91 percent of those records fell within plus or minus one-tenth inch of each other, for each 20.0 inches of d.b.h. observed. This percentage is referred to as the observed compliance rate. MQOs for each variable consist of two parts: a compliance standard and a measurement tolerance, and can be compared to the observed compliance rate to determine that variables performance.

Discussion—The information in tables 7 and 8 shows variables with varying degrees of repeatability. For example, one condition-level regional variable that appears fairly repeatable is "percent crown cover." At the 1X tolerance level, its observed compliance rate was 91 percent for 67 paired observations that were within plus or minus 10 percent of each other. In contrast, the compliance rate for "habitat type 1," which has no tolerance variability, was only 66 percent for the same observations. Habitat types are an important variable for forest management. Accurate determination could provide an insight to successional status when combined with existing vegetation (such as tree numbers, size class, and species by habitat types or series) thus warranting further investigations into the potential repeatability issues associated with evaluating habitat type.

The tree-level variable "d.b.h.," as mentioned above, is more repeatable when compared to the regional variable "breast height tree age," which has a 1X tolerance compliance rate of 70 percent. This is probably due to the difficulty of obtaining accurate tree ages. Several factors that might affect inconsistent tree ages are (1) tree too large to reach the center, (2) rings too close or faded to read accurately, (3) variation in age estimation when not hitting tree center (pith). Although not much can be done about the first two situations, QA data can be used to develop better field procedures for the last, especially for critical variables such as tree age.

As more blind check information becomes available, it might become apparent that a variable's MQO needs to be adjusted accordingly to better reflect the realistic expectation of quality for that variable. As a result, MQO's should be used not only to assess the reliability of FIA measurements and whether current standards are being met, but also to provide data collection experts with the information necessary to improve the current data collection system. This process can improve repeatability, or lead to elimination of variables that prove to be unrepeatable.

In 2010, Interior West FIA will begin re-measurement of the first panel of annual plots in Utah. Given the typical slow-growing nature of woodland trees, the difficulty in marking qualifying stems for future d.r.c. measurements, and the general inferior repeatability of d.r.c. compared to d.b.h. and single-stemmed d.r.c.s compared to multi-stemmed d.r.c.'s (table 8); it's been questioned whether re-measurement of d.r.c.s is the best approach for assessing growth on woodland trees. QA data may play a key role in helping answer these kinds of questions.

USDA Forest Service Resour. Bull. RMRS-RB-10. 2010

29

30

USDA Forest Service Resour. Bull. RMRS-RB-10. 2010

V. Current Issues

As FIA responds to the requests and concerns of its users and clients, questions are often asked about bringing FIA data to bear upon many issues. FIA's unbiased, systematic sampling approach and the broad-scale strategic nature of FIA data provides a unique and appropriate framework for initial investigations. Discussions of the following current issues and potential associated FIA indicators (Section VI) serve as a setup for further in-depth analyses at national, regional, State, or sub-State scales. Sources of data for the following issues sections are from 2000 through 2005.

Other Wooded Land

Background — Other wooded land, an important ecotone between forest and nonforest land, is defined in Appendix A as land with low tree crown cover densities of 5 to 9 percent, or 40 to 199 seedlings per acre. In Utah, other wooded land is most commonly the arid, low elevation pinyon-juniper and juniper forest types that are typical of the southwestern United States. The relatively recent expansion of pinyon-juniper and juniper types into sagebrush and other vegetation types since Euro-American settlement of the West has been widely documented (see "Expansion of Pinyon and Juniper Woodlands" in this section for more details). This has been attributed to many factors, such as livestock grazing, climatic shifts, reduced fire frequency, and increases in atmospheric carbon dioxide (Miller and Wigand 1994; Weisberg and others 2007). What is less well documented and not fully understood is the diversity of historical conditions and ecological processes that have shaped the distribution of pinyon and juniper in the distant past (Romme and others 2007). This makes it difficult for land managers and policy-makers to compare current to "historical" conditions.

The dynamics of pinyon and juniper expansion and contraction are often associated with forest/nonforest boundaries. Therefore, monitoring other wooded land may prove particularly useful for assessments of future trends and historical context related to fluctuations in pinyon and juniper types. By definition, other wooded land plots occur in low cover situations and need to be checked in the field to determine whether they meet the definition of forest land. Because they have low cover, the cost of field data collection is small compared to the cost of accessing the plot. In addition, although somewhat insignificant in terms of area, considering other wooded land as simply forest or nonforest ignores its ecotonal value, and potentially eliminates an important land classification.

Inventory Results — About 3 percent (1.6 million acres) (table 2) of Utah's total area meets the definition of other wooded land, which consists mostly of juniper woodland forest type (34 percent), followed by pinyon-juniper woodland (32 percent), and nonstocked land (29 percent). Stocking, an expression of the extent to which growing space is effectively utilized by live trees, is a calculated variable based on the subplot and microplot tree tally. Nonstocked stands are commonly disturbed lands that have not yet regenerated. In addition, naturally sparse stands often get classified as nonstocked. Stockability is an estimate of the stocking potential of a given site; for example, a stockability factor of 0.8 for a given site indicates that the site is capable of supporting only about 80 percent of "normal" stocking as indicated by yield tables (Pfister and others 1977; Steele and others 1983).

Prior to the implementation of mapped-design inventories, woodland forest types were assigned in the field and were not calculated using stocking. Beginning with mapped-design, IWFIA calculated all forest types and used stockability factors based on habitat

USDA Forest Service Resour. Bull. RMRS-RB-10. 2010

31

types to adjust stocking to "normal" for some low-yield timber and woodland types. Figure 10 is a comparison of area of stocked versus nonstocked other wooded land using two stocking calculation methods: one with stockability factors (annual inventory method) and one without (periodic inventory method). This shows that over 71 percent of all other wooded land is stocked using stockability factors, and 54 percent is stocked when not using stockability factors. Since stocking often connotes some management objective, and other wooded land denotes naturally sparse cover, it's probably unrealistic to assume that large portions of these lands need regeneration. This is somewhat embodied by the fact that only 5 percent of other wooded lands have been classified as recently disturbed or chained using FIA's disturbance variable.

The lack of sample trees on other wooded land often results in plots being classified as nonstocked. Figure 11 displays percent of "field-recorded" stand-size class by "calculated" stand-size class, which demonstrates that only 10 percent of the calculated nonstocked stand-size class is considered nonstocked by field crews on the ground. Also, 81 percent of the calculated nonstocked other wooded land had a "field-recorded" forest type of pinyon-juniper woodland or juniper woodland; the remaining 19 percent consisted of small amounts of various timber and woodland types (fig. 12).

As discussed in Section IV, elevation is a major factor in the spatial distribution of forest, other wooded, and nonforest land in Utah (fig. 2). The juxtaposition of other wooded land in relation to nonforest and forest land is displayed in figure 13. This shows the area distribution within each land type by 1,000-ft elevation classes. Other wooded land in Utah, of which 48 percent occurs at the 5,000-ft to 6,000-ft elevation class, is sandwiched between predominantly nonforest land at 4,000 ft to 5,000 ft and forest land occurring mostly at 6,000 ft and above. If climate changes occur, this elevation zone

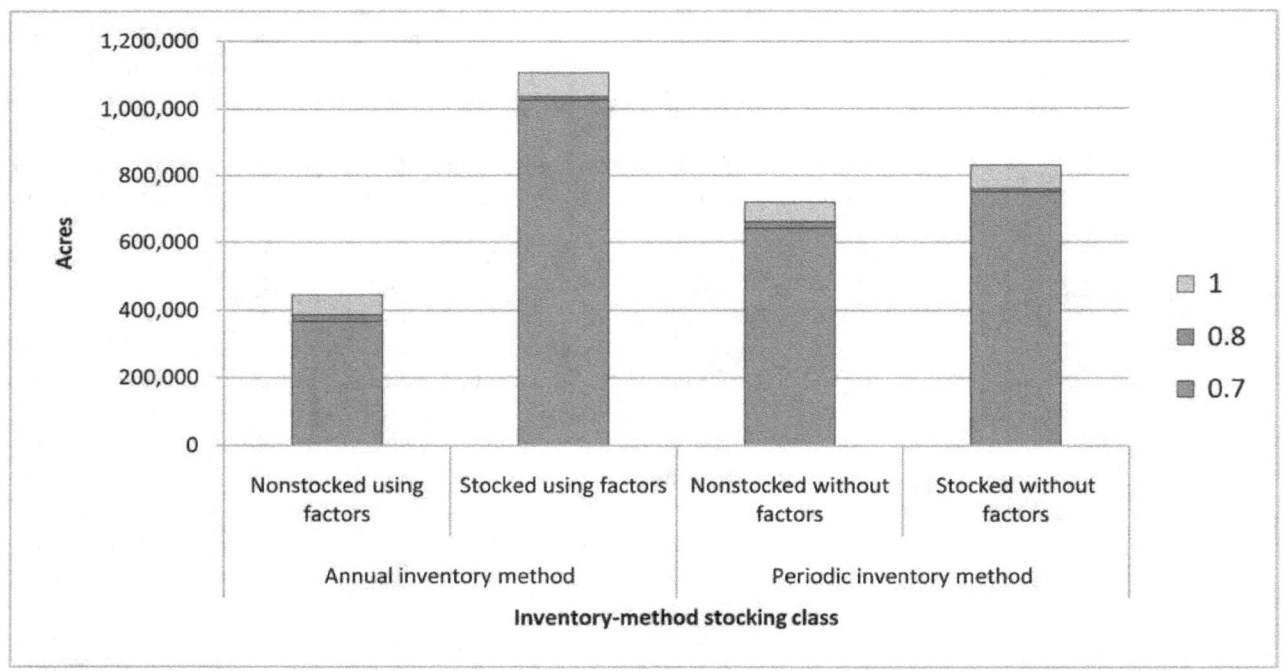

Figure 10—Acres of other wooded land by stocking class, inventory method, and stockability factor, Utah, cycle 2, 2000-2005.

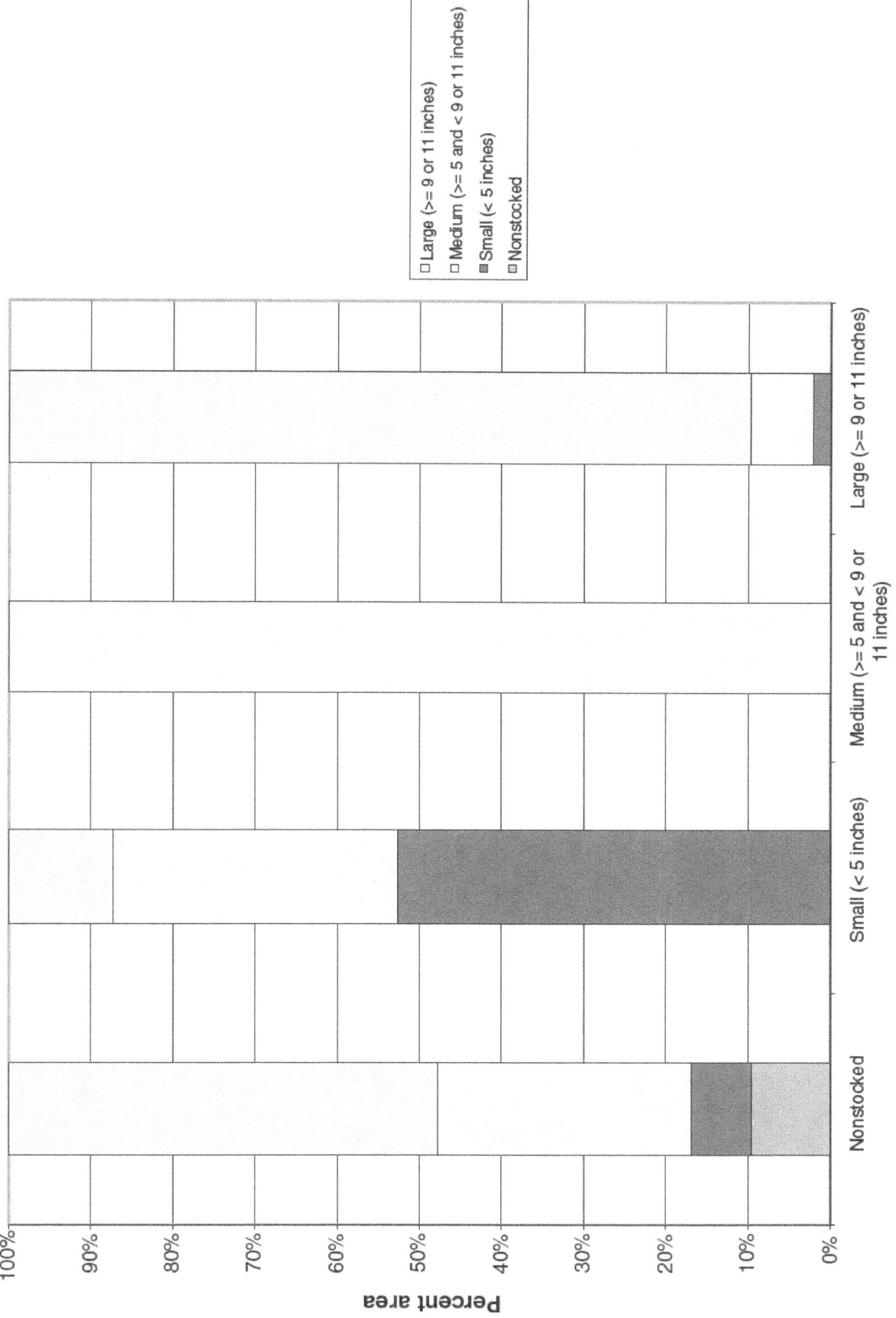

Figure 11—Percent area distribution of four "field" stand-size classes within the same four "calculated" stand-size classes for other wooded land, Utah, cycle 2, 2000-2005.

USDA Forest Service Resour. Bull. RMRS-RB-10. 2010

33

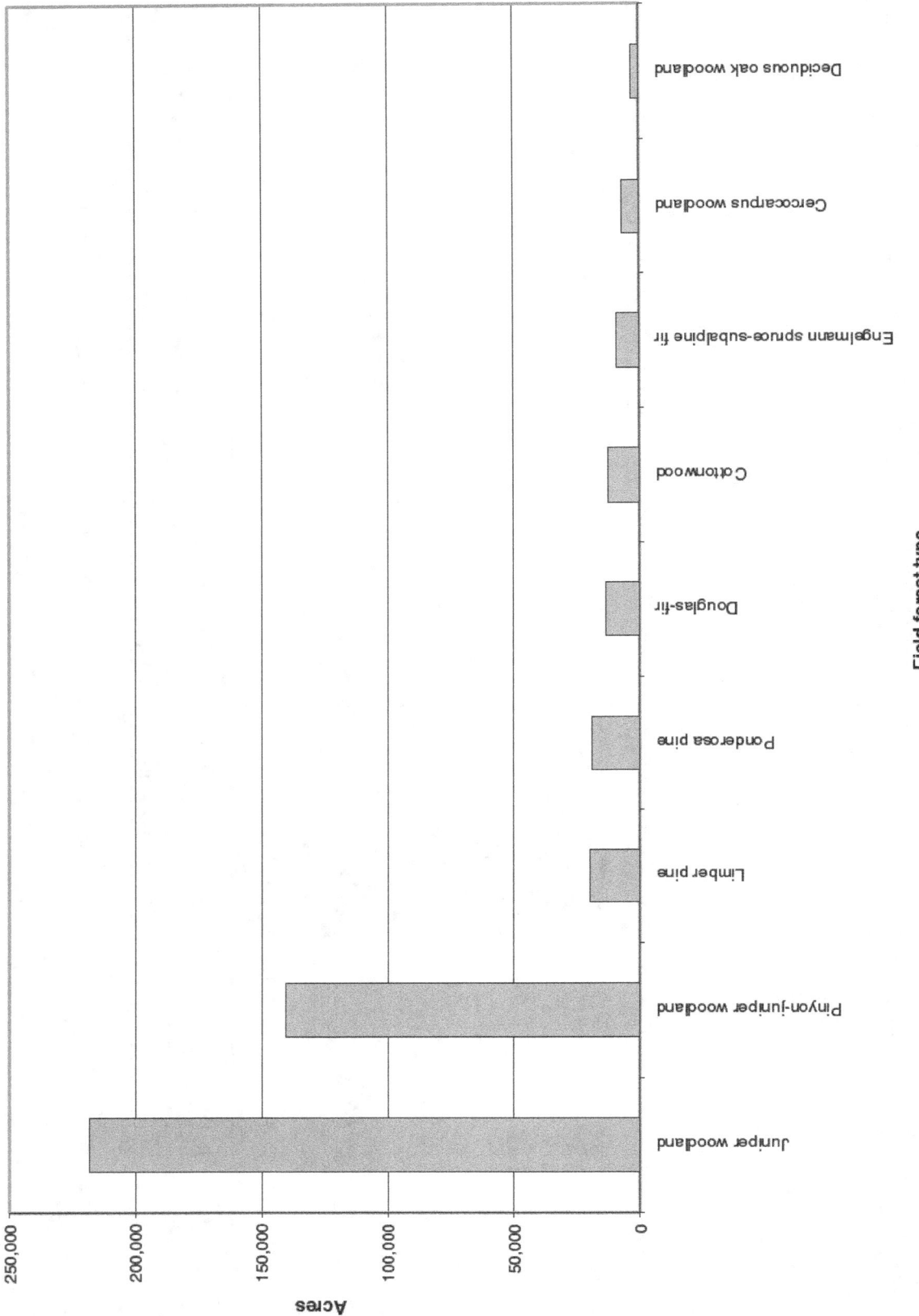

Figure 12—Acres of other wooded land by field forest type where calculated forest type is nonstocked, Utah, cycle 2, 2000-2005.

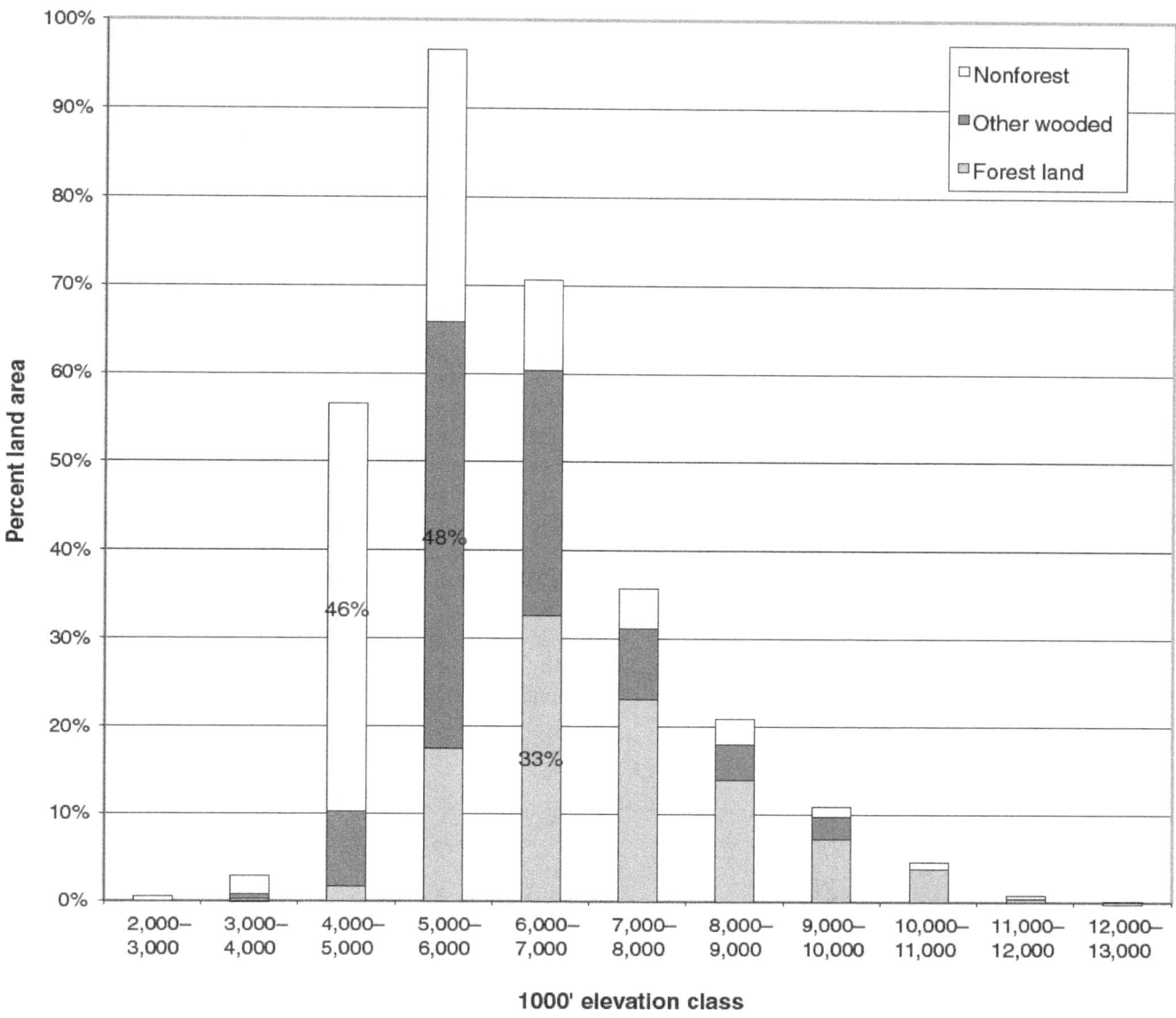

Figure 13—Percent of land area within each land type by 1,000-foot elevation class, Utah, cycle 2, 2000-2005.

could become a key area for future land type changes.

Three factors that influence FIA's forest and other wooded land definitions are currently described in the field by measuring three condition-level field variables as surrogates (see "Plot-filtering and the definition of forest and other wooded lands" in Appendix A). Any combination of these variables can be used to demonstrate why plots were called forest land or other wooded land. Nonforest plots that are not field visited are also similarly evaluated with remotely sensed imagery for land use and cover. Potentially, users could apply various thresholds of cover, disturbance, or regeneration on these land types to test the effects of changing definitions, from the densest of forest land to the most sparsely treed of other wooded and nonforest land. It should be noted that cover

USDA Forest Service Resour. Bull. RMRS-RB-10. 2010

35

estimates greater than approximately 20 percent using these variables are probably not as accurate. Figure 14 shows the area of other wooded land by cover (live), disturbance (live plus missing cover), and regeneration (seedlings per acre). Based on these variables, over 69 percent of other wooded land meets the definition due to live cover alone, almost 23 percent due to a combination of live cover and regeneration, about 3 percent due to regeneration alone, about 4 percent due to some level of past disturbance, and about 1 percent due to a combination of past disturbance and regeneration.

Discussion—Generally, forest type is calculated from trees sampled on the subplots. Due to the sparse nature of other wooded land, some condition-defining attributes like forest type and stand-size class are best described on the sample acre, rather than calculated from the tree tally. Field forest type and field stand-size class are assessed at the condition-level and account for anomalies between the tree tally and observations on the sample acre. Field crew assessments also take into account the effects of disturbance and regeneration. Since field forest type and stand-size class consider both past (disturbance) and present (regeneration) influences, perhaps these variables would be more useful for monitoring the expansion and contraction of other wooded lands over time, rather than a calculated forest type based on tally-tree stocking.

Other wooded land usually occurs on the edge between forest and nonforest, and has a narrow ecological niche but plays an important role in land type dynamics. Monitoring other wooded land should prove particularly useful for assessments of future trends and historical context related to fluctuations in forest area, particularly in pinyon and juniper types. Perhaps the best way to monitor these marginal lands accurately is by measures of cover. This requires a classification system that is efficient, accurate, standardized, and easily implemented on the ground. Cover-based definitions of other wooded land has

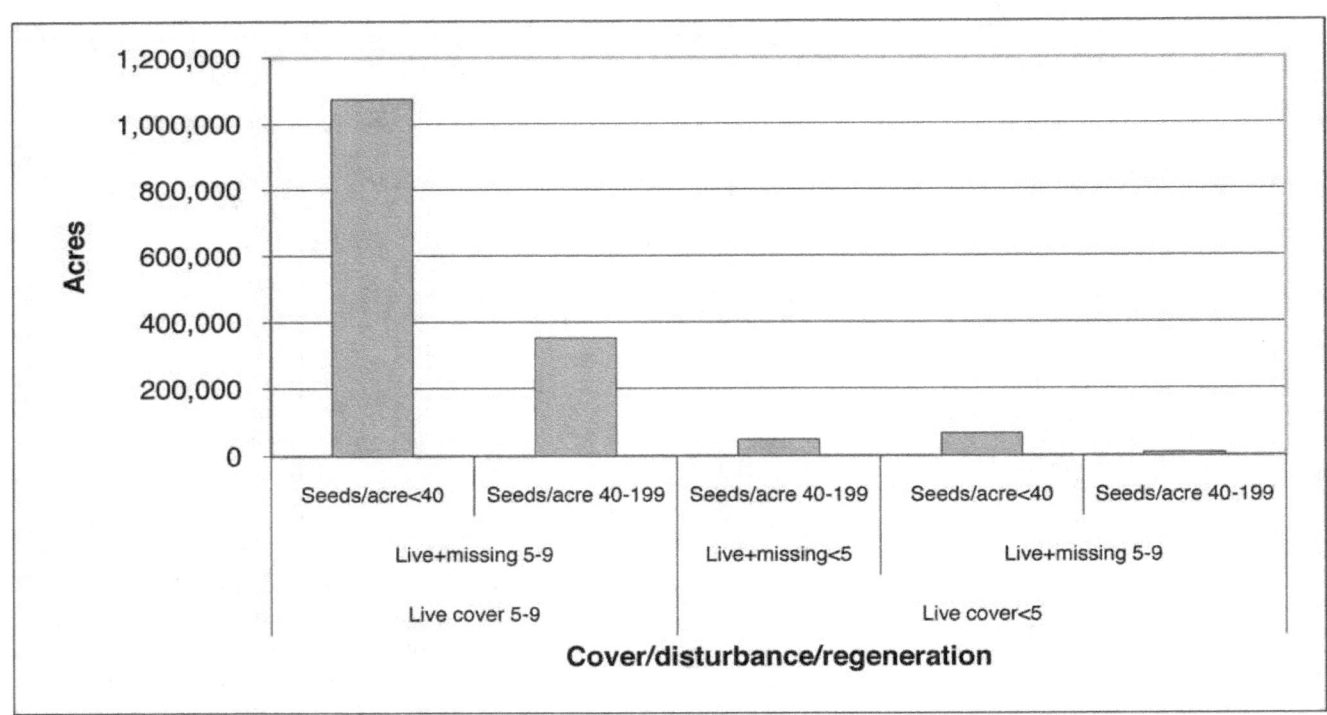

Figure 14—Area of other wooded land by live cover, disturbance, and regeneration, Utah, cycle 2, 2000-2005.

several advantages over stocking-based definitions: (1) direct measurement of complete tree crown cover is quick and accurate at low cover levels; (2) assessments of stocking on the subplot or sample acre are often cumbersome, for example, recording many stem measurements on woodland trees; (3) cover-based definitions are recognized internationally, while stocking-based definitions are mostly inherent to FIA; and (4) cover-based definitions are more directly related to remotely sensed imagery.

Aspen Mortality

Background—Aspen is the widest-ranging species in North America. It is present in all States in the Interior West and occupies a wide elevational range—from 2,000 ft in northern Idaho to 11,700 ft in Colorado. It is also found on a wide range of sites, and occurs in 26 of the forest types that occur in the Interior West. The species is intolerant of shade and relatively short-lived, which makes it prone to replacement by conifers through successional change. In the Interior West, it also reproduces infrequently by seeding, relying mostly on root sprouting for reproduction. However, aspen responds well to fire and cutting, and it is able to dominate heavily disturbed sites for many years following severe disturbance. In addition, there is some evidence that aspen is able to persist in conifer-dominated forests by exploiting gaps in the conifer canopy that are caused by insects, disease, windthrow, and other smaller-scale disturbances.

In recent years, there has been concern about the future of aspen on the landscape, primarily due to the characteristics of aspen and how they relate to changes in disturbance regimes. The earliest concerns were related to successional change in the Interior West where fire suppression has decreased disturbance rates and, as a result, decreased aspen regeneration rates. In addition, it has been shown that large populations of herbivores can inhibit aspen regeneration where it occurs spontaneously or after disturbance (e.g., Hessl and Graumlich 2002). The lack of disturbance allows conifers to gain dominance where they are present, and in pure aspen stands, consumption of regeneration by ungulates could lead to loss of senescing overstory trees without replacement. More recent concerns are related to a period of drought that has had an impact on aspen and other forest types (e.g., Shaw and others 2005; Thompson 2009). Drought appears to have contributed to mortality in many low-elevation stands (Worrall and others 2008), and in some of these regeneration is either lacking or suppressed by herbivores.

Johnson (1994) suggested that the acreage of aspen-dominated stands had declined as much as 46 percent in Arizona since the 1960s, with most of these acres becoming dominated by mixed conifer forest types. Kay (1997) and Bartos and Campbell (1998) suggested that similar changes had occurred in Utah. All of these assessments of "lost" aspen acres were based on the assumption that forested acres with a minority aspen component were, at one time in the recent past, dominated by aspen in pure, or nearly-pure stands. This assumption may not be reasonable because there are many situations where aspen may persist normally as a minor stand component.

Assessing changes in the aspen forests of Utah over time is possible because a periodic inventory of Utah was conducted by FIA in 1993 (O'Brien 1999). Although changes in methodology limit the ability to compare some aspects of the 1990s inventory with current data, many characteristics of aspen forests are possible to compare at the population scale.

Inventory Results—Current inventory data show that there are just over 1.64 million acres (table 2) of the aspen forest type in Utah, as compared to nearly 1.43 million acres found during the previous inventory in 1993 (O'Brien 1999). When considering all forest land where at least one live aspen 1.0-inches diameter or greater was sampled, the current inventory data shows just over 2.66 million acres, while the previous inven-

USDA Forest Service Resour. Bull. RMRS-RB-10. 2010

37

tory showed live aspen present on just over 2.57 million acres.

Statistics on live trees may overlook "relict" aspen stands, and both inventories show that some stands had only standing dead aspen present at the time of inventory. The 1993 periodic inventory showed that only standing dead aspen 1.0 inch diameter and greater were found on approximately 42 thousand acres, or about 1.7 percent of all acres with aspen present. The current inventory shows an apparent increase to nearly 132 thousand acres, or about 5.0 percent of all acres with aspen present.

The 1993 periodic inventory showed just over 925 million live aspen with diameter 1.0 inches and greater, while the current estimate is over 733 million trees. Although the total number of trees has apparently decreased, the net volume found in trees 5.0 inches diameter and greater has increased. The 1993 inventory found over 1.74 billion cubic feet of volume in live aspen 5.0 inches diameter and greater, giving an average volume per tree of nearly 5.2 cubic feet. The estimate of volume from the current data is over 1.95 billion cubic feet, or over 6.9 cubic feet per tree.

Gross volume growth of aspen at the time of the 1993 inventory was estimated to be over 49.5 million cubic feet per year, with annual mortality estimated to be nearly 17.9 million cubic feet; this resulted in net annual growth of nearly 31.7 million cubic feet. The gross volume growth estimate from current inventory data is very close to the 1993 estimate—49.6 million cubic feet per year—but annual mortality is somewhat lower at slightly more than 14.3 million cubic feet. As a result, current inventory data indicate somewhat higher net annual growth of just over 35.3 million cubic feet. When net growth is expressed as a percentage of live volume, the results of both inventories are the same—net growth is 1.8 percent of live volume.

Discussion—Comparisons between the 1993 periodic inventory results (O'Brien 1999) and the current data suggest that there has not been a detectable decline in the acreage of the aspen forest type or in the total number of acres with live aspen present. The estimates of acres having only standing dead aspen present appear to show that there has been a small increase in the area where there has been complete mortality of the aspen component, although the presence of seedling-sized aspen on many of these acres suggests that aspen is reproducing on most of them. Because the lack of successful reproduction in some aspen stands is an issue of concern, this situation warrants continued monitoring.

Comparisons of standing live volume, growth, and mortality likewise do not indicate any negative trends in the aspen resource. Although there are currently fewer trees than there were in 1993, the total standing volume is greater and, as a result, the mean volume per tree is greater. This is consistent with what would be expected from an aging population of trees. Aspen have a relatively short life expectancy as compared with many other tree species, so with a mean stand age of approximately 85 years, and a large proportion of stands in the 80- to 100-year age class (fig. 15), it is clearly an aging population. Because the rate of disturbance is relatively low, resulting in few regenerating stands, the existing trees are getting larger and fewer. However, the population is relatively stable in the sense that it is able to maintain, and even increase, its live volume over time. Even though some areas have suffered substantial mortality related to drought, the quantity of drought-affected acres has not been high enough to make a large change in population-scale trends.

There have been many studies that have shown aspen to be in decline at local scales (e.g., Bartos and Campbell 1998; Di Orio and others 2005; Worrall and others 2008), while other analyses have shown increased dominance of aspen in some landscapes (Kulakowski and others 2004). It is not surprising that studies documenting loss are more numerous, because unexplained or unexpectedly high mortality events tend to attract the attention of managers, researchers, and the public. Because these changes are

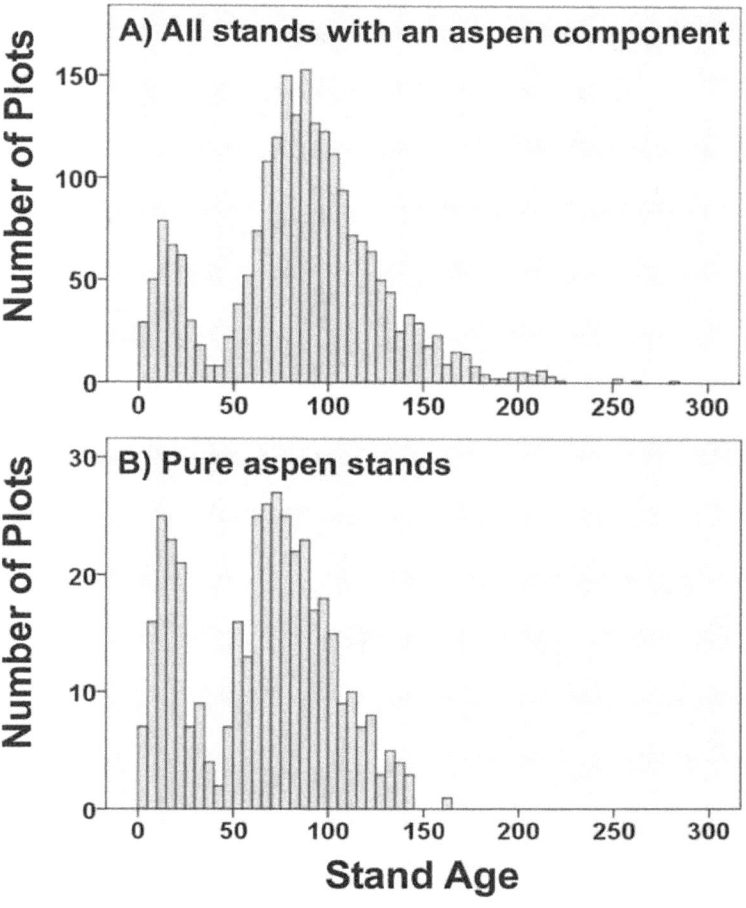

Figure 15—Stand age class distributions for (A) all stands in the Interior West with an aspen component, and (B) pure aspen stands (95 percent or more aspen by basal area), cycle 2, 2000-2005. Mean age of all stands with aspen is 84.8 years (stdev. 42.3) and mean age of pure aspen stands is 64.6 years (stdev. 35.9 years).

obvious to a wide range of observers, there is a tendency to extrapolate local conditions to larger areas. However, the current FIA inventory data show that in recent years aspen has both gained and lost dominance at the stand level (fig. 16), resulting in little net change for the species by most measures. This suggests that factors other than succession and drought-related mortality are affecting the aspen resource; fire affects all species and forest insects have had substantial impacts on conifer species. These widespread changes will be followed as monitoring of FIA plots continues.

Expansion of Pinyon and Juniper Woodlands

Background—The pinyon-juniper forest type group in Utah consists of three forest types: pinyon-juniper woodland, juniper woodland, and Rocky Mountain juniper. It is by far the most common group in Utah, covering 10.2 million acres, or 57 percent of the forest land (Appendix E, tables 3-7). The pinyon-juniper group also dominates Utah's other wooded lands, covering over one million acres, or 68 percent of the other wooded land ("Area" in Section IV; table 2). In addition, 78 percent of the nonstocked area,

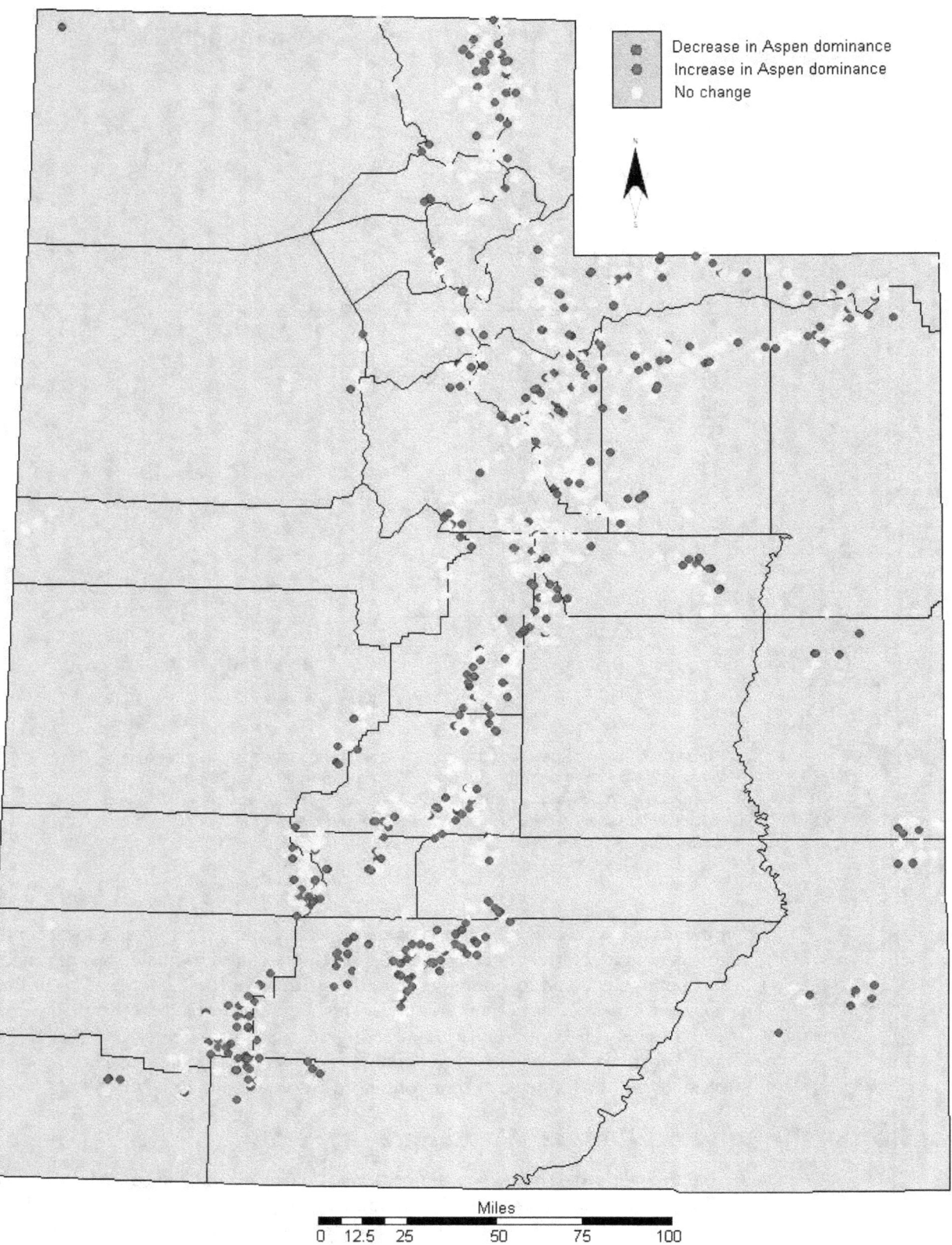

Figure 16—Map of annual FIA plots in Utah with aspen present, showing change in the aspen component based on recent mortality, cycle 2, 2000-2005. Red symbols represent plots where aspen has decreased in dominance, green represents plots where aspen has increased, and yellow indicates no change.

both forest and other wooded lands, were identified by field crews as formerly and/or potentially stocked by pinyon-juniper group forest types. In total, over 12 million acres are either now, were recently, or will soon be pinyon-juniper forest type group, or 62 percent of the forest and other wooded land combined. The dominant species are Utah juniper, Rocky Mountain juniper, common or two-needle pinyon, and singleleaf pinyon.

There has been concern that, since Euro-American settlement of the West, pinyons and junipers have been expanding their ranges dramatically, encroaching on and degrading grasslands and shrublands. This expansion has been well documented in many parts of the pinyon-juniper range (Burkhardt and Tisdale 1976; Tausch and Hood 2007). Generally, expansion has been attributed to direct or indirect alterations of pre-settlement fire regimes. These fire regimes are theorized to be of three general types (Baker and Shinneman 2004; Romme and others 2009):

1. **Low intensity, frequent fires that tend to "thin from below."** These would occur in pinyon-juniper stands where the understory is dominated by grasses and forbs, and the tree density should be comparatively low. This type is most common in the extreme southwestern United States and northern Mexico. It should be rare to non-existent in Utah.

2. **Less frequent, high intensity stand replacing fires**. This regime occurs in pinyon-juniper stands where the understory is dominated by shrubs, notably sagebrush. This type is common in the Great Basin, and would be expected in parts of Utah.

3. **Very rare, mostly localized fires that occur under only the most extreme conditions, and that may only burn small areas**. These are pinyon-juniper stands with rocky substrates or cryptobiotic crusts, that support little, if any, understory. The topography is often rugged with features such as cliffs and bare bedrock, which prevent or inhibit the spread of fires. This type is documented on the Colorado Plateau (Romme and others 2003), so it would be expected in southeastern Utah.

Inventory data were used to evaluate the age, structure, and potential status of pinyon-juniper stands. The age chosen to represent pre-settlement stands was 150 years. The first estimate was stand age, but since this is based on the age of the trees in the dominant size class rather than the oldest trees in the stand, the maximum ages were also evaluated, along with the proportion of trees over 150 years old. Since tree and stand ages are determined from a few live trees on a plot, the presence of very large dead trees (14.5 inches diameter) and dead basal branches (12.4 inches diameter) were evaluated as evidence that the stand was in existence at least 150 years ago. More recently disturbed stands with few or no live trees were classified as disturbed. Understory cover and layering, along with tree cover were evaluated to characterize fire regimes (Scott and Burgan 2005) and estimate fine fuel loading (Caratti 2006).

Inventory Results—About 2.4 percent of the pinyon and juniper dominated land in Utah has been recently disturbed. Of the remaining, about 62 percent (7.3 million acres) was classified as older than 150 years. The remaining 38 percent (4.4 million acres) was characterized as having established within the last 150 years. The younger stands tended to be more prevalent in the northern and western parts of the State, while the older stands occurred more frequently in the southeastern part of the State (fig. 17).

In terms of fire regime and fuel loading, a larger proportion of the older stands were found to have very low fuel loadings, indicating a low probability of severe fire. Sixty-one percent of older stands had very low fuel loadings, while 45 percent of younger stands did. A higher percentage of younger stands had understories dominated by shrubs or shrub-grass mixtures (22 percent) than did older stands (12 percent). Less than 0.5 percent of stands of any age had grass-dominated understories.

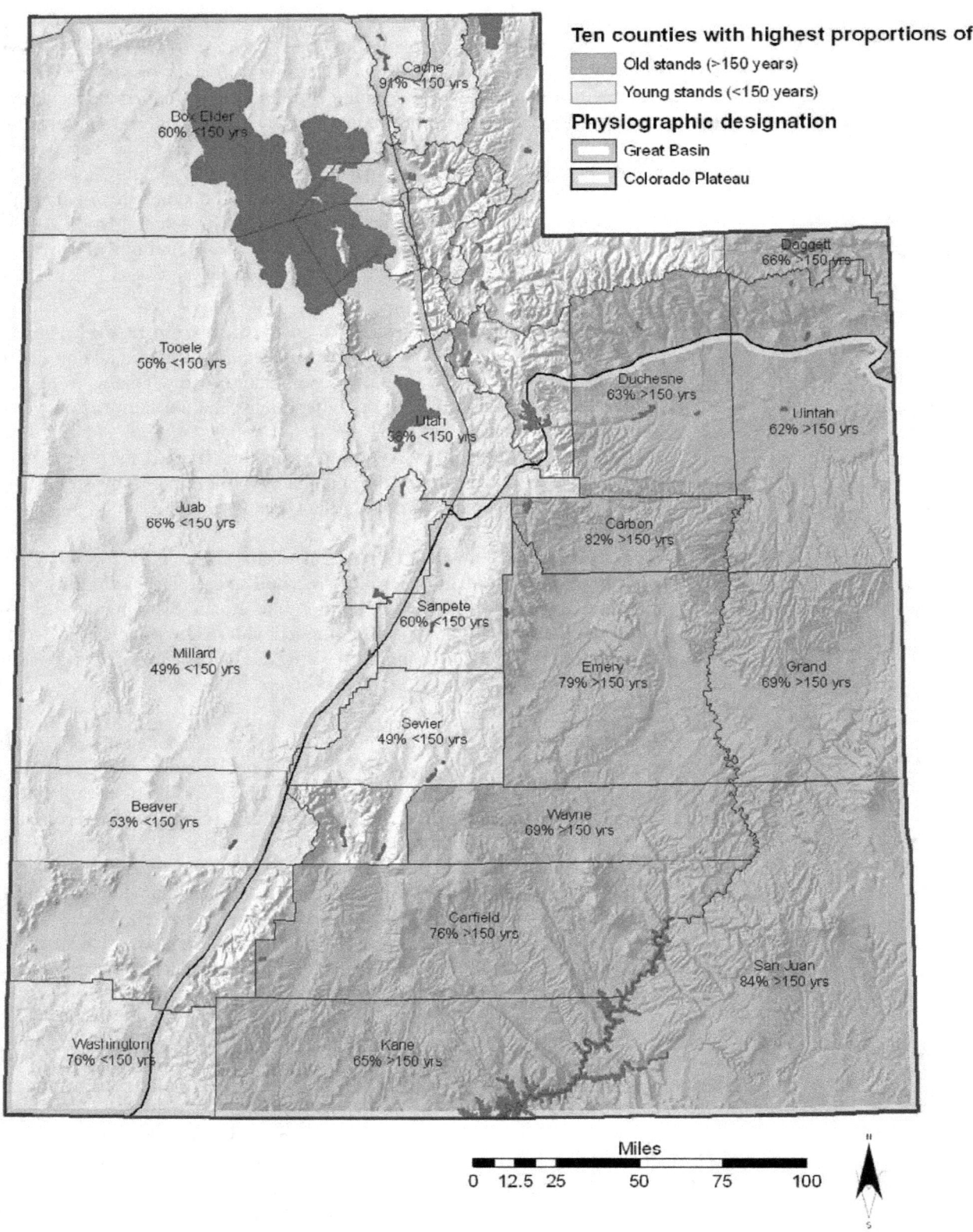

Figure 17—Counties with the ten highest proportions of young and old pinyon and/or juniper stands, showing percentages over or under 150 years, Utah, cycle 2, 2000-2005. Note: Physiographic boundary of the Great Basin is slightly different than the hydrologic boundary.

Discussion—Ten Utah counties with the highest proportions of pinyon and juniper dominated stands older than 150 years (fig. 17) are all in the area of the Colorado Plateau in the southeastern part of the State. This distribution, combined with the finding that a greater proportion of older stands than younger stands have very sparse understories, supports the expectation that the third fire regime—characterized by very rare, localized fires—is operating in this area. This situation results in most pinyon-juniper stands having existed in similar densities, structures, and age classes as they have been found for hundreds, if not thousands, of years (Romme and others 2003).

On the other hand, the ten Utah counties with the highest proportions of pinyon and juniper dominated stands younger than 150 years are all in the Great Basin in the western and northern part of the State (fig. 17). The common occurrence of younger stands, along with younger stands having more shrub dominated understories than older stands, tends to support the expectation that this part of the State is dominated by the second fire regime. In this situation, pinyon and juniper populations are maintained by relatively small areas with fire-resistant properties, similar to those in the third fire regime (Weisberg and others 2008). When conditions favor tree growth, pinyons and junipers expand from these refugia into mostly shrub-dominated areas, where eventually they experience high intensity stand replacing fires that halt tree expansion. If the fire frequency is artificially lengthened, trees can increase uninterrupted, displacing shrublands. In the Great Basin, this process is well documented (Tausch and Hood 2007), with many, if not most, pinyon and juniper landscapes younger than the advent of European-American settlement (Miller and others 2008). Evidence of high intensity fire regimes is also supported by the distribution of disturbed stands: 71 percent of them occur in the ten counties with the highest proportions of young stands, especially Juab and Millard counties. Some younger pinyon-juniper stands probably represent recovery from severe human-caused disturbances, such as early chaining or harvest for charcoal to support the mining and railroad industries (Romme and others 2009).

Drought-Related Effects on Pinyon-Juniper Woodlands

Background—Collectively, pinyon-juniper and juniper woodlands make up the most common forest type in the American Southwest and covers over 54.4 million acres in the western United States (Smith and others 2009), extending well into Mexico. In Utah, these types account for approximately 11.3 million acres of forest land and other wooded land, or nearly 58 percent of the area with 5 percent or more cover in trees. The pinyon-juniper type is defined by the presence of one or more pinyon species—usually common or singleleaf pinyon—and one or more juniper species; pure stands of pinyon are not considered a separate type by the FIA program. Juniper types are dominated by various juniper species, but other species, exclusive of pinions, may be present as a minor component. In this section, and to most laypersons and many managers, the term pinyon-juniper woodland (or P-J, for short) includes all lands dominated by pinyons, junipers, or both. Note that the results for individual years discussed below are based on IWFIA's definition of mortality (see "Growth and Mortality" in Section IV) for the panel of plots measured in that year.

The IWFIA program operates in Arizona, Colorado, Idaho, Montana, Nevada, New Mexico, Utah, and Wyoming; these States include most of the range of the pinyon-juniper type in the United States. Annual inventory was implemented in Utah in 2000. At about that time, forest managers and researchers began to notice an increase in the incidence of insects and disease in several forest types, including pinyon-juniper. At that time, drought was beginning to move across much of the Southwest, including Utah (fig. 18). As the drought progressed, tree mortality appeared to be increasing and there was increasing interest in using FIA data to quantify the effects of drought, insects, and disease on pinyon-juniper woodlands.

USDA Forest Service Resour. Bull. RMRS-RB-10. 2010

43

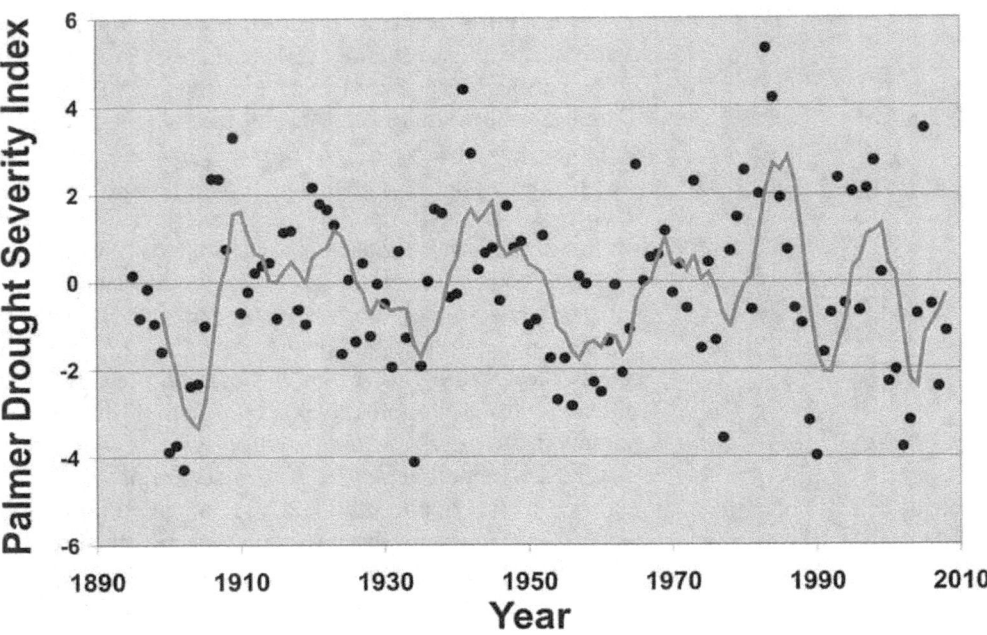

Figure 18—Palmer drought severity index (PDSI) for Utah, 1895-2008. Positive values indicate relatively moist conditions and negative values indicate drought. Points are average for all climate divisions in Utah (National Climatic Data Center 1994) and red line is the 5-year moving average.

Because the FIA sample is unbiased with respect to plot location and covers a wide area and extended time period, it provides a unique view of pinyon-juniper woodlands. The systematic sample reduces the likelihood of producing erroneous conclusions that may come from surveys conducted only in known areas of mortality. Therefore, this drought-related mortality episode provided an opportunity to test the utility of the FIA annual inventory system for quantifying rapid change in pinyon-juniper woodlands over a large geographic area (Shaw 2006).

Inventory Results—Since 2000 there has been a substantial upward trend in mortality for pinyon species in Utah (fig. 19A). In 2000 and 2001, when mortality was at "background" rates and most pinyon mortality was due to fire, annual mortality was only about 7 and 17 percent of annual gross growth, respectively. This resulted in a net annual increase in volume of just over 0.8 percent. Starting in 2003, annual mortality started to exceed gross growth. In 2005, about 8 percent of the pinyon volume that was live in 2000 had died from all causes combined, and mortality was over 159 percent of gross growth. As a result, there was a net annual decrease of just under 0.6 percent of live volume. Although there is currently a negative trend in net growth, for the period 2000 to 2005 there was still a net increase (0.17 percent) in pinyon volume overall.

Juniper species have shown to be much more resistant to drought-related mortality than pinyon species. From 2000 to 2005, the mortality rate of juniper species in Utah has been steady to slightly declining over time (fig. 19B). Compared to pinyon species, the annual mortality of juniper species is typically a higher percentage of gross growth—about 43 percent on average. Slightly more than 1 percent of juniper species volume has been lost to mortality, and net volume growth has been a relatively slow, but steady 0.34 percent per year. Most juniper mortality is attributable to fire rather than drought, insects and disease. As a result, the mortality of junipers has not shown the sharply upward trend that has been seen in pinyon species during the drought years.

44

USDA Forest Service Resour. Bull. RMRS-RB-10. 2010

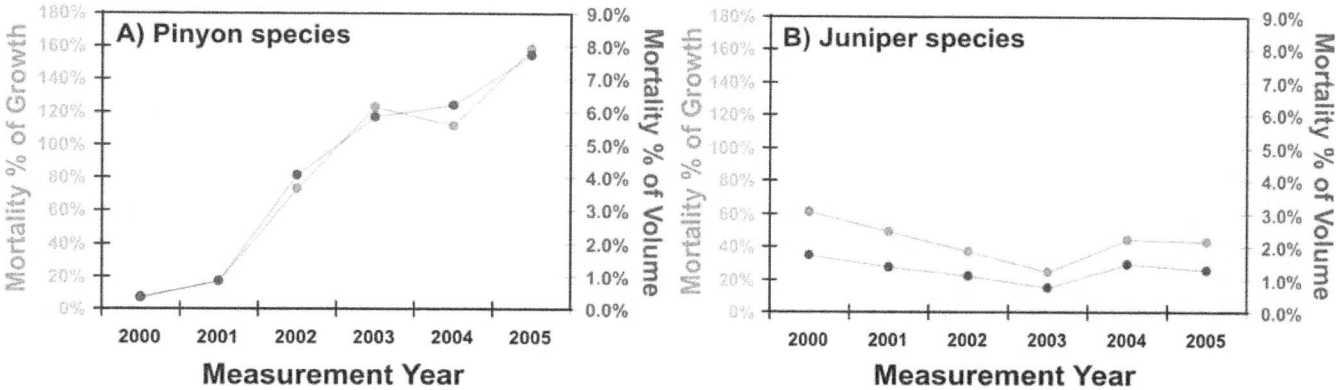

Figure 19—Mortality trends for (A) pinyon and(B) juniper species in Utah, cycle 2, 2000-2005. Left axis on each panel represents annual mortality as a percentage of annual growth on a volume basis. For values greater than 100 percent, mortality exceeds growth. The right axis on each panel represents recent mortality as a percentage of live volume.

Discussion—The dramatic visual effect of drought-related mortality of pinyon species—dying trees with reddened foliage covering entire landscapes—brought much public and media attention to the event. Because there were typically local "hot spots" of mortality that were surrounded by large areas of relatively low mortality, it was difficult to obtain unbiased, quantitative estimates of the true extent of mortality. In some cases, mortality estimates were extrapolated from local sites to entire States. For example, one account reported that 90 percent of the pinyon trees in Arizona had been killed (Society of American Foresters 2004). However, a preliminary analysis of the available data in Arizona, Colorado, and Utah (Shaw and others 2005) showed that while there was clearly an upward trend in pinyon mortality, population-level mortality was not nearly as high as initially feared. Today it appears that mortality remains above the background rate that would be expected for pinyon species during "normal" times, but the year-to-year increase in mortality appears to be occurring at a decreasing rate.

One persistent question about the current episode of drought-related mortality is: "How does the current episode compare with previous drought-related die-offs?" The climatic record shows that similar droughts occurred in the Southwest during the early 1900s and mid-1950s (National Climatic Data Center 1994). Breshears and others (2005) characterized the recent mortality event as response to "global-change-type drought," and suggested that recent conditions have been hotter than in the 1950s. Some of the conclusions about the relative magnitude of mortality in the 1950s are based on the lack of evidence of widespread mortality in the form of remaining dead woody material from the 1950s. However, despite the perceived long-term persistence of woody material in the arid Southwest, pinyons may decay or physically break down relatively quickly. Although Kearns and others (2005) found that pinyon snags could persist as long as 25 years, it only took an average of 16.2 years for dead trees to become extremely fragmented. Because the impacts of the 1950s drought were not well studied and there is a great deal of uncertainty surrounding the possible surviving evidence of pinyon mortality, the relative magnitude of the two mortality episodes remains uncertain.

The recent drought has undoubtedly impacted the pinyon-juniper resource in Utah, but the magnitude of impact varies widely between the pinyon and juniper components. Differential mortality among species on the same site has been shown by Mueller and others (2005), who found mortality of common pinyon to be 6.5 times higher than

USDA Forest Service Resour. Bull. RMRS-RB-10. 2010

45

oneseed juniper mortality during two drought events in northern Arizona. Collectively, pinyon-juniper woodlands in Utah have maintained positive net growth—about 2.3 percent of live volume–in the face of serious drought conditions. This suggests that as relief from drought conditions occurs, as it appears to have done in recent years (fig. 18), the live volume may begin to recover at an increasing rate. The dynamics of this forest type have important implications for carbon storage, because dead trees have released growing space to the survivors and new regeneration. Although there has been a short-term loss in living biomass, there may be a long-term increase in carbon storage while dead wood persist and new growth accumulates. It will be possible to determine the actual trends as FIA continues to monitor these woodlands into the future.

Spruce Beetle Mortality

Background—Engelmann spruce forests are widespread in Utah, occurring at higher elevations. In Utah, most stands with an Engelmann spruce component occur between 8,000 and 11,200 ft elevation, with a mean of about 9,800 ft. Engelmann spruce forests are commonly multi-aged, exhibiting a wide range of tree sizes (Aplet and others 1988). Many other species co-occur with spruce; its most common associates are subalpine fir, Douglas-fir, aspen, limber pine, whitebark pine, and lodgepole pine. Subalpine fir is unique among the associates because it is the only one that is commonly co-dominant with spruce—spruce and fir frequently account for large, nearly equal proportions of total stand basal area. Both low- and high-severity disturbances influence the structure and composition of Engelmann spruce forests (Veblen and others 1994). Windthrow, root and butt rots, and endemic spruce beetle (*Dendoctronus rufipennis*) all act locally to create canopy gaps in spruce forests, and contribute to the development of structural diversity. In contrast, crown fires, wind storms, and spruce beetle outbreaks, while infrequent, are high-severity disturbances that occur at much larger scales. These disturbances have the potential to decrease the diversity of classes and structure at stand to landscape scales.

The spruce beetle is a host-specific bark beetle native to Engelmann spruce forests across the Intermountain West (Holsten and others 1999). Endemic populations of the beetle can build to epidemic (outbreak) levels in recently downed material such as logging slash, wind throw, or avalanche debris (Schmid 1981). Transition from endemic to epidemic population levels can be facilitated by warmer-than-average summer temperatures (Hansen and others 2001). It is commonly thought that composition and structure of Engelmann spruce-dominated stands influence the potential for spruce beetle activity. For example, a commonly used stand-level spruce beetle risk-rating (Schmid and Frye 1976) suggests dense (high basal area), pure (greater than 65 percent Engelmann spruce), old (large diameter) stands on well-drained creek bottoms (high site productivity potential) are most likely to be attacked by the spruce beetle. The Schmid and Frye (1976) risk-rating, in effect, quantifies the view that compositionally and structurally diverse stands have less potential for spruce beetle activity, including the shift from endemic to epidemic population-levels.

Beginning in the late 1980s, spruce beetle activity began to increase in several parts of Utah. Epidemic population levels were reached in some areas, particularly the Wasatch (Dymerski and others 2001) and Markagunt Plateaus, by the late 1990s. For example, mortality of overstory spruce was over 90 percent on the Manti-LaSal National Forest in just a few years (Dymerski and others 2001) and 95 percent of overstory and understory spruce were killed on the Markagunt Plateau (Dixie National Forest) during the late 1990s (DeRose and Long 2007; fig. 20). Some successful beetle suppression was conducted on the Wasatch-Cache National Forest (Bentz and Munson 2000), but beetle-induced mortality has gone unchecked in most of Utah for the past 10 years. Although the spruce beetle is a natural part of Engelmann spruce forest disturbance, the regionally

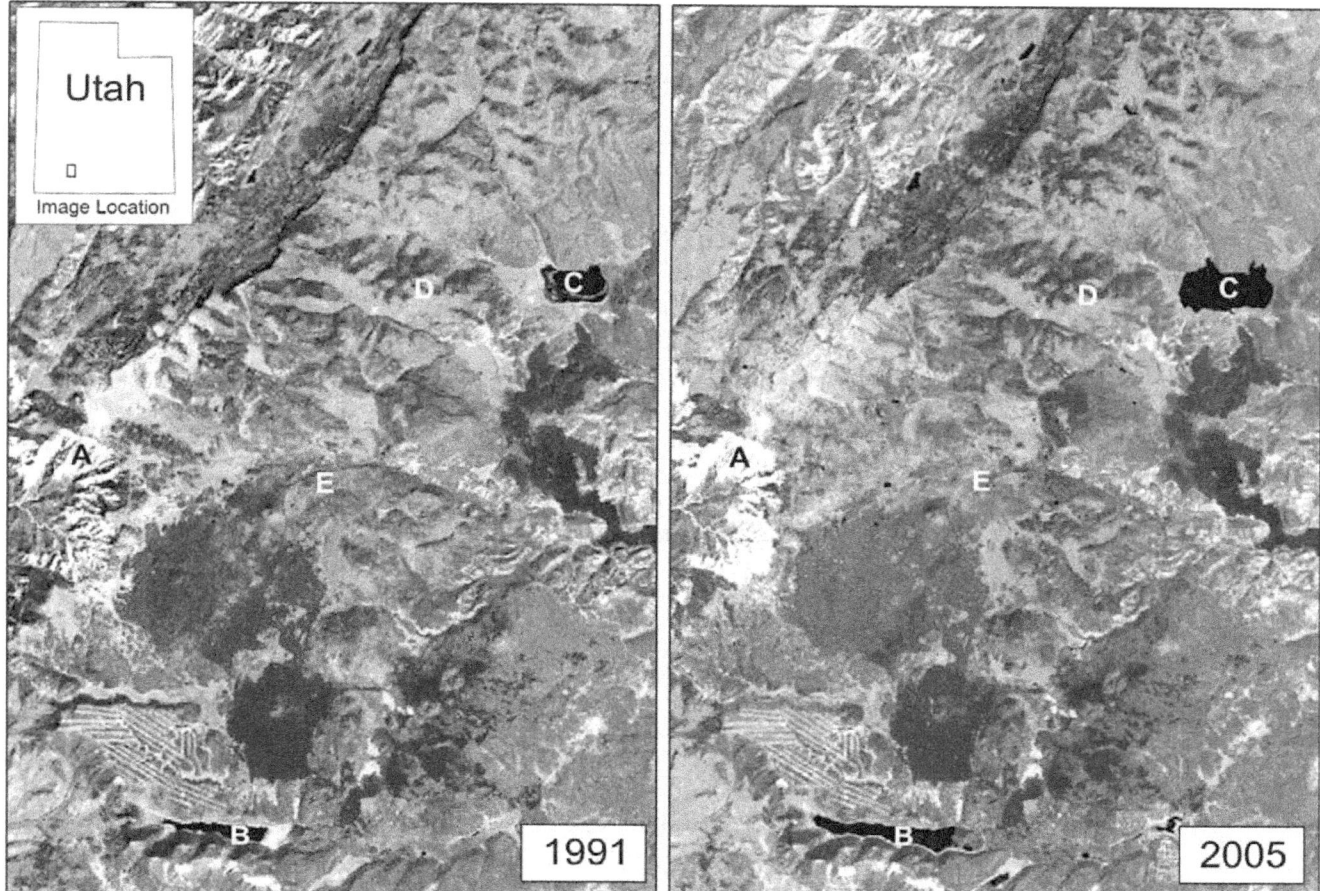

Figure 20—Comparison of Landsat images from 1991 and 2005 showing expansion of spruce beetle infestation. Reference points are (A) Cedar Breaks National Monument, (B) Navajo Lake, and (C) Panguitch Lake. Vegetated areas appear in shades of green, with the darkest greens indicating conifer forest. Dark purple-magenta areas, such as north of Navajo Lake and south of Panguitch Lake are unvegetated lava flows. Pink-violet areas, such as the area north of Panguitch Lake are low vegetation (typically sagebrush). Areas of spruce beetle mortality are those that appear dark green in 1991 and appear pink to dark magenta in 2005 (e.g., areas D and E). The shift in color is due to mortality of the overstory and increased exposure of understory vegetation or soil.

high levels of mortality suggest that the recent outbreaks may be unprecedented in Utah (DeRose and Long 2007; Dymerski and others 2001). However, localized surveys and studies cannot quantify the statewide impact to the spruce resource. Because surveys conducted by FIA are systematic and geographically unbiased, they have the potential to quantify changes to the spruce resource over time and space.

Inventory Results—FIA's periodic statewide inventory of Utah in 1993 (O'Brien 1999) serves, for the most part, as baseline data since it generally preceded the majority of spruce beetle epidemic. The current, annual inventory began late in the epidemic period (2000) and, therefore, captured mostly the post-beetle forest conditions. However, because the annual inventory protocol includes trees killed during the 5 years prior to the plot visit as "recent" mortality, annual data effectively capture much of the mortality that occurred during peak mortality years. Although there have been changes in plot design and some definitions between the periodic and annual inventories, we are able to use the most comparable figures from both inventories to assess change to the Engelmann spruce resource over the past 10 to 15 years.

O'Brien (1999) reported that there were 452,567 acres of the Engelmann spruce forest type and 735,851 acres of the Engelmann spruce-subalpine fir forest type in Utah, for a total estimate of 1,188,418 acres. With the implementation of the annual inventory, the forest type algorithm was changed such that these two forest types were split into three types—Engelmann spruce, Engelmann spruce-subalpine fir, and subalpine fir—with the separations between types dependent on the relative abundance of spruce and fir. Under the new forest type classification, annual inventory data show 491,425 acres of Engelmann spruce, 397,054 acres of subalpine fir, and 172,942 acres of Engelmann spruce-subalpine fir, for a total of 1,061,421 acres (table 2). This change in area is consistent with the compositional changes that have been documented in spruce-dominated stands affected by spruce beetle; many stands shift to dominance of subalpine fir (thereby remaining in the Engelmann spruce-subalpine fir type group), and others shift to dominance of other common associates (DeRose and Long 2007; DeRose and others 2008).

The live volume of Engelmann spruce also appears to have decreased. O'Brien (1999) reported approximately 1.711 billion cubic feet of volume in all live Engelmann spruce in Utah, while the current estimate is 1.594 billion cubic feet (fig. 5). In the last decades of the 20th century, removals and mortality were typically lower than growth, so the expectation would have been for total live volume to increase. The loss of live volume can be explained by looking at the estimated rates of volume change during each inventory period. O'Brien (1999) reported average annual gross growth of Engelmann spruce at approximately 26.5 million cubic feet. For the same time period, average annual mortality was estimated to be 12.6 million cubic feet, giving a net annual growth of approximately 13.9 million cubic feet. The current estimate of average annual gross growth is approximately 24.3 million cubic feet. However, average annual mortality is estimated to be 39.4 million cubic feet, over three times the mortality reported in the previous inventory. This results in a negative net annual growth of approximately 15.1 million cubic feet.

Discussion—The widespread mortality observed in Engelmann spruce forests will affect stand structure and dynamics for many years to come. In some stands the presence of a small residual spruce component, which is commonly made up of trees smaller than 2.0 inches d.b.h., means that spruce will remain a minor component until the residual trees reach reproductive maturity and suitable conditions for reproduction occur. In some parts of Utah, spruce reproduction is a rare event, which may further delay spruce dominance (DeRose and Long 2007).

DeRose and Long (2007) hypothesized that stands in the areas that experience the highest mortality may have been regenerated by a similar mortality event in the past, thereby setting up a cycle in which large areas of forest become susceptible to spruce beetle at about the same time. However, their investigation revealed that stands that recently experienced mortality were regenerated through a series of events that were separated in time. As a result, the recent mortality event appears to have created a situation where future spruce forests in Utah may be less structurally diverse than in the past. In the near term, though, forest structure and composition may be more diverse because stands formerly dominated by spruce will be dominated by one or more spruce associates.

Indicators of risk, such as stand composition and structure, and various site attributes were found to be marginally useful predictors of spruce beetle activity at the stand level (DeRose and others 2008). It is commonly difficult to associate particular stand conditions with risks to insect attack, because epidemic populations may build in high-risk stands and later overwhelm stands with conditions that would not ordinarily allow populations to expand. This "contagion" phenomenon tends to mask the conditions in which population expansion occurred. FIA data showed that mortality occurred across the entire range of Engelmann spruce in the Intermountain West, separated by distances that rule out a fire-like contagion spread of mortality. This suggests that other factors, such as widespread weather and climate patterns, have been as important or more important factors leading to mortality than stand and site attributes. Climate and weather are known to affect bark beetle populations (Hansen and others 2001; Logan and Bentz 1999), so the widespread mortality was likely a result of tree stress induced by heat and drought, as well as favorable conditions for the spruce beetle.

One question that commonly occurs after large mortality events is "What will be the effect on fire behavior?" Using simulation methods, DeRose and Long (2009) found that projected fire behavior in post-outbreak conditions is affected by pre-outbreak stand composition and structure and spruce beetle impacts. In stands with lower spruce composition, the spruce beetle did not change canopy structure sufficiently to alter the potential for crown fire. In stands sites with high spruce composition spruce beetle activity substantially reduced canopy fuel and, therefore, subsequent crowning potential for at least several decades. They concluded that extreme fire behavior is not an inevitable consequence of spruce beetle outbreaks. Although canopy fuels have been reduced in these stands, there has been a considerable increase in the amount of fuel on the forest floor. As this fuel load changes over time, FIA will continue to monitor its quantity and characteristics.

Although the spruce beetle has made a substantial impact on the Engelmann spruce resource in Utah, the vast majority of spruce-dominated stands and stands with a spruce component remain relatively unaffected. Whether these stands remain unaffected or continue the trend of mortality remains to be seen through continuous inventory. The long-term outlook will depend on composition and structure of the remaining stands, weather and climate conditions, and spruce beetle population trends.

Old Forest

Background—One goal of managing for ecological sustainability is to maintain diverse ecosystems that are composed of both biological and physical components. The structure and function of these components are important for ecosystem health, diversity, productivity, and resiliency following disturbances. Diversity of forest vegetation both in terms of composition and structure is of primary concern. In 1996, the Forest Service Intermountain Region assigned a team to establish a process, including criteria and indicators, that would allow identification of areas not currently in a properly functioning condition (USDA Forest Service 1996).

Properly functioning conditions were defined as conditions that are "dynamic and resilient to perturbations to structure, composition, and processes of their biological or physical components." Structure is a means to express the balance of age and size classes related to vegetation types. In order to sustain a forest type in the long term it is necessary to define a balance of size/age classes that will ensure adequate recruitment of size/age classes over the long term. For some of Utah's conifer types, a suggested approximate range of classes includes 10 percent Grass/Forb; 10 percent Seedling/Sapling; 20 percent Young Forest; 20 percent Mid Aged Forest; 20 percent Mature Forest; and 20 percent Old Forest (Williams 2009). These percentages are estimates or approximations and are not presented as absolute values but are suggested general proportions. The basis for using these vegetative structural stages is the work of Reynolds and others (1992). The relative amount of old forest in particular is often of interest to many land managers. Previous studies of old forest in Utah have used a stand age of 150 years or greater as a surrogate for mature stand structure (USDA Forest Service 2005). For this analysis, tree or stand age of 150 years or greater was used for identifying old forests.

Inventory Results—Although this analysis focuses on the timber types of Utah, figure 21 displays the total area of forest land in Utah for all timber, woodland, and nonstocked forest types by two stand age classes. This shows that woodland types have a much higher relative amount (38 percent) of stands 150 years and greater than timber types (16 percent). This makes sense since woodland types are comprised of species that are generally longer-lived. See "Expansion of Pinyon and Juniper Woodlands" in Section V for a similar stand age analysis of pinyon and juniper woodlands.

Figure 22 shows the 4.6 million acres of forest land timber types in Utah by forest type. Fifty-one percent (250 thousand acres) of the acreage in the Engelmann spruce type are 150 years and greater based on stand age, followed by white fir at 34 percent (122 thousand acres), ponderosa pine at 26 percent (99 thousand acres), lodgepole pine at 21 percent (82 thousand acres), and aspen at almost none. Although only four plots were sampled, the foxtail/bristlecone forest type had the largest percentage (100 percent) of 150 year and greater stands based on stand age.

Stand age is generally calculated as the mean age of trees from the stand-size class that has the plurality of stocking. This tends to diminish the significance of older trees by averaging tree ages of both old and young trees. Another method of using FIA data for describing stand structure is by calculating the number of trees per acre that are at

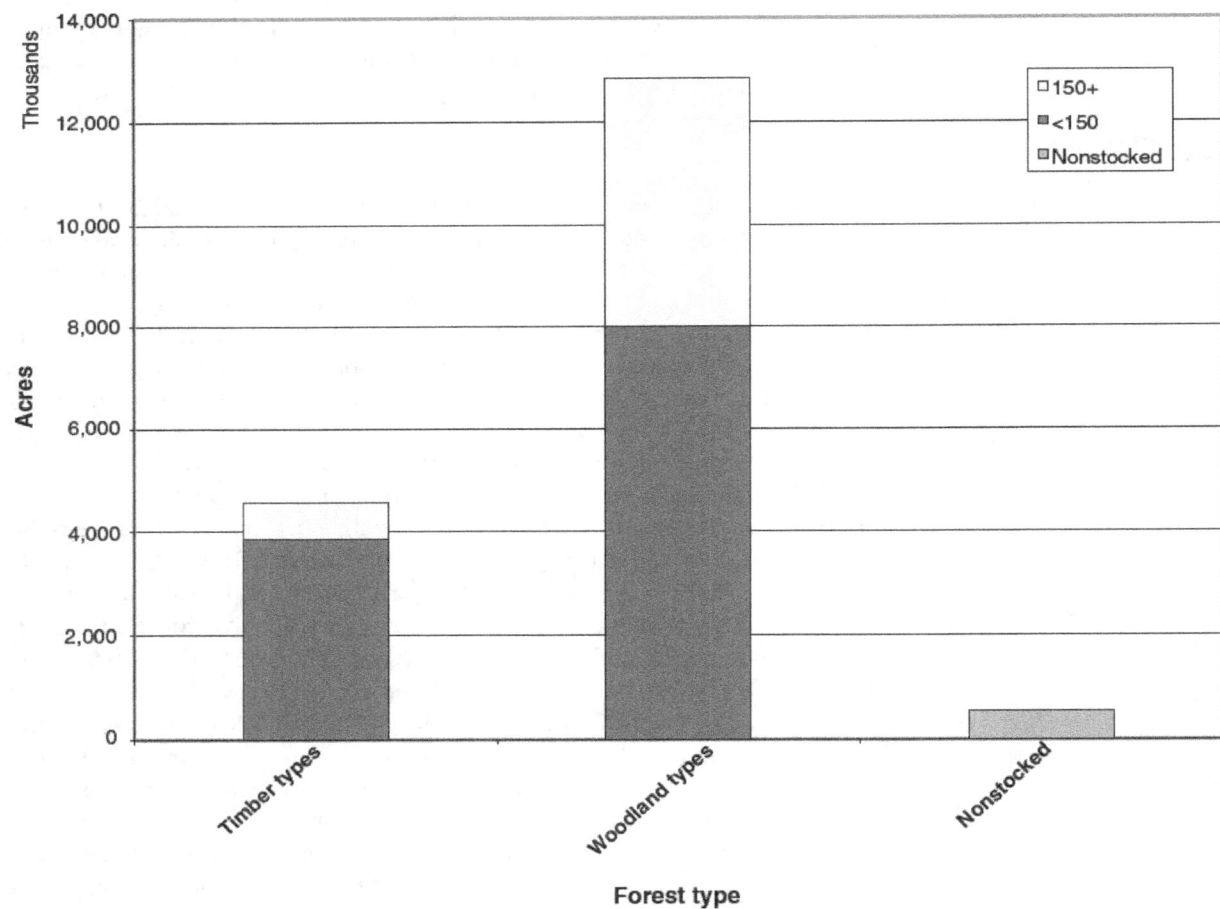

Figure 21—Total area of forest land for timber, woodland, and nonstocked forest types by stand age class, Utah, cycle 2, 2000-2005.

50

USDA Forest Service Resour. Bull. RMRS-RB-10. 2010

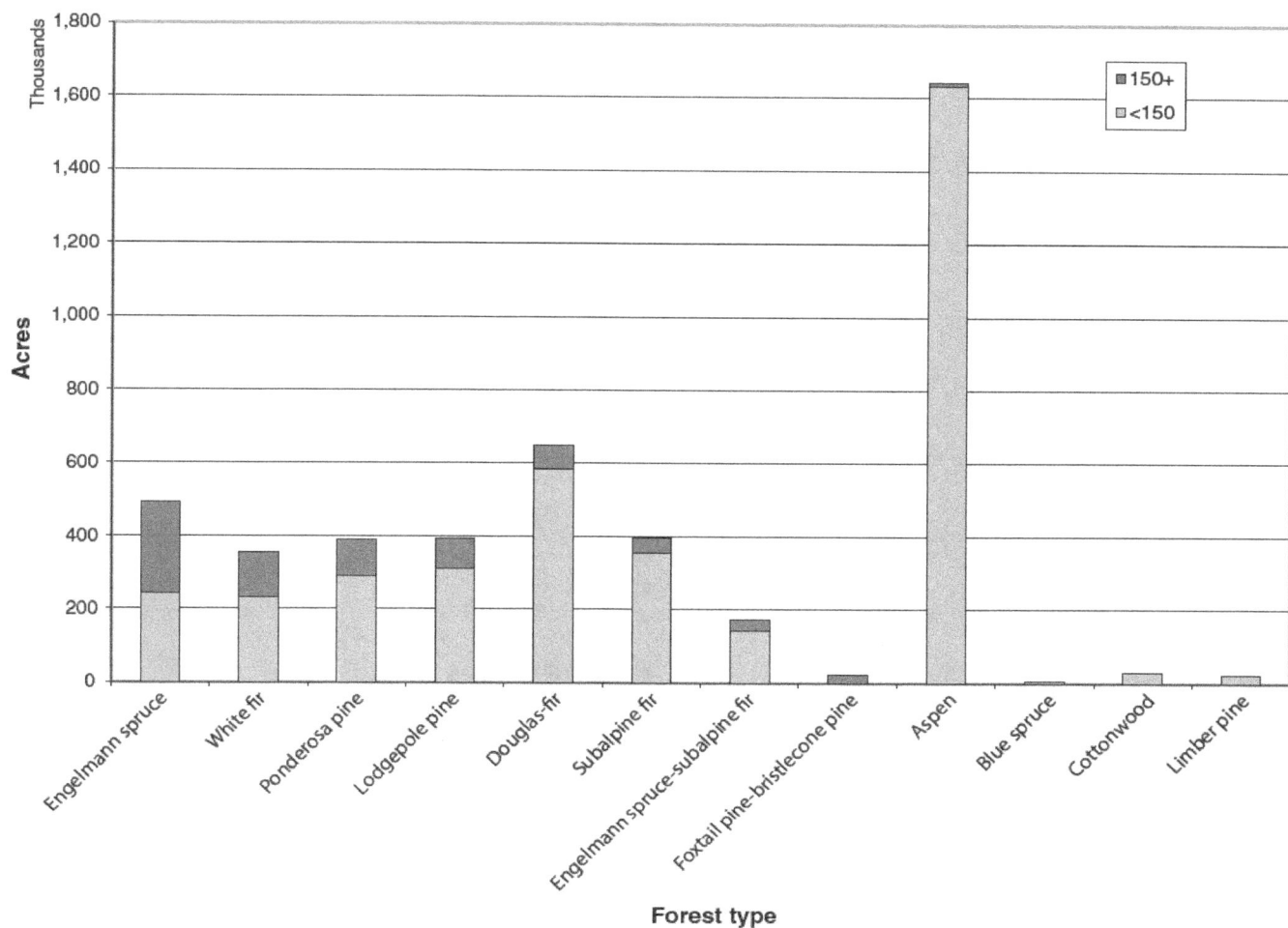

Figure 22—Total area of forest land by timber forest types and stand age class, Utah, cycle 2, 2000-2005.

least 150 years old breast height age, based on sample core trees. Area of old forest by forest type using thresholds of 10 trees per acre and 5 trees per acre at least 150 years old is shown in figure 23. Compared to an overall figure of 16 percent (719 thousand acres) using stand age, 22 percent (1 million acres) of all forest land timber type acreage in Utah would meet the old forest criteria at 10 old trees per acre, and almost 37 percent at 5 old trees per acre.

Aspen, Douglas-fir, and Engelmann spruce-subalpine fir forest types had the largest percent increases in old forest area at 10 trees per acre; and aspen, Douglas-fir, and subalpine fir had the largest percent increases at 5 trees per acre. At the 10 trees per acre threshold, the forest land timber types with 20 percent or greater stands in old forest structure are foxtail/bristlecone pine at 100 percent, Engelmann spruce at 56 percent, white fir at 40 percent, Engelmann spruce-subalpine fir at 34 percent, lodgepole pine at 29 percent, and Douglas-fir at 26 percent. The rest of the timber types have less than 20 percent in old forest. Comparing all three methods for all forest types excluding foxtail/bristlecone, the amount of old forest Engelmann spruce forest type was the least impacted by the different methods for classifying stand structure.

USDA Forest Service Resour. Bull. RMRS-RB-10. 2010

51

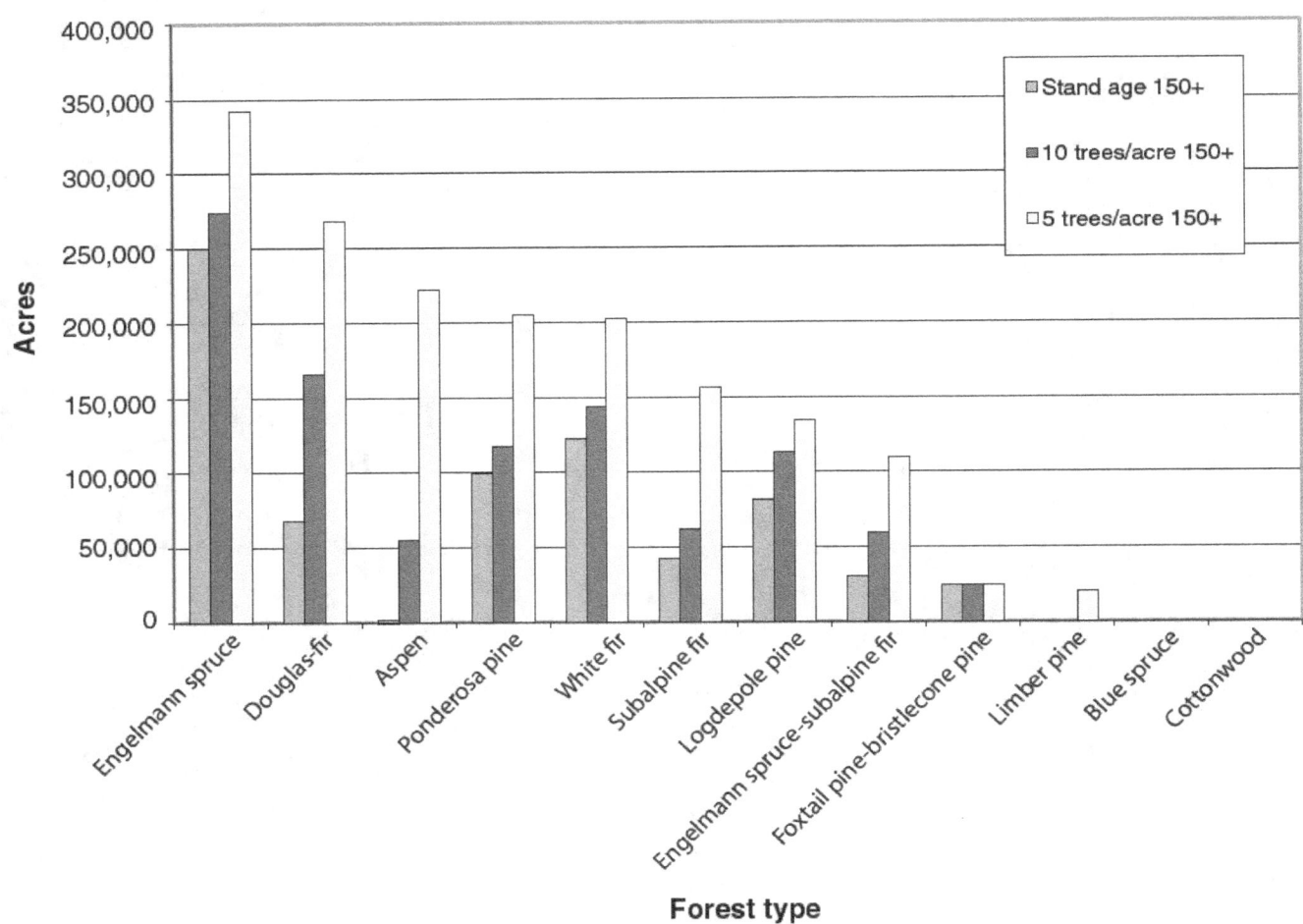

Figure 23—Area of old forest stand structure by timber forest type and stand age method, Utah, cycle 2, 2000-2005.

Discussion—As discussed in Section IV ("Quality Assurance Analysis"), tree age is an important but sometimes difficult variable to collect accurately, although table 8 showed that breast height age for timber trees is much more repeatable than root collar age for woodland trees. Some aspects of this analysis have made the estimates of old forest somewhat conservative. First, the ages of trees are not total age, but breast height age. Total tree age could be significantly greater in some stands. Second, only a subset of trees present on FIA plots are bored for age, so possibly many more trees greater than 150 years are present on the FIA plots. A more robust analysis could assign tree age to non-sampled core trees by species and diameter class, possibly based on the age and height of core trees on the plot. This could potentially increase the per acre estimates of 150 year old and greater trees.

From an ecological perspective, if stand origin is more important for describing old forest structure than average age of trees by stand-size class (stand age), then perhaps a variable other than stand age, such as trees per acre by age threshold, would be more appropriate. Since the surrogates used to categorize old forest structure can give varying results for different forest types, it is important to align size/age structure definitions with the methods or variables intended for monitoring them. It is also important that the desired measure for monitoring be able to address the full range of size/age structural categories included in the definitions so that categories are mutually exclusive and cumulative.

Noxious Plants

Background—Noxious plant species can have many negative effects on forest communities: displacing native flora, altering fire regimes, reducing diversity in plant and pollinator communities, and generally reducing the diversity and resiliency of forest ecosystems. FIA field crews record any instance where a noxious species is found on a plot that contains a forested condition. Only those plant species listed by the State of Utah as noxious are recorded, which will allow for the spatial and temporal extent of these species to be documented as plots are revisited. Although cheatgrass (*Bromus tectorum*) is not listed as noxious in Utah, it is a non-native annual grass that is quickly invading many areas of the State. There is considerable interest in the occurrence of cheatgrass on Utah's forests, but since it is not considered noxious by the State, cheatgrass data are collected in a different manner and will be discussed in a separate section.

Inventory Results—A total of 2,236 sample conditions were used to assess the occurrence of noxious plant species in Utah. These samples represent plots that had a forested condition recorded somewhere within the boundaries of the four subplots. Eight different noxious species were documented on these forested plots, with one or more found on 90 (4.0 percent) of the sampled plots. Canada thistle (*Cirsium arvence*) and Musk thistle (*Carduus nutans*) were by far the most common species, accounting for 78 percent of the noxious plant occurrences (fig. 24).

The elm-ash-cottonwood forest type group had the highest percentage of locations infested with at least one noxious species (fig. 25), although this type had a low sample size. Conversely, the most frequently sampled forest group, the pinyon-juniper group (n = 1349), had a smaller proportion of infested locations (1.8 percent) than any other group except the ponderosa pine group (n = 59) in which no noxious species were found.

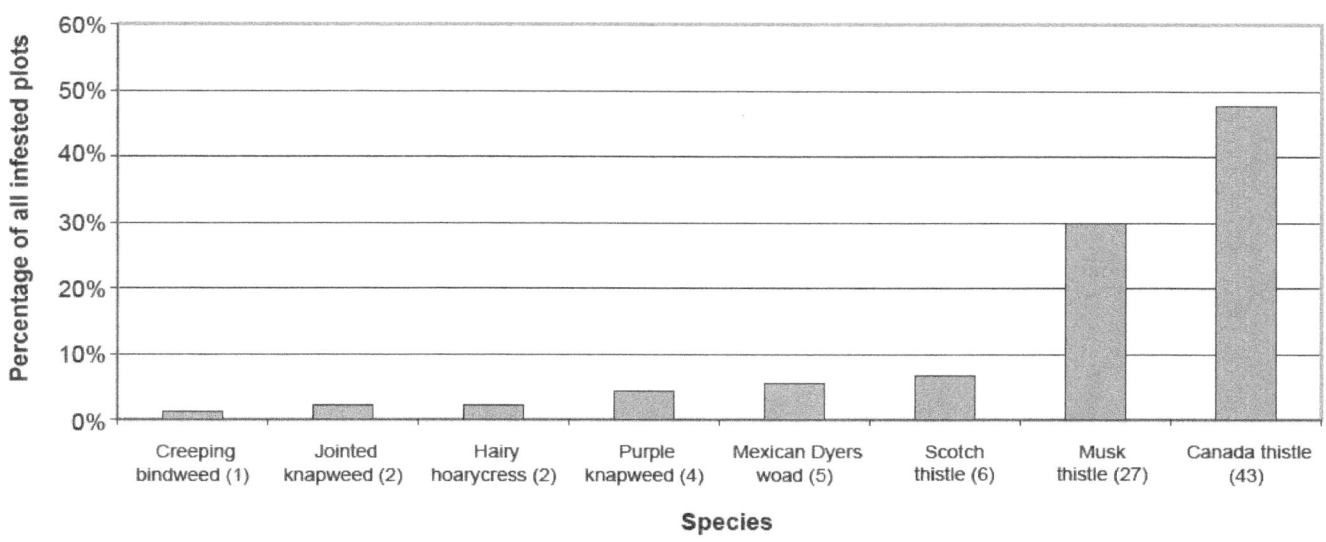

Figure 24—Distribution (as a percentage of total occurrence) of noxious species. Number of detections of each species in parentheses, Utah, cycle 2, 2000-2005.

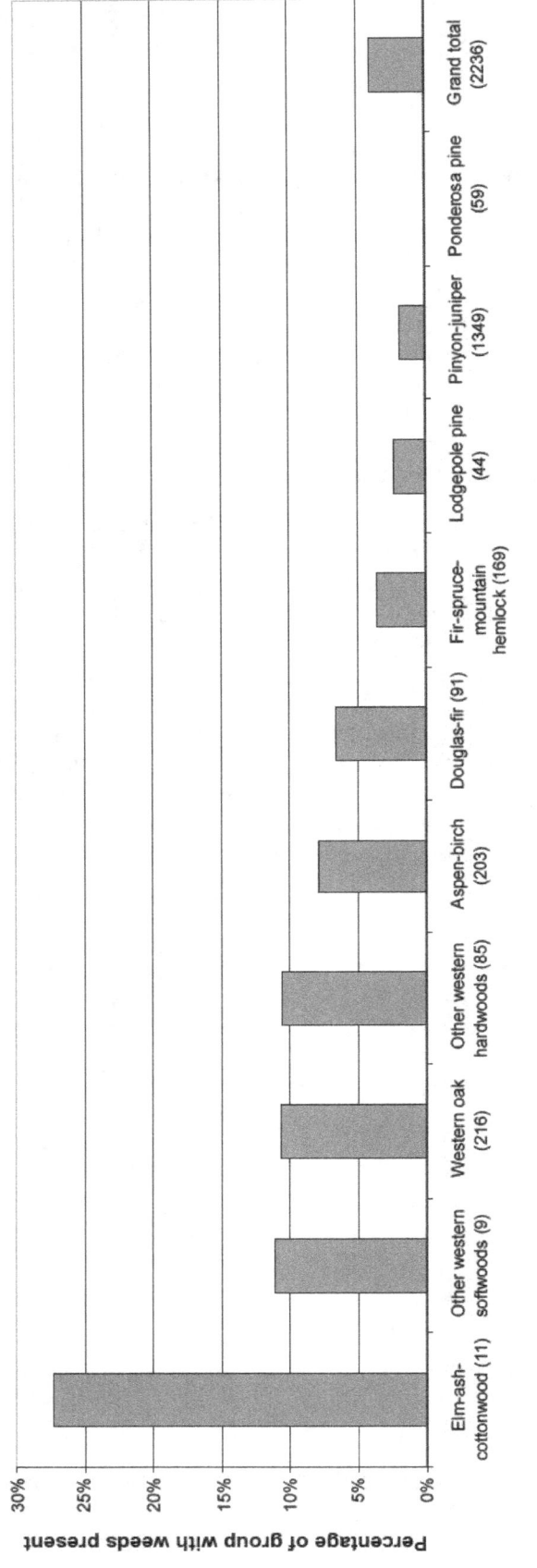

Figure 25—Distribution of noxious species (as a percentage of total occurrence) by forest type group. Number of sampled conditions for each group in parentheses, Utah, cycle 2, 2000-2005.

Stand age appeared to correlate with the frequency of noxious species occurrence, with 63 percent of the observations located in stands less than 100 years old and 88 percent found on stands less than 151 years old (fig. 26). Forty-eight percent of all sampled plots were in stands less than 100 years old and 72 percent were in stands less than 150 years old. Locations that had more than one condition (more than one forest type or a portion of the plot was non-forest) had more than twice the occurrence of noxious species than did those locations where only a single forested condition represented the entire plot (fig. 27). Twenty-four percent of all sampled plots in Utah had multiple conditions.

Discussion — The paucity of noxious plants found in the pinyon-juniper forest group suggests that these forest types are less susceptible to invasion and/or persistence of plants designated as noxious. The intense competition of overstory species found in these xeric forest types may limit the opportunities for infestation and establishment. On the other hand, oak, aspen, and other western hardwood species appear to be most susceptible to invasion. This may be due to one or more factors, including soil conditions, accessibility to livestock grazing, road and foot traffic, high frequency of both natural and man-induced disturbance, and/or which plants have been determined "noxious."

Plant communities in young forest stands may not be fully established when noxious species are introduced to the area. Therefore, conditions may favor introduction and establishment in presently unfilled niches in the system. Communities in older and undisturbed stands are generally stable and thus more resistant to invasion. Multiple conditions on a plot indicate transition zones between forest types and between forest and non-forest conditions. These "edge" areas are often dynamic in terms of site occupation, utilization, and species composition. This makes them more susceptible to occupation by noxious plants than the more stable interior of the stands. However, it should be noted that stand-age and condition proportion are correlated (older stands tend to be one condition more often than younger stands) so one would expect this trend, given the stand-age relationship discussed above.

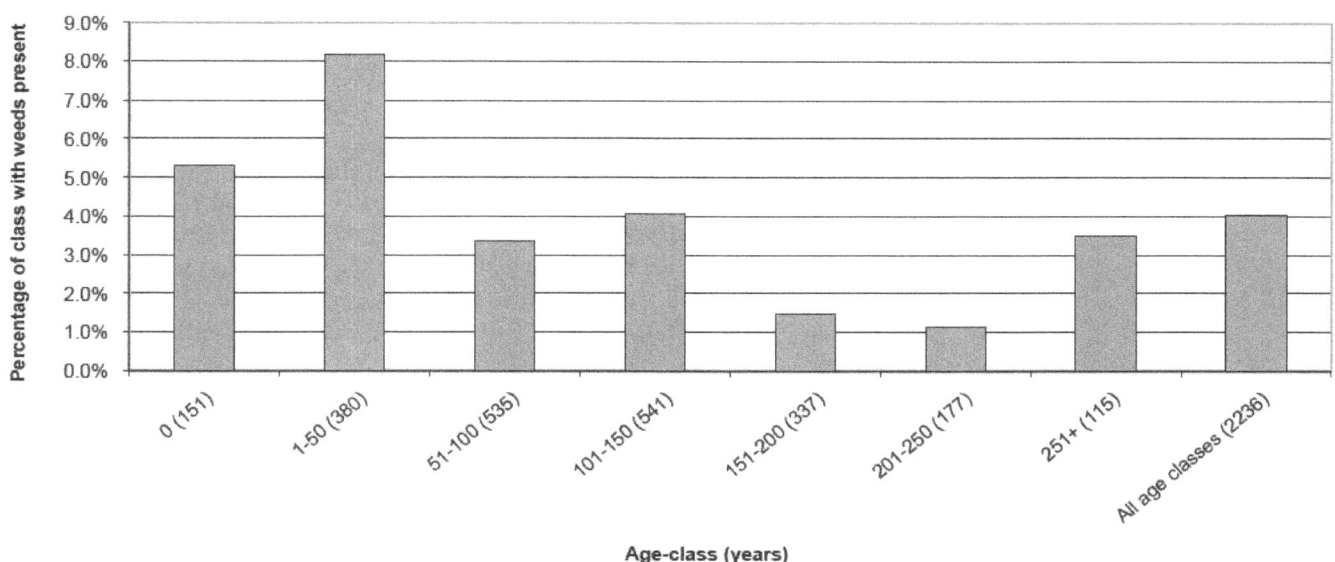

Figure 26—Distribution of noxious species (as a percentage of total occurrence) by age-class. Number of sampled conditions for each group in parentheses, Utah, cycle 2, 2000-2005.

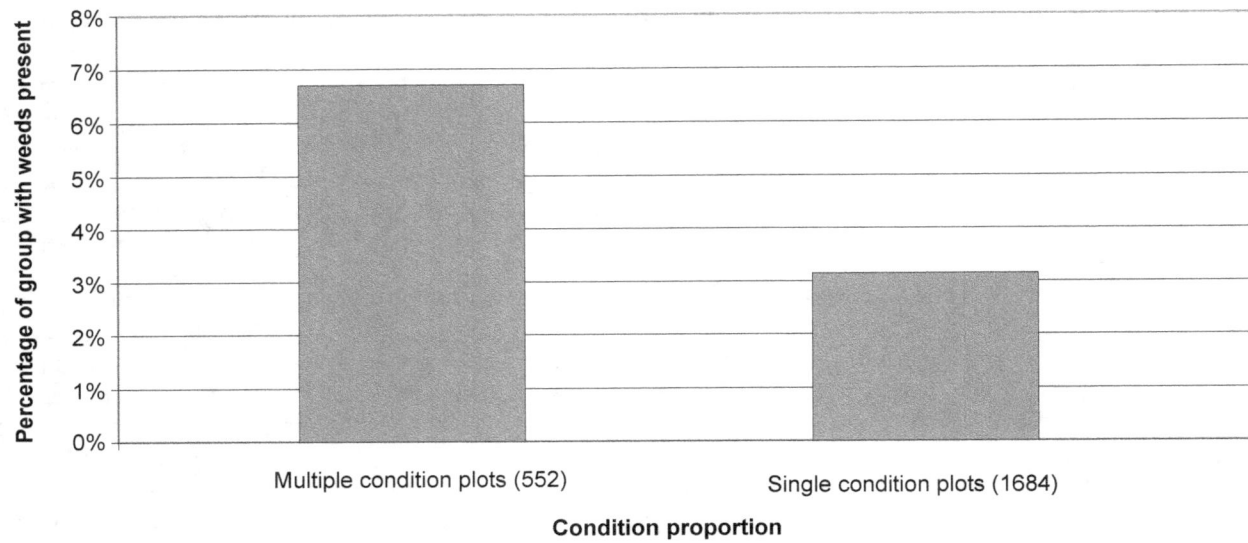

Figure 27—Percentage of single and multi-condition plots with noxious species. Total sample size for each group in parentheses, Utah, cycle 2, 2000-2005.

Snags as Wildlife Habitat

Background—Standing dead trees (snags) provide important habitat in forest ecosystems. Numerous organisms use snags at some point in their life history. These include, but are not limited to bacteria, fungi, insects, rodents, cavity-nesting birds, bats, mustelids, and black bear. The height and diameter of standing dead trees largely determine the utility of snags as a nesting, roosting, or den sites. Individual tree data collected by FIA field crews allow for population level analysis of the availability and quality of individual snags that meet criteria important to wildlife.

Most species within the guild of cavity-nesting birds found in Utah utilize snags that are greater than 9 inches d.b.h. and 34 feet or taller (Harestad and Keisker 1989; Lawler 1999; McClelland 1977). Silver-haired bats (*Lasionycteris noctivagans*) have been associated with trees 12 inches or greater d.b.h. and taller than 25 feet (Campbell and others 1996). Although black bears (*Ursus americanus*) do not require snags for den sites, pregnant females or those with cubs select them over ground dens where they are available. Bears prefer snags 30 inches or greater d.b.h. and taller than 16 feet (Kolenosky and Strathearn 1987;, Oli and others 1997). This section describes how FIA variables such as d.b.h., actual height, live or dead status, and lean code can be used to quantify potential den, nest, and roost sites for black bears, cavity-nesting birds, and silver-haired bats. Data are from plots found on forest and other wooded land.

Inventory Results—An estimated 56.5 million snags meet the size preferences of most cavity nesting birds found in Utah (fig. 28). An estimated 33.1 million trees have the potential t o be suitable roost sites for silver-haired bats (fig. 28), and approximately 685,000 trees have the potential for black bear den sites (fig. 29).

Engelmann spruce contributes the most potential snags for all three wildlife species combined, with aspen and subalpine fir being available in abundance for both bats and cavity-nesting birds (figs. 30 and 31). Douglas-fir and lodgepole pine also contribute significantly to birds' and bats' needs (fig. 30) while ponderosa pine provides the bulk of the remaining potential den sites for black bear (fig. 31).

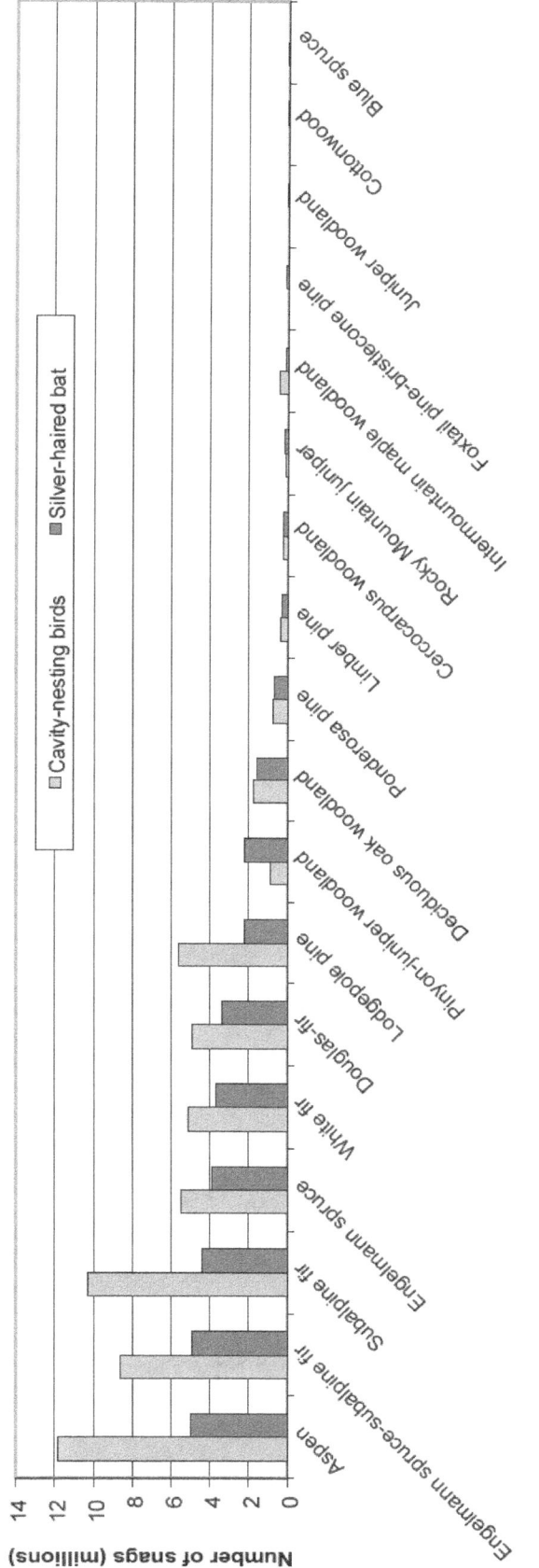

Figure 28—Number of suitable snags for cavity-nesting birds and silver-haired bats by forest type, Utah, cycle 2, 2000-2005.

USDA Forest Service Resour. Bull. RMRS-RB-10. 2010

57

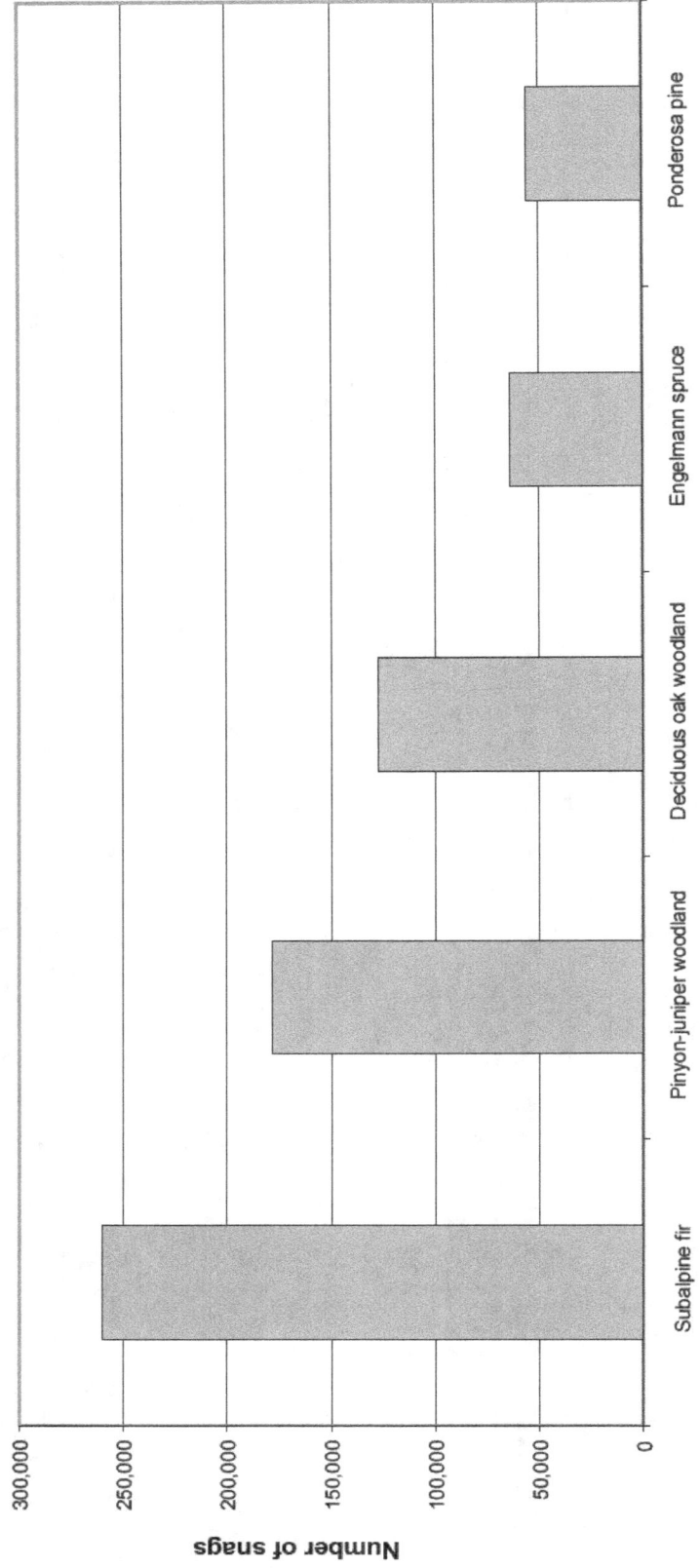

Figure 29—Estimated snags potentially suitable as black bear den sites by forest type, Utah, cycle 2, 2000-2005.

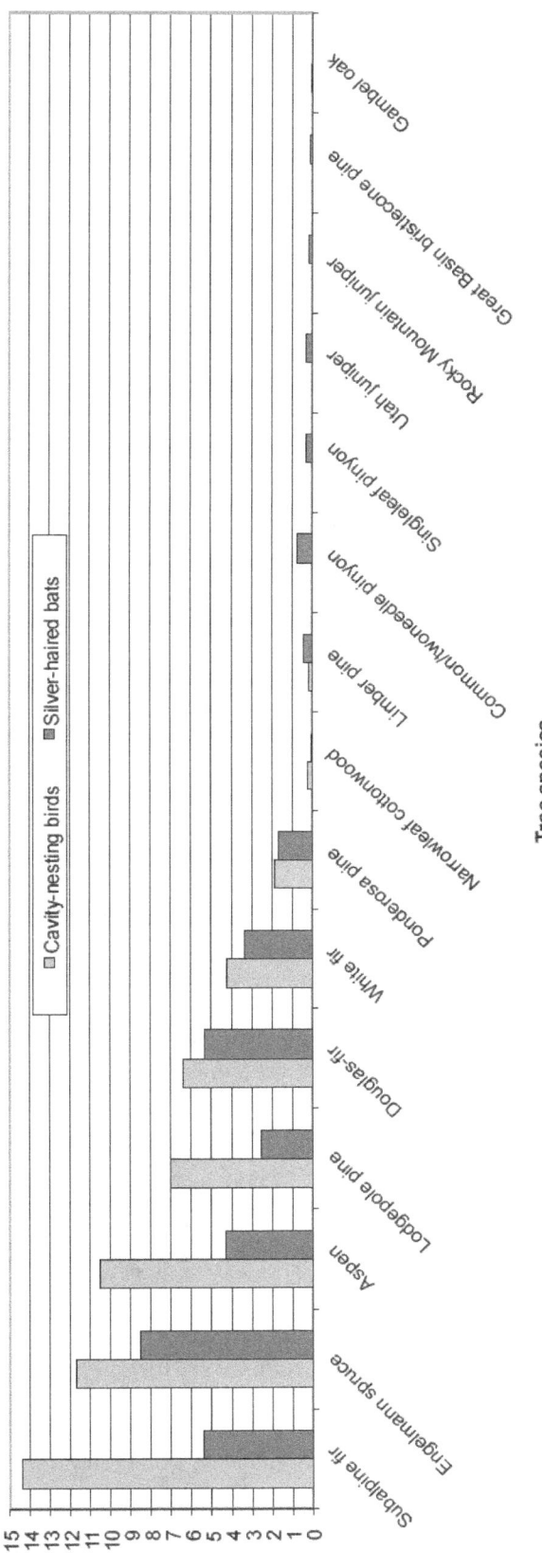

Figure 30—Number of snags suitable to cavity-nesting birds and silver-haired bats by tree species, Utah, cycle 2, 2000-2005.

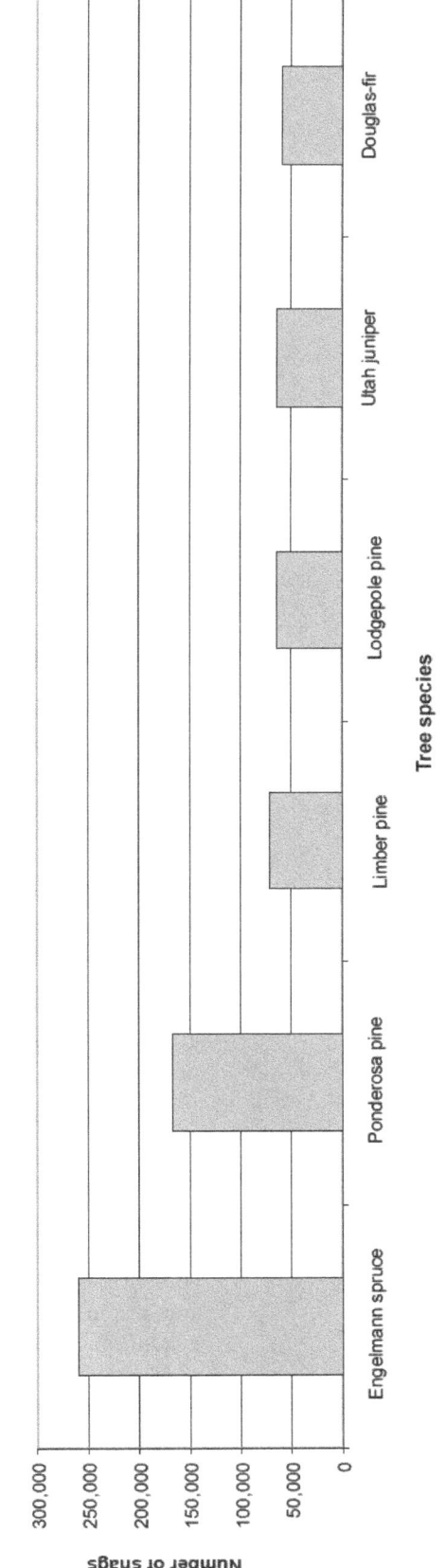

Figure 31—Estimate of snags potentially suitable as black bear den sites by tree species, Utah, cycle 2, 2000-2005.

USDA Forest Service Resour. Bull. RMRS-RB-10. 2010

59

Available snags for cavity-nesting birds are predominantly found in the aspen forest type, but several other types contribute potential habitat (fig. 32). These are the same forest types that provide the majority of snags preferred by silver-haired bats. However, the suite of forest types that have black bear den site potential is much smaller, including subalpine fir, pinyon-juniper woodland, ponderosa pine, and deciduous oak woodland.

Discussion—Aspen, Engelmann spruce, and subalpine fir are valuable snag species for several forest birds and mammals, even when found in other forest types (mixed stands). Depending on where they are located on the landscape, ponderosa pine snags can be utilized by black bears. Variables other than snag dimensions and numbers need to be considered when predicting suitable wildlife habitat for forest-dwelling species. For example, proximity to forest edge and stand density of live trees is important to many cavity-nesting birds. The state of decay of a tree and its distance to water are important to silver-haired bats and bears. Proximity to hard mast resources (juniper berries and acorns in Utah), slope, aspect, presence of a cavity, and the amount and timing of snow-pack are important in determining the relative value of trees as den sites for black bear. FIA data can address many of these factors and there are current efforts to build predictive models for these species in Utah by using IWFIA data collected by our field crews. These models can be valuable tools for Federal and State land managers, as over 90 percent of the suitable snags measured by FIA occur on public lands.

Cheatgrass

Background—Cheatgrass (*Bromus tectorum*) is a non-native annual grass that has invaded and displaced native vegetation throughout the West. Cheatgrass grows and produces seed earlier than most native species, thus gaining a competitive advantage for the limited resources in the arid environments of Utah and other States. The fine fuels created by cheatgrass alter fire frequency in the areas where it is found in abundance. These fuels can perpetuate the spread of the species by creating new areas to invade after a fire disturbance. Both public and private land managers are interested in understanding the spatial and temporal patterns of cheatgrass and any other information that can be used to curb infestation. Cheatgrass is not listed as noxious by the State of Utah. However, FIA field crews document it in the understory vegetation procedure if it reaches a threshold of 5 percent or greater ground cover. However, only those plots with a forested condition present have understory vegetation recorded (USDA Forest Service 2000-2005a); therefore, these data do not reflect cheatgrass on non-forested portions of plots. This analysis used all plots found on forest and other wooded land.

Inventory Results—Cheatgrass was measured at 5 percent or greater cover on 259 out of 1,537 conditions (plots or parts of plots) in Utah, or 17 percent of the conditions. The pinyon-juniper forest type group had the most instances of cheatgrass at 199, which represents 77 percent of the total number of cheatgrass indices sampled in Utah (fig. 33). The western oak forest type group had the next highest occurrence with 41 records (16 percent), followed by other western hardwoods, represented by cercocarpus woodland and intermountain maple woodland types, with 17 records (7 percent). There were two instances where cheatgrass was located in a non-stocked cottonwood forest type.

Most of the cheatgrass sampled occurs on plots below 7,000 feet elevation (fig. 34). When examined as a percentage of plots infested within an elevation group, the 4,001-5,000-ft elevation class appeared to be most susceptible to infestation, with almost 64 percent of plots infested (fig. 35).

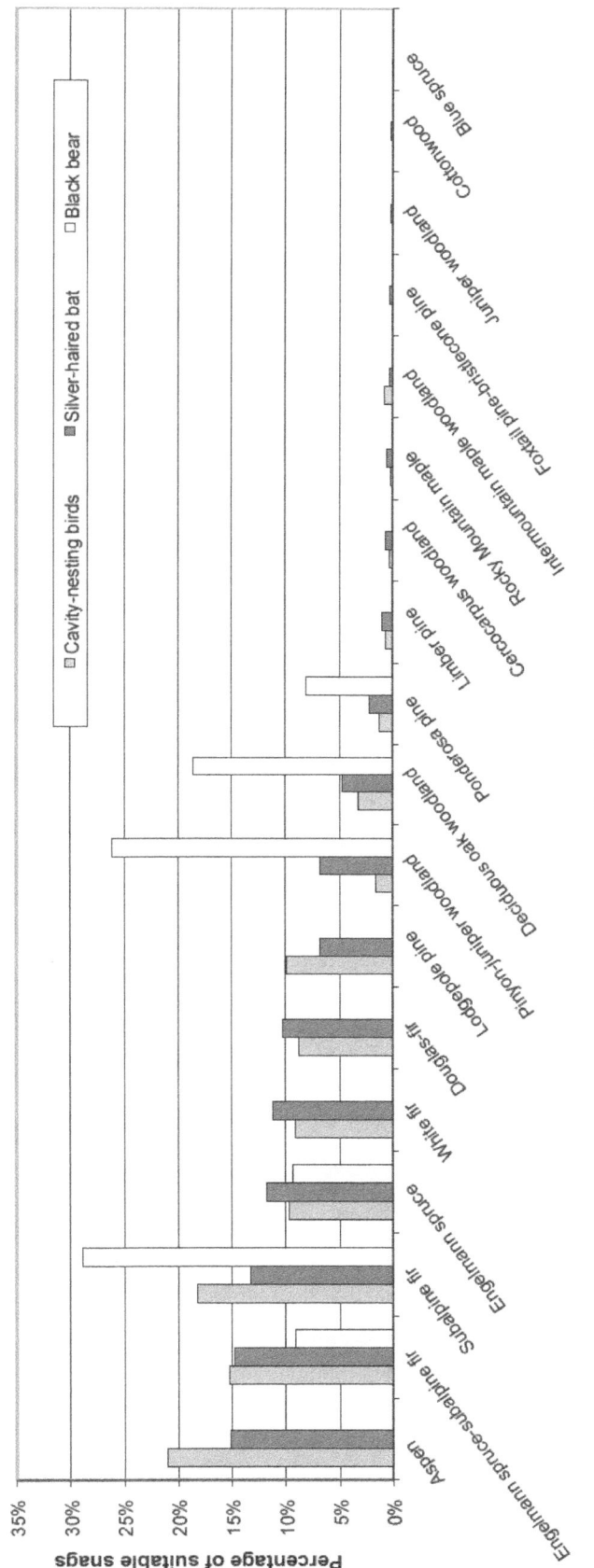

Figure 32—Distribution (by percentage) of suitable snags by wildlife guild/species and forest type, Utah, cycle 2, 2000-2005.

USDA Forest Service Resour. Bull. RMRS-RB-10. 2010

61

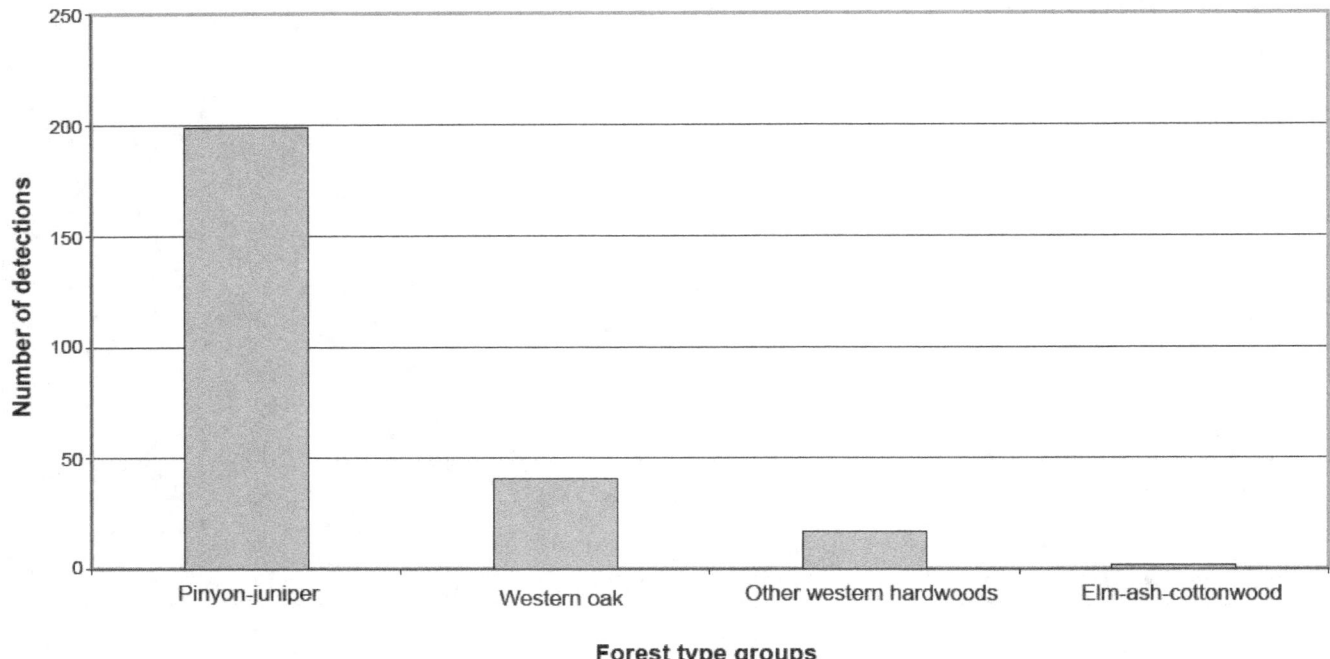

Figure 33—Number of cheatgrass detections (≥ 5 percent cover on subplot) by forest type group, Utah, cycle 2, 2000-2005.

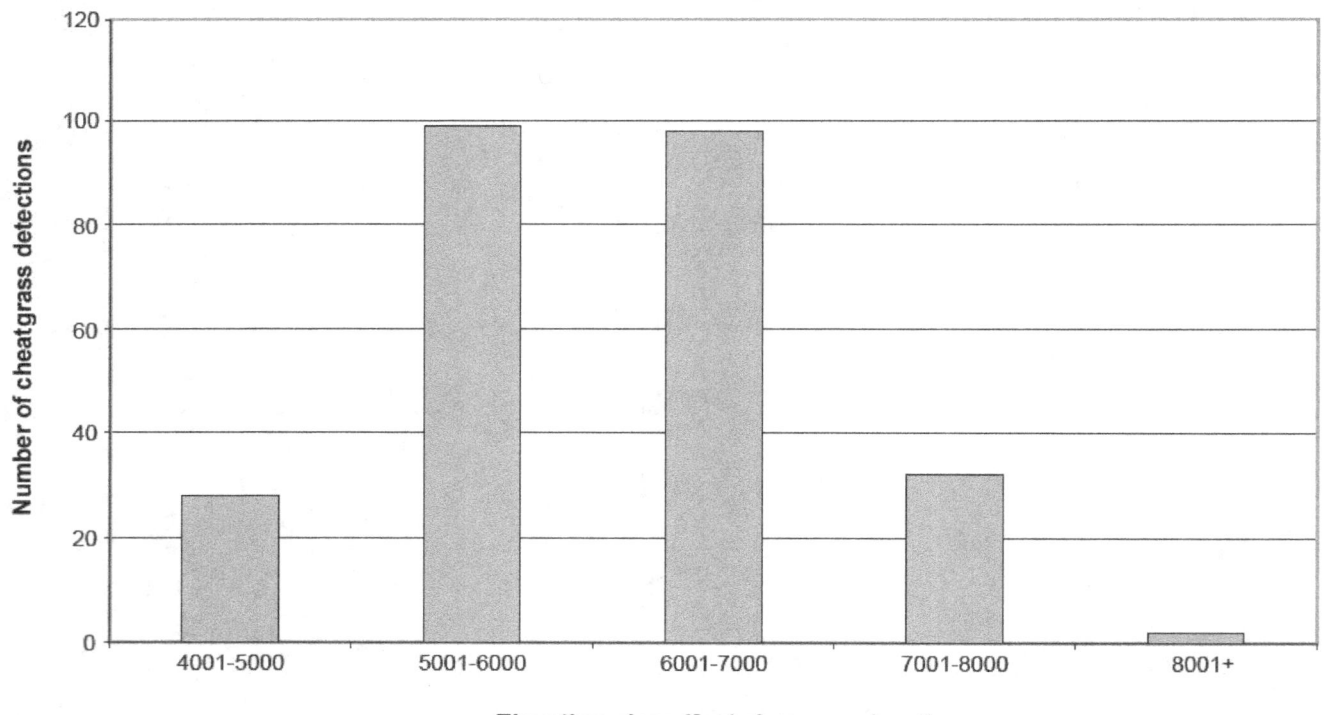

Figure 34—Number of cheatgrass detections by elevation class, Utah, cycle 2, 2000-2005.

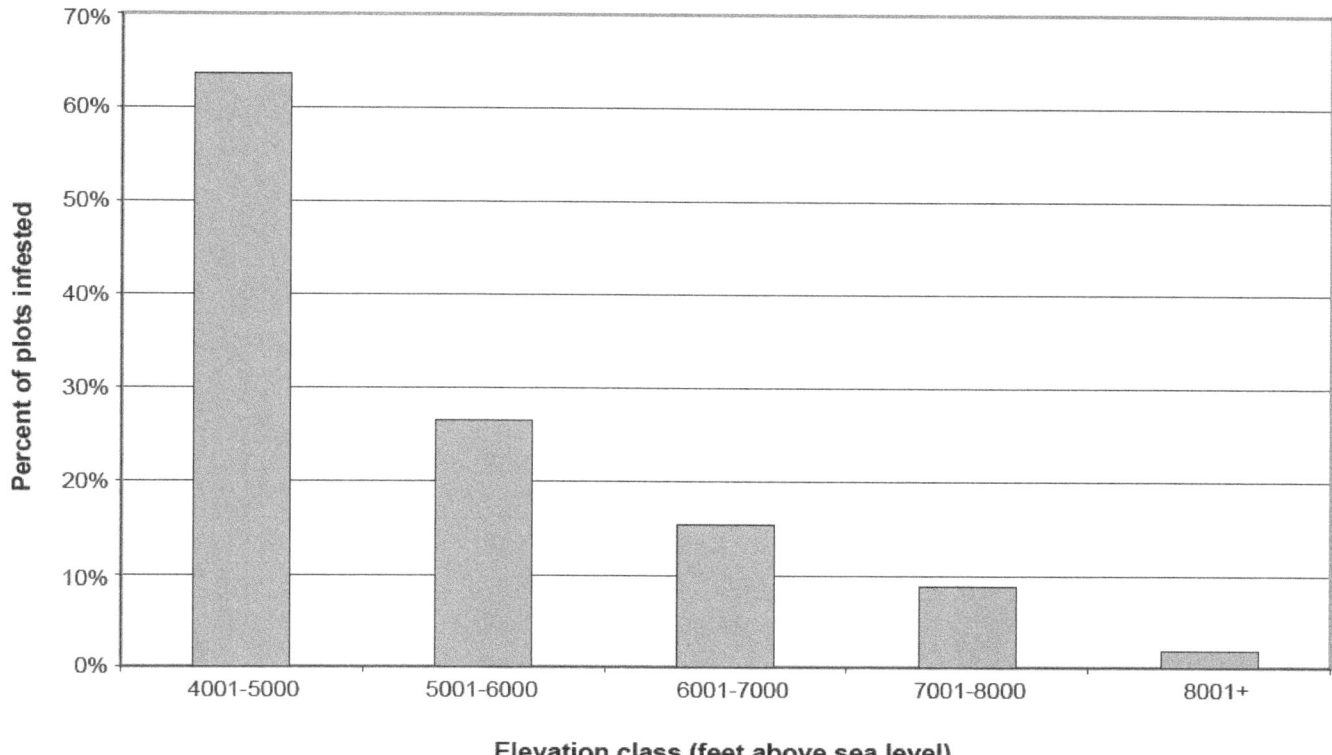

Figure 35—Percent of plots infested with cheatgrass by elevation class, Utah, cycle 2, 2000-2005.

Discussion—In contrast to species officially listed as noxious in Utah, cheatgrass is not found in abundance in any timber forest type. The vast majority of plots with cheatgrass were in the pinyon-juniper forest type group, with the rest in hardwood forest type groups. These forest types often occur in areas that have lower soil moisture and understory species diversity than higher elevation sites. These may be factors that affect an area's susceptibility to invasion. Other possible factors include the type, level, and frequency of disturbance (natural and human-induced) in these areas.

The pattern of cheatgrass across the elevation gradient may be driven by the corresponding moisture gradient. Plots located at higher elevations typically have more soil moisture, cooler temperatures, and a shorter growing season. These factors may impede the introduction and/or establishment of cheatgrass in these areas.

Cheatgrass presents a threat to western ecosystems and a challenge to those that manage the lands where it has become established. FIA data can be used to identify areas infested and/or most susceptible to infestation. This information can also be used to test cheatgrass models currently being developed or refine those already being implemented.

VI. FIA Indicators

As discussed in Section II, the forest monitoring component of the FIA program consists of a three-stage systematic sample of sites across all forested lands of the United States. Phase 3 plots, a one-sixteenth subset of Phase 2 sample plots, are measured for a broader suite of forest health attributes including tree crown conditions, lichen community composition, understory vegetation, down woody materials, and soil attributes. An associated sample scheme exists to detect cases of ozone damage occurring adjacent to forest vegetation.

This suite of Phase 3 attributes are often referred to as FIA indicators, although in a broader sense FIA indicators could be any national or regional field-collected or derived variable used for monitoring purposes. In addition, some of the Phase 3 indicators are currently being developed at the Phase 2 intensity, such as down woody materials and tree damage. Due to the extensive plot intensity of Phase 3 data, or due to changes in data collection procedures, some indicators may have limited information or may only include a subset of years of data between 2000 and 2005. The following indicator topics, not discussed in any of the issues sections, are included here as an introduction for future Utah reporting, as these indicators undergo further development.

Soils

Background—Soils on the landscape are the product of five interacting soil forming factors: parent material, climate, landscape position (topography), organisms (vegetation, microbes, other soil organisms), and time (Jenny 1994). Many external forces can have a profound influence on forest soil condition and forest health. These include agents of change or disturbances to apparent steady-state conditions, such as shifts in climate, fire, insect and disease activities, land use activities, and land management actions.

The Soil Indicator was developed to assess the status and trend of forest soil resources in the United States across all ecoregions, forest types, and land ownership categories. For this report, data were analyzed and are reported by forest type groups. This forest type aggregation not only reflects the influence of forest vegetation on soil properties, but also the interaction of parent material, climate, landscape position, and time with forest vegetation and soil organisms. A complete list of mean soil properties in Utah organized by forest type is in Appendix F, tables 1 to 4. Some key soil properties were graphed by forest type group in Utah and were placed side by side with regional data for comparison.

Inventory Results—With the exception of the western oak type, soil C (carbon) and N (nitrogen) percentages generally increase from drier to wetter forest environments (fig. 36). Generally, soil moisture increases with elevation and latitude (cooler temperatures) and forest types reflect this climatic gradient. When expressed in as megagrams of C or N per hectare of forest area, C stocks also generally increase with elevation and latitude (fig. 37), with the exception of western oak and western softwoods. Soil N stocks show a more mixed response to climatic gradients in Utah and the Interior West.

Aspen forests store more N in the mineral soil than any other forest type group in the Interior West (fig. 37, right side). Aspen forests store significantly more N than Engelmann spruce-subalpine fir forests, which often intermingle with aspen. The high N levels in aspen forest floor and soils leads to lower C/N ratios than those found in forest floor and soils under spruce/fir. Since low C/N is a good indicator of relative organic matter decomposition rate, nutrient-rich aspen leaves decompose quickly and easily compared to conifer needles.

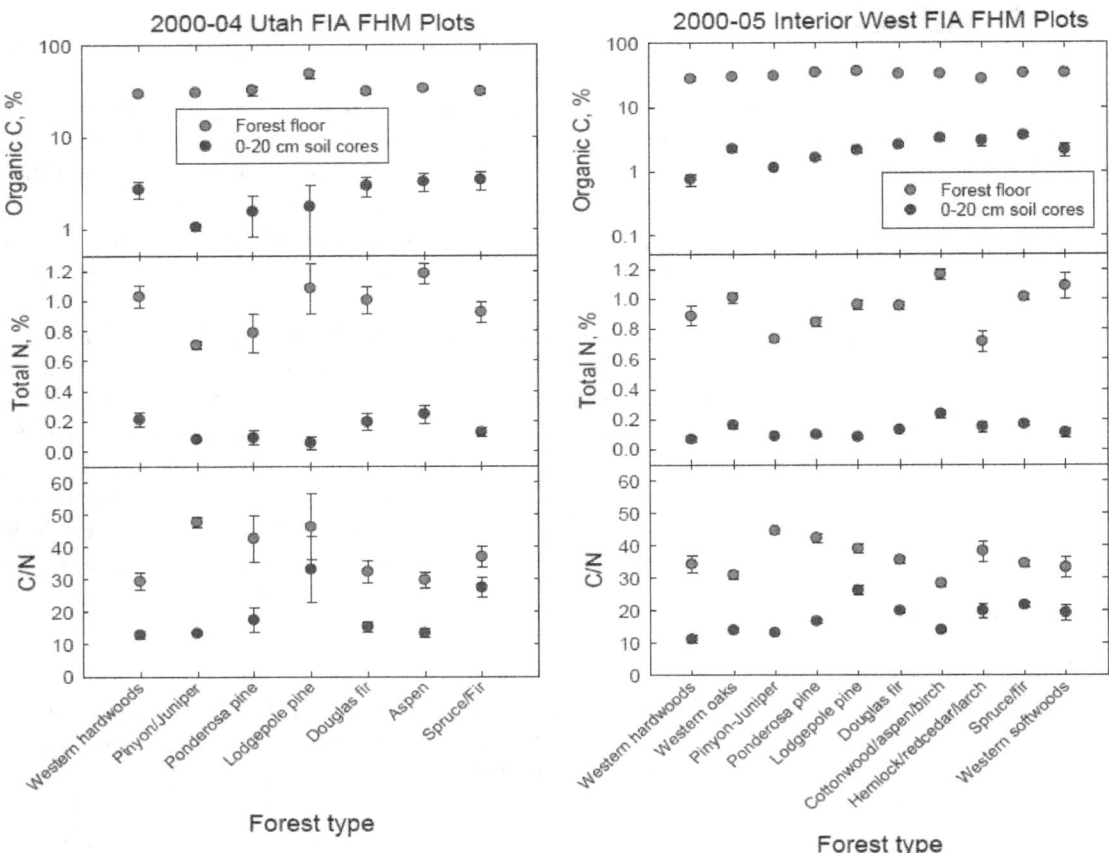

Figure 36—Forest floor and 0-20 cm mineral soil percent C, percent N, and C/N arranged by forest type groups in Utah (left side) and in five Interior West States (Arizona, Colorado, Idaho, Montana, and Utah) (right side). The forest type groups are arranged left to right in order of increasing latitude, elevation, and precipitation with some overlap among forest types. The other western hardwoods group in Utah includes *Cercocarpus* woodland and deciduous oak woodland. For the Interior West as a whole, the western oak group (deciduous and evergreen oak woodlands) was separated from the other western hardwoods (mesquite and *Cercocarpus* woodlands). The pinyon-juniper group in Utah includes Rocky Mountain juniper, juniper woodland, and pinyon-juniper woodland. For the Interior West, this group also includes western juniper. The spruce-fir group in Utah includes white fir, Engelmann spruce, subalpine fire, and mixed Engelmann spruce-subalpine fire. For the Interior West, this group also includes grand fir and blue spruce. The western softwoods group includes western white pine, foxtail pine-bristlecone pines, limber pine, and whitebark pine.

Soil pH generally decreases with increasing elevation, latitude, and precipitation (fig. 38) with more acidic soils found in wetter high-elevation forest types. Higher levels of exchangeable Al (aluminum) also are found in wetter high-elevation forest soils (fig. 38). In both Utah, and the Interior West as a whole, much higher levels of Al are found in spruce/fir than aspen soils. Aspen are intolerant of high levels of exchangeable Al. In the Interior West as a whole, aspen soils store more K (potassium) than other forest type groups (fig. 38). In Utah, western hardwoods, ponderosa pine, Douglas-fir, and aspen forests store comparable amounts of soil K. High levels of exchangeable Ca are found in the calcareous, high-pH soils under western hardwoods (including oaks) and pinyon-juniper group woodlands (fig. 38).

66

USDA Forest Service Resour. Bull. RMRS-RB-10. 2010

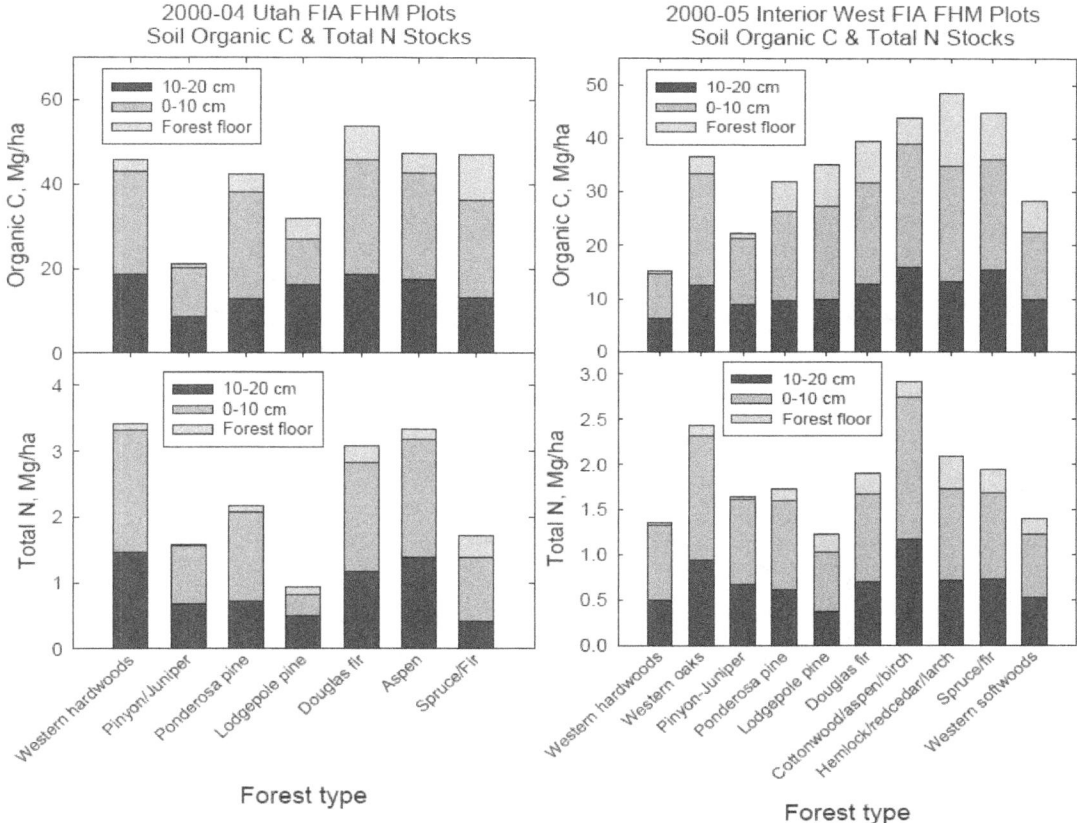

Figure 37—Soil organic carbon (top) and total nitrogen (bottom) stocks (Mg/ha) in the forest floor and 0-10 and 10-20 cm soil layers arranged by forest type groups in Utah (left side) and in five Interior West States (Arizona, Colorado, Idaho, Montana, and Utah) (right side).

Discussion—Common causes of aspen mortality include fire suppression, overbrowsing by native ungulates and domestic livestock, and forest succession in which aspen are replaced by invading conifers (Bartos and Campbell 1998). Loss of aspen on the landscape can lead to decline or loss of ecosystem benefits provided by aspen. Since aspen soils store large amounts of N and K and maintain moderate soil pH levels, conifer replacement of aspen can lead to nutrient loses and soil acidification. If these soil changes are permanent, aspen may be unable to re-colonize areas where they formerly thrived.

Phase 3 Down Woody Material

Background—Down woody material (DWM) is an important component of forests that greatly impacts fire behavior, wildlife habitat, and carbon sources. Some examples of DWM are fallen trees, branches, and leaf litter commonly found within forests in various stages of decay. The main components of DWM include fine woody debris (FWD), coarse woody debris (CWD), litter, and duff. FWD comprises the small diameter (1 to 3-inch) fire-related fuel classes (1-hr, 10-hr, 100-hr), and CWD comprises the large diameter (3-inch +) 1000-hr fuels. This DWM analysis used Phase 3 (P3) data collected on 181 plots from 2001 to 2004 (Woodall and Williams 2005).

USDA Forest Service Resour. Bull. RMRS-RB-10. 2010

67

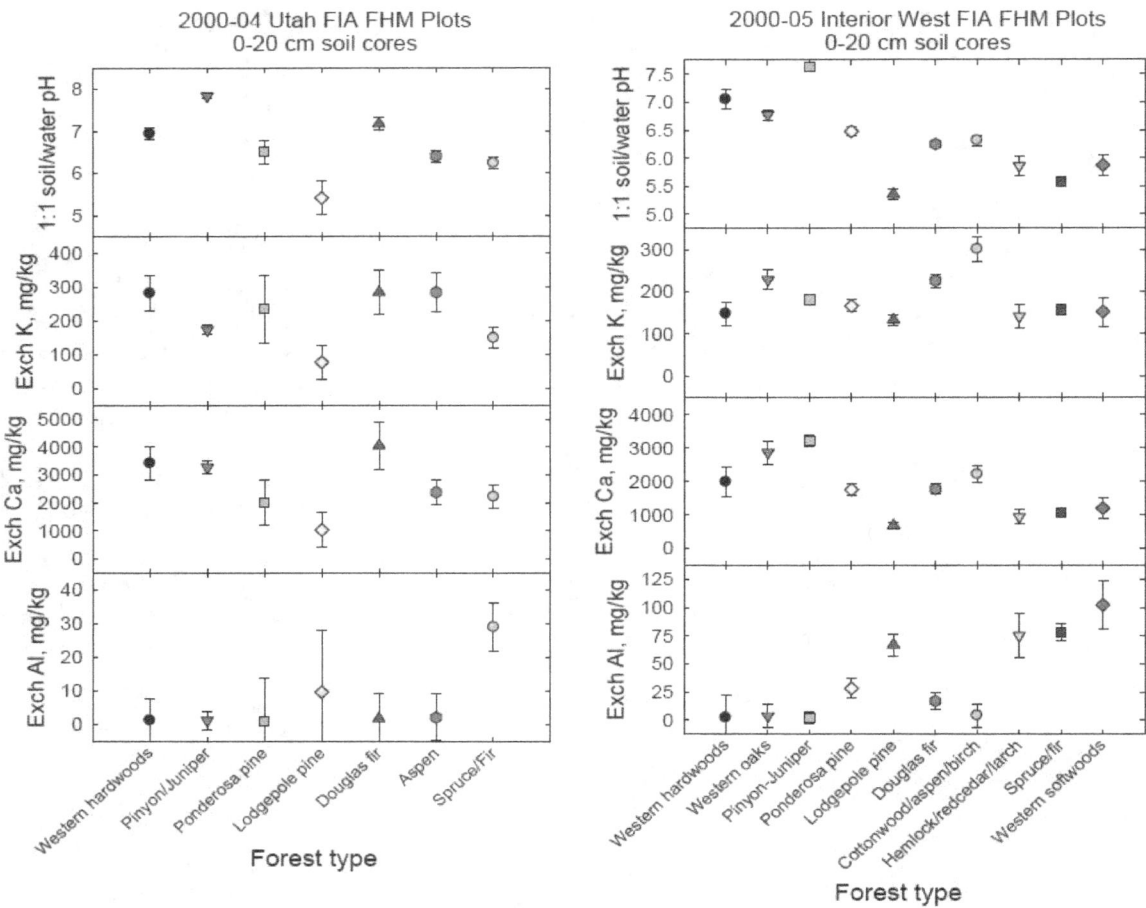

Figure 38—Soil pH and exchangeable potassium, calcium, and aluminum in the 0-20 cm soil layers arranged by forest type groups in Utah (left side) and in five Interior West States (Arizona, Colorado, Idaho, Montana, and Utah) (right side).

Inventory Results—The mean forest fuel loading in Utah for all fuel classes combined is over 8 tons per acre. Figure 39 shows the mean tons per acre of DWM by fuel classes. CWD and duff have the highest mean fuel loadings at around 2 tons per acre each, and FWD (1Hr) has the lowest at 0.22 tons per acre.

A closer look at mean fuel loadings in Utah by forest type (168 plots) and fuel class reveals a wide variation (fig. 40). The Engelmann spruce and subalpine fir forest types have the highest total fuel loadings at 32 and 27 tons per acre, respectively, while juniper and nonstocked forest types have the lowest at about 4 tons per acre each. Lodgepole pine, white fir, and Rocky Mountain juniper forest types each had less than three plots sampled and were combined into the "other" category. The Engelmann spruce-subalpine fir forest type was not sampled. As expected, wetter forest types have much higher total fuel loadings than drier ones, and possibly greater fire hazard potential depending on the current environmental conditions. Also, fuel loading variation among forest types in the three FWD classes is not as great as in the CWD, duff, and litter classes.

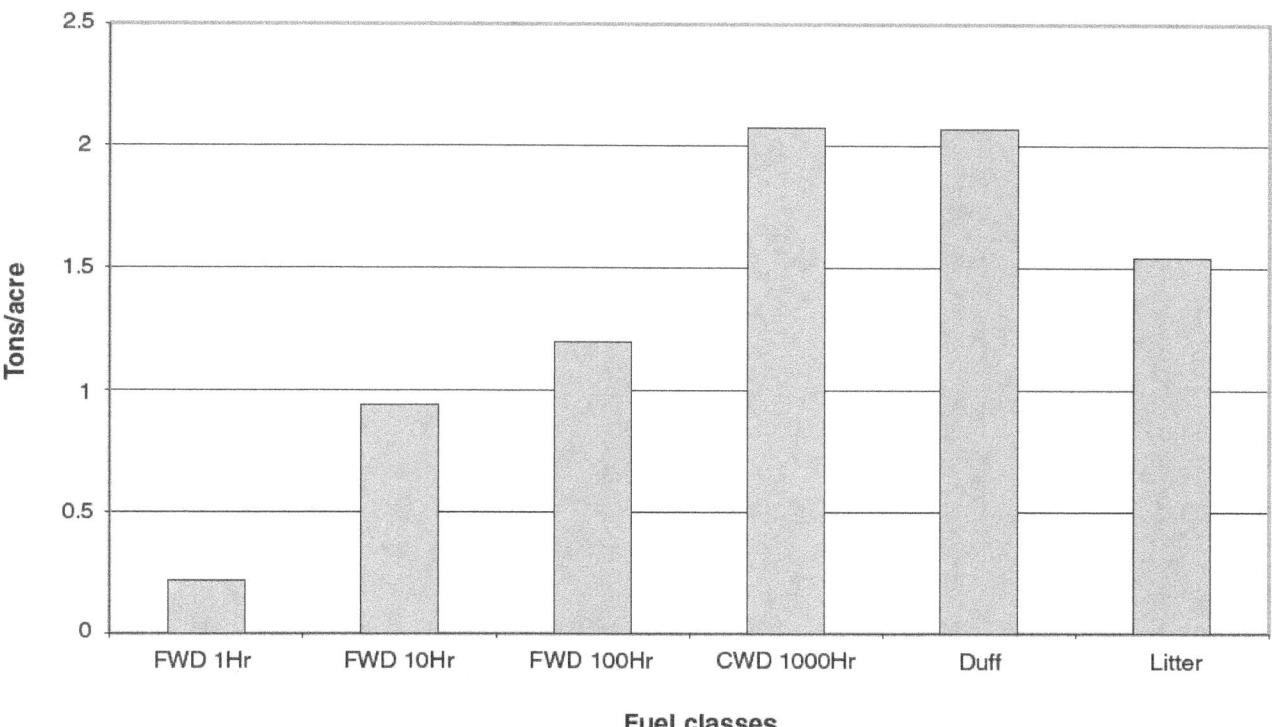

Figure 39—Mean tons per acre of down woody material by fuel class, Utah, cycle 2, 2001-2004.

Structural diversity in terms of CWD diameters and decay classes are an important consideration for wildlife habitat. Figure 41 displays the mean number of logs per acre by forest type and transect diameter class. Although the overall mean in the 18-inch and greater class is 0.66 per acre, some forest types such as subalpine fir, aspen, and Douglas-fir have as many as 5.6, 2.5, and 2.3, respectively. This could be critical for wildlife species that use large diameter logs for habitat. Another consideration other than size is the degree of decay of individual logs. Decay classes can range from class 1, which are newly fallen trees with no decay, to class 5, which still resemble a log but often blend into the duff and litter layers. Figure 42 shows the mean number of logs per acre by forest type and decay class. The most common decay classes in Utah for all forest types combined is class 3 and 4, with a mean of 55 and 38 logs per acre, respectively.

Discussion—The current annual FIA system supports live and standing dead tree inventories but does not include down dead trees as did some past periodic inventories. The current P3 DWM protocols and estimation procedures (Woodall and Monleon 2008) include improvements, such as population estimation, and are designed to capture some important aspects that will hopefully serve as a better surrogate for answering relevant questions about other material in forests. Pacific Northwest FIA and IWFIA are jointly investigating a national Phase 2 inventory version of DWM to support a more robust dataset for future fire fuel, wildlife structure, and carbon assessments.

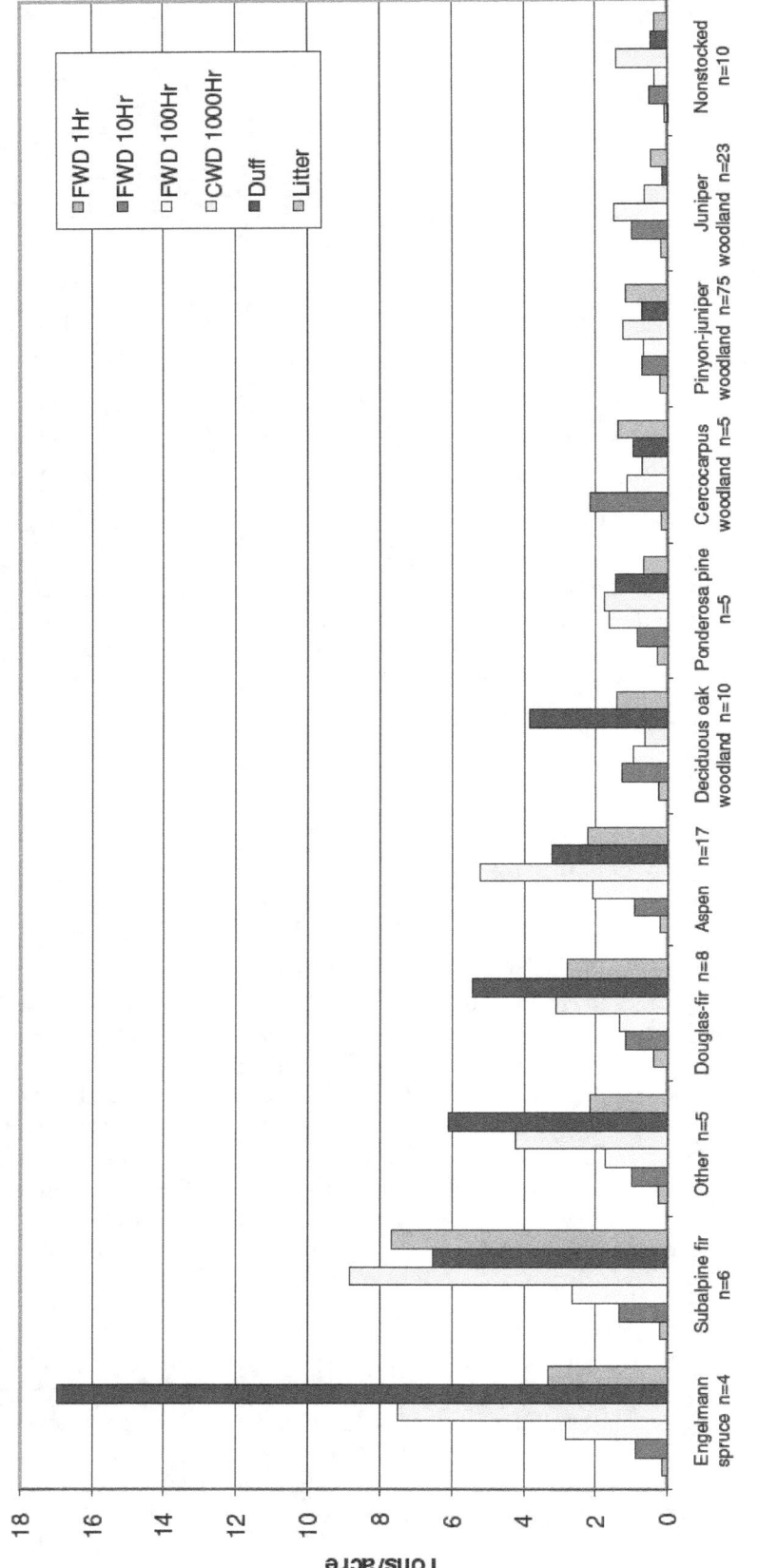

Figure 40—Mean tons per acre of down woody material by forest type and fuel class, Utah, cycle 2, 2001-2004.

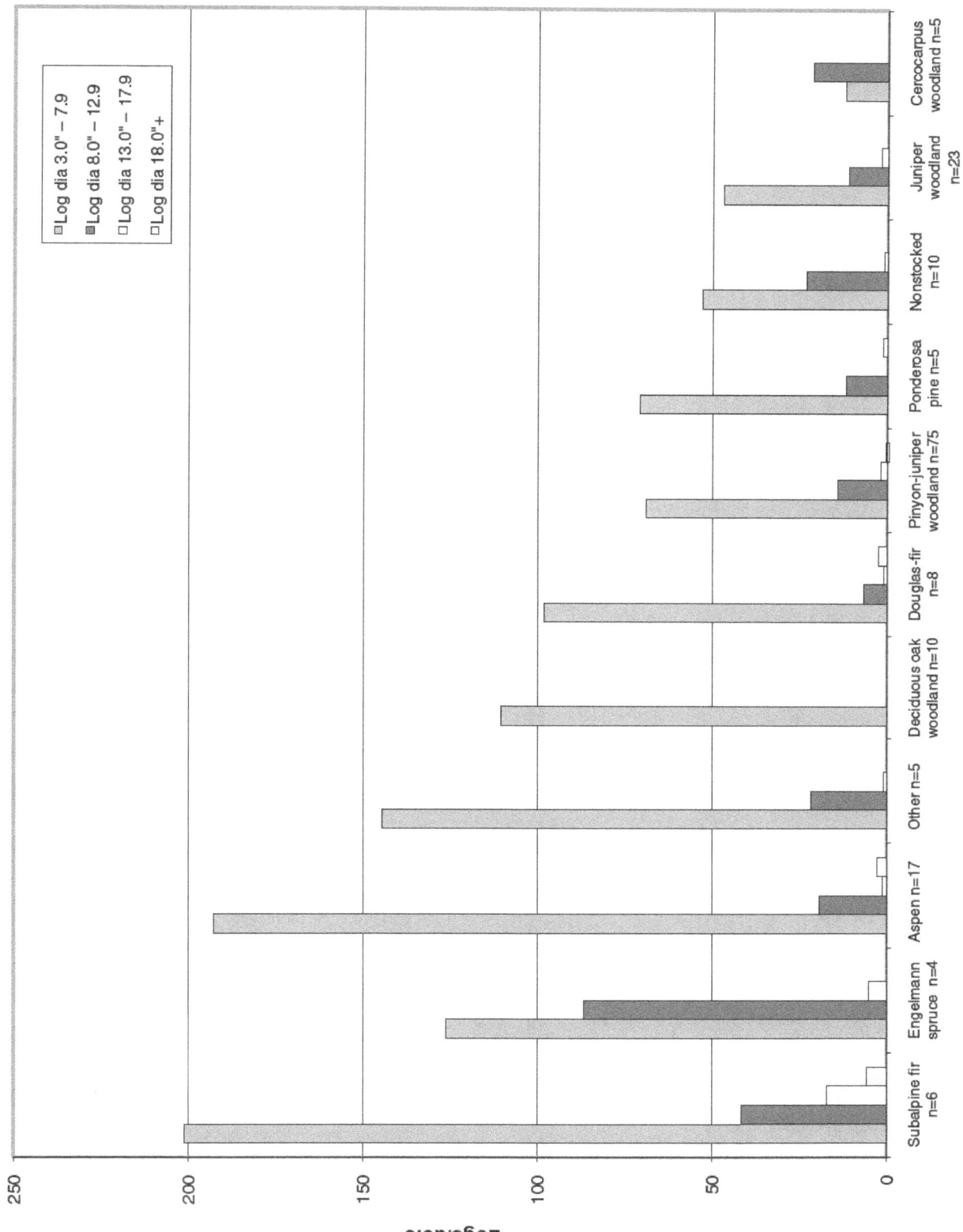

Figure 41—Mean number of CWD logs per acre by forest type and transect diameter class, Utah, cycle 2, 2001-2004.

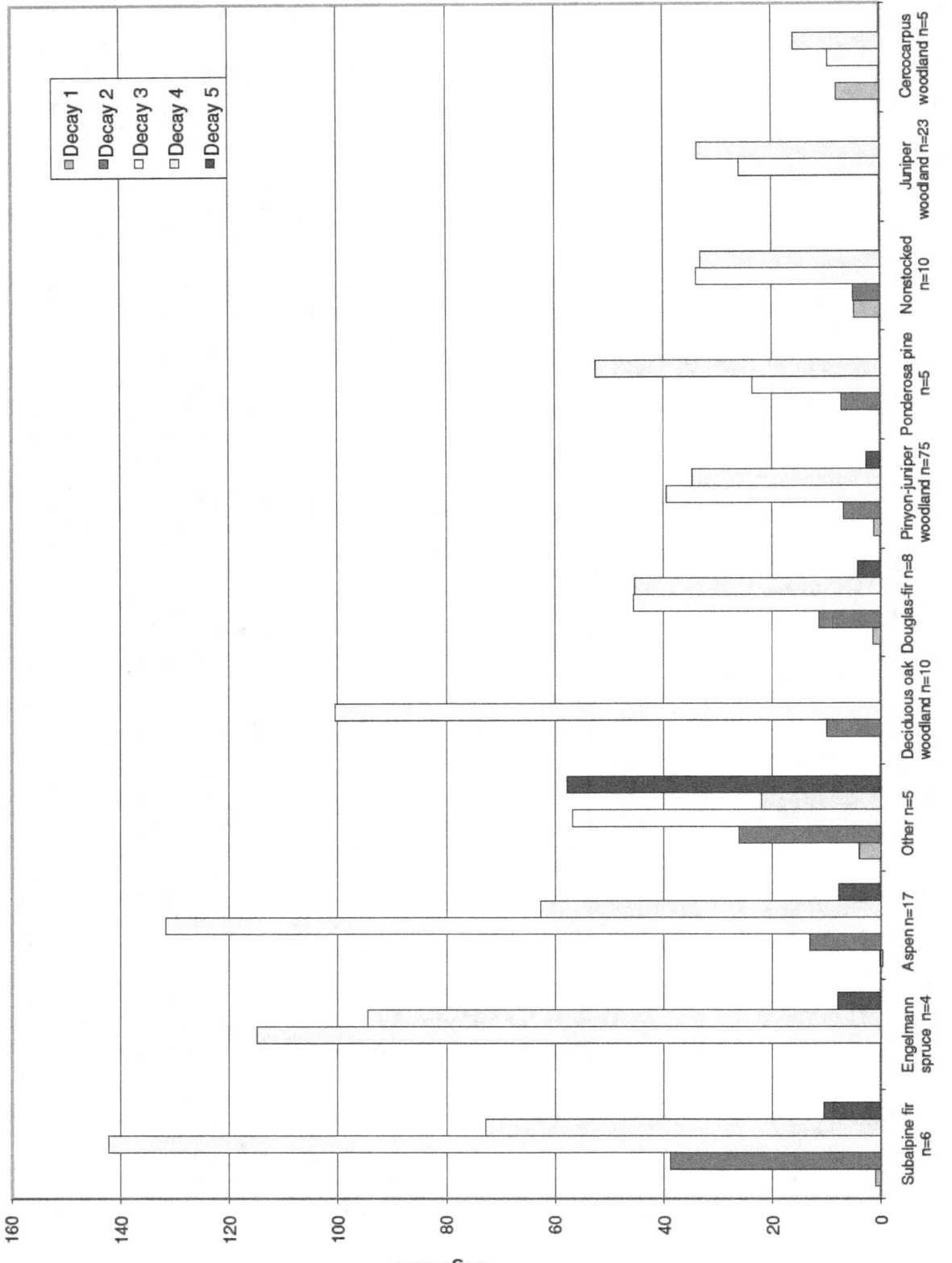

Figure 42—Mean number of CWD logs per acre by forest type and decay class, Utah, cycle 2, 2001-2004.

72

USDA Forest Service Resour. Bull. RMRS-RB-10. 2010

Forest Lichens

Background—Lichen communities are used by FIA as biomonitors of air quality, climate change, and the impacts of change in the structure of the forest vegetation on other members of the forest community. Over time, lichen communities may change in response to stressors, such as air pollutants, and other factors, such as successional change. For example, Rogers and Ryel (2008) found that in an aspen-to-conifer successional sequence, certain lichens favored an aspen conifer mix, while others became more abundant in later successional stages. Some of the differences in lichen communities across the successional sequence appeared to be related to the age of the trees (more time for lichens to become established) and to the quality of substrate available for colonization (rougher bark more likely to be colonized than smooth bark).

Because the lichen community indicator measures change over time, it is implemented in two phases. A calibration phase, which uses data from standard FIA plots and supplemental plots from sites with poor air quality, is used to develop a lichen gradient model for a specific geographic region (Neitlich and others 2001; Will-Wolf 2010). Once the gradient model is developed, changes in lichen communities can be assessed in the application phase. In this phase, lichen community data from standard FIA plots are fitted to the gradient models to generate lichen community scores. These scores are then interpreted to evaluate lichen community status and trends, and their possible relationship to environmental changes such as increasing pollution or warming climate.

The lichen community gradient model has not yet been developed for Utah, so Utah is currently in the calibration phase. Until the calibration phase is complete, lichen species richness and abundance are the only lichen indicator statistics available for standard FIA plots. There are three measures of lichen community richness and abundance calculated during the calibration phase: richness, diversity, and evenness. Richness is simply the number of lichen species on a plot. Lichens identified only to genus are included in this count, because a lichen listed by genus only is known to be different from all other species found on the plot. Diversity is expressed using the Shannon-Weiner Diversity Index, which is calculated as:

$$H' = -\sum(P_i * \ln(P_i))$$

where H' is the Shannon-Weiner index, and

P_i is the proportion of total abundance of species i on the plot.

Evenness is a measure of how evenly abundance is distributed among species. It is calculated as:

$$E = H'/\ln(Richness)$$

where E is evenness and the other variables are defined as above.

Evenness is scaled from zero to 1, with 1 indicating equal abundance of all species.

Inventory Results—Figure 43 shows richness, diversity, and evenness for lichen plots in Utah. On most of the plots with lichen present, there are three or more lichen species. As expected, the diversity index tends to be highest where there are more species present. However, evenness appears to be unrelated to richness or diversity, because most plots have approximately equal evenness.

Discussion—Use of the lichen indicator in Utah is currently limited to relatively simple measures, but the establishment of an environmental gradient model will enable more detailed analysis in the future. Other lichen studies have found that lichens in Utah, for the most part, have not been significantly impacted by air pollution. For example, pilot biomonitoring studies in the Manti-LaSal National Forest (St. Clair 2000) and the

USDA Forest Service Resour. Bull. RMRS-RB-10. 2010

73

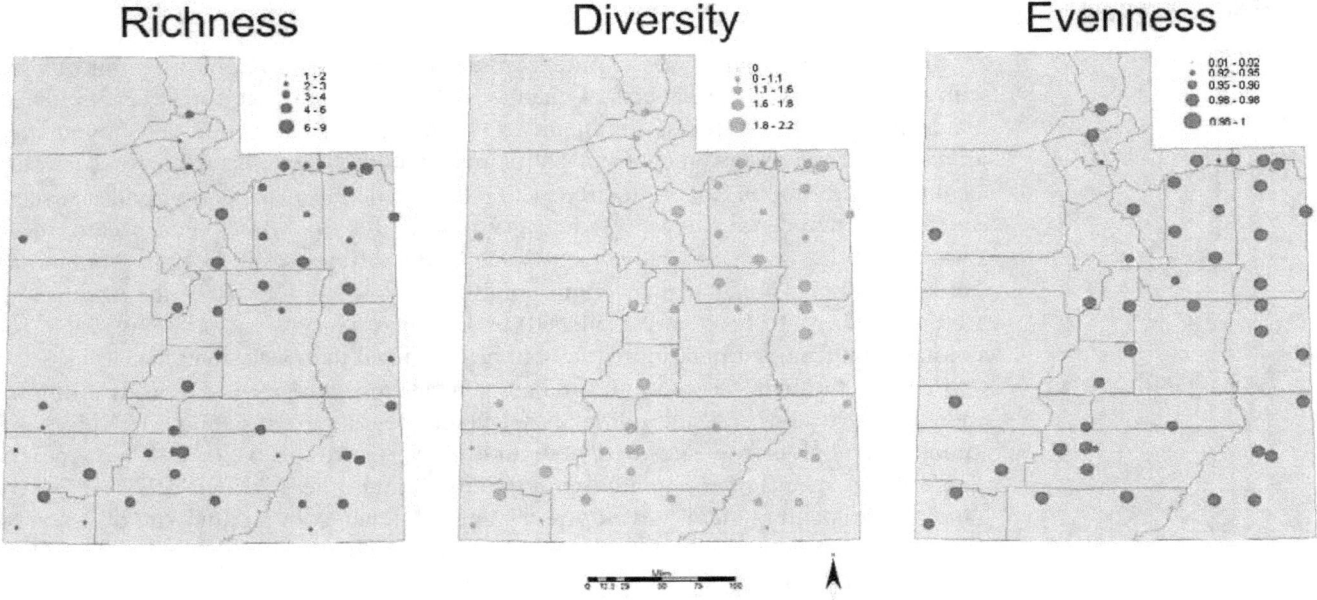

Richness   Diversity   Evenness

Figure 43—Lichen richness, diversity, and evenness measures for FIA plots in Utah, cycle 2, 2000-2005. Larger symbols indicate higher values for each measure.

Uinta Mountains (St. Clair and Newberry 1994) found little pollution-related damage on lichens, but noted that some potentially harmful elements were found in relatively high levels in lichen tissue. Because there has been little impact to lichen communities to date, it is expected that the application phase will be able to detect environmental change as lichen monitoring in Utah continues.

Phase 2 Damage

Background—As field crews measure live trees on subplots (trees 5 inches diameter and greater), they carefully examine those trees for the presence of damaging agents (USDA Forest Service 2000-2005a). They record up to three damaging agents if the damages meet one or more of the following three criteria:

1. The damage will prevent the tree from living to maturity, if immature, or living 10 more years, if mature.
2. The damage will prevent the tree from producing marketable products.
3. The damage will seriously reduce (or has reduced) the quality of the tree's marketable products.

Since the last two criteria are less applicable to woodlands species that produce few marketable products, results from damage data can be quite different between woodland type species and timber type species.

Damaging agents are grouped into several general classes: insects, diseases, fire, animals, humans, and miscellaneous. The miscellaneous group includes suppression, some symptomatic groups whose ultimate causation can be difficult to determine in the field (unhealthy foliage and heartwood scars), unknown causes, and timber form defects that affect commercial products (forking, excessive lean, broken tops, and excessive crook, sweep, or taper). Crews also estimate cull volume percentages (missing top, dead wood, rotten and missing wood, and timber form). When these percentages exceed specific thresholds, although these thresholds can vary by timber or woodland species type, the damaging agent must be recorded.

Inventory results—Of the estimated 2.1 billion live trees 5.0 inches diameter and greater in Utah, about 844 million, or 40 percent, are estimated to have at least one damage meeting one or more of the three damage evaluation criteria above. Of these, 634 million have only one damaging agent, 179 million have two, and 31 million have three (table 9). Timber species had a damage agent recorded more frequently than did woodland species (56 percent versus 30 percent), mostly due to loss of marketable products, although there were other differences between damages to timber and woodland species. The species with damages most frequently recorded were quaking aspen, white fir, limber pine, Great Basin bristlecone pine, narrowleaf cottonwood, and Fremont/Rio Grande cottonwood—all of which are measured and evaluated as timber species. Great Basin bristlecone and the cottonwood species were measured on few plots, so the actual estimates of numbers of trees may not be completely reliable, but they all have growth form and/or ecological characteristics that would lead to an expectation of frequent damage. The most frequently damaged woodland species was Utah juniper.

Discussion—The most common damage category was the miscellaneous group, followed by diseases. Figure 44 shows the percentages of trees with at least one damaging agent recorded by damage agent group and timber/woodland species group. Most groups show differences between timber species and woodland species.

Damages to timber species in the miscellaneous group are mostly growth form defects affecting merchantability, led by excessive crook, sweep, or taper and forking below the merchantable top. The most important health-related miscellaneous damages in timber species were heartwood scars on the bole and dead tops. The most frequent miscellaneous damage in woodland species was "unidentified or unknown." Woodland species frequently have dead branches that remain on the tree long after the cause(s) can be identified, and damage agents are required when volume deductions are made for dead wood. Heartwood scars on the bole are the second most common damage on woodland species.

Disease damaging agents are more frequent in timber species than in woodland species, with aspen being the most affected common timber species. Other species with common disease damage agents were subalpine fir, Douglas-fir, white fir, and lodgepole pine. The most common diseases in timber species were cankers and stem and butt rots, which were particularly abundant in aspens. Also frequent in timber species were broom rusts. Woodland species were most affected by stem and butt rots. Dwarf mistletoe was frequently found on common and singleleaf pinions; true mistletoe was found on Utah juniper and, to a lesser extent, on Gambel oak.

Two damaging agents that were found relatively infrequently, but merit mention, are insects and fire, because they are the most common causes of tree mortality (see "Growth and Mortality" in Section IV). Insect damage, particularly bark beetles, can be difficult to see in live trees, but can rapidly lead to tree death; thus, insect damage would be more commonly recorded as a mortality agent than a damage agent. Bark beetles were the most common insects recorded in timber species. In Utah, fire tends to kill trees rather than damage them, although two fire-resistant species, ponderosa pine and Douglas-fir, did have the highest rates of fire damage.

USDA Forest Service Resour. Bull. RMRS-RB-10. 2010

75

Table 9—Number of live trees 5.0 inches diameter and greater by species and number of damages, Utah, cycle 2, 2000-2005.

Species		No damage	One damage	Two damages	Three damages	All trees
				*Thousand trees (%)**		
Timber species	Aspen	81,016 (29)	128,747 (45)	59,764 (21)	13,783 (5)	283,311
	Lodgepole pine	68,675 (52)	48,882 (37)	11,516 (9)	2,425 (2)	131,498
	Subalpine fir	54,378 (51)	38,511 (36)	11,998 (11)	1,554 (1)	106,441
	Douglas-fir	47,005 (48)	39,695 (41)	8,382 (9)	1,920 (2)	97,001
	Engelmann spruce	53,415 (61)	28,462 (32)	5,028 (6)	1,371 (2)	88,276
	White fir	21,665 (40)	25,159 (46)	6,808 (13)	735 (1)	54,367
	Ponderosa pine	18,648 (60)	10,034 (32)	2,331 (7)	119 (0.4)	31,132
	Limber pine	2,610 (38)	3,099 (45)	1,048 (15)	176 (3)	6,933
	Blue spruce	2 345 (87)	165 (6)	56 (2)	126 (5)	2,691
	Great Basin bristlecone pine	565 (29)	796 (40)	504 (26)	111 (6)	1,975
	Narrowleaf cottonwood	304 (26)	759 (65)	111 (9)	0 (0)	1,174
	Fremont cottonwood, Rio Grande cottonwood	0 (0)	285 (43)	296 (45)	76 (12)	657
Timber species Total		**350,625 (44)**	**324,594 (40)**	**107,841 (13)**	**22,396 (3)**	**805,456**
Woodland species	Utah juniper	402,541 (64)	169,395 (27)	46,558 (7)	6,405 (1)	624,898
	Common or twoneedle pinyon	240,816 (73)	70,425 (21)	15,100 (5)	1,801 (0.5)	328,142
	Gambel oak	77,036 (75)	23,812 (23)	2,231 (2)	122 (0.1)	103,201
	Curlleaf mountain-mahogany	67,958 (74)	20,923 (23)	3,194 (3)	55 (0.1)	92,129
	Singleleaf pinyon	60,129 (78)	14,627 (19)	2,569 (3)	172 (0.2)	77,498
	Rocky Mountain juniper	40,698 (88)	4,074 (9)	1,130 (2)	171 (0.4)	46,073
	Bigtooth maple	25,761 (80)	5,731 (18)	491 (2)	129 (0.4)	32,112
Woodland species Total		**914,938 (70)**	**308,988 (24)**	**71,273 (5)**	**8,855 (0.7)**	**1,304,054**
All species		**1,265,564 (60)**	**633,582 (30)**	**179,114 (8)**	**31,251 (1)**	**2,109,510**

*Numbers and percents may not add to totals due to rounding.

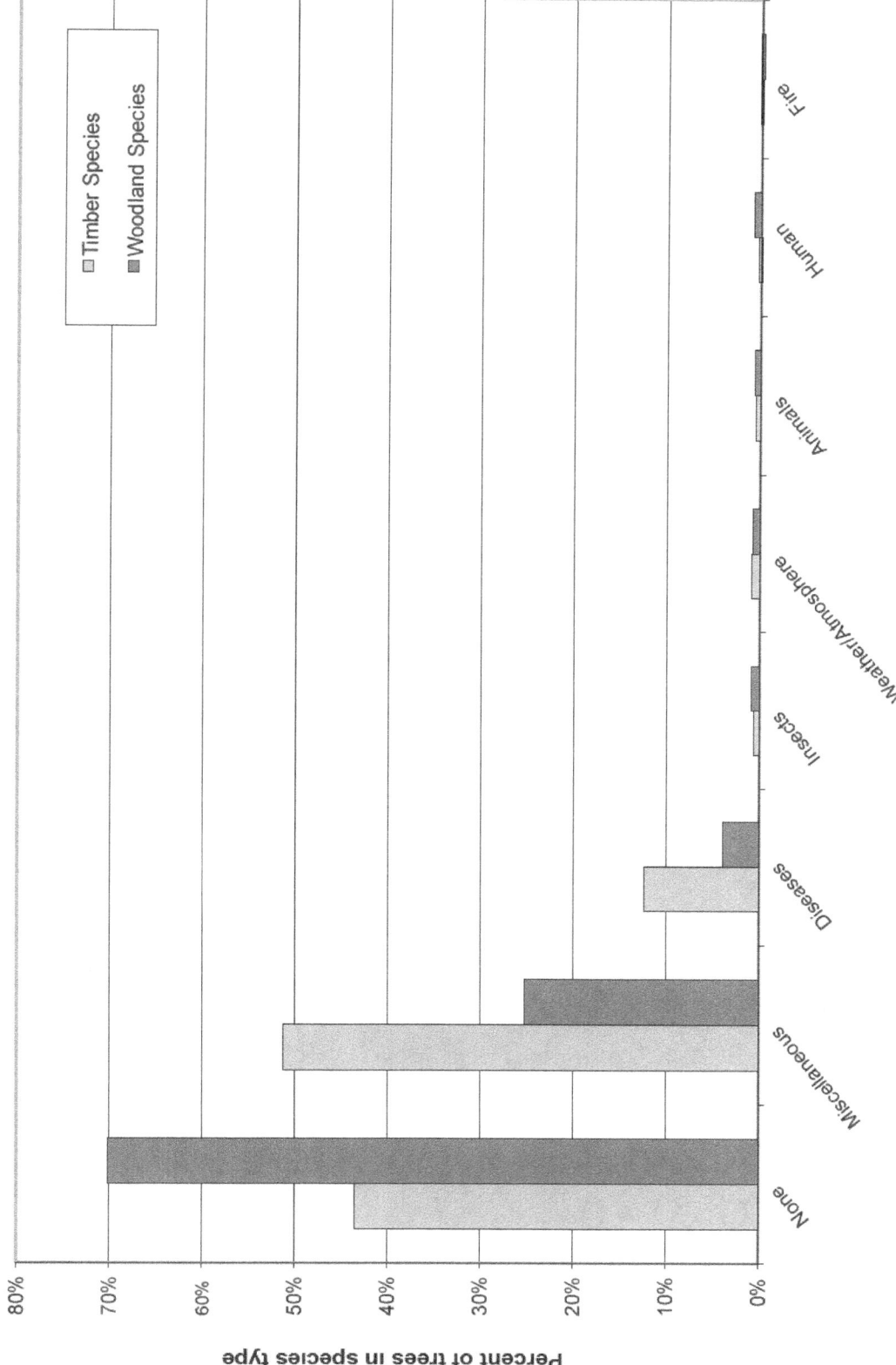

Figure 44—Percent of live trees 5.0 inches diameter by species type and damage agent group, Utah, cycle 2, 2000-2005

USDA Forest Service Resour. Bull. RMRS-RB-10. 2010

77

VII. Timber Products

Removals

The net volume of growing-stock trees removed from the inventory by harvesting, cultural operations, land clearing, and changes in land use is generally known as "removals." As State annual inventory cycles are completed, future reports will assess removals through remeasurement of the permanent annual field plots. In this report, removals, which are measured periodically, are based on data from 2002, and deal only with removals for timber products. Utah's 2002 industrial timber harvest was 41.3 million board feet Scribner, and dead trees accounted for nearly 17.6 million board feet (43 percent) of the harvest (Morgan and others 2006). Dead trees are not considered growing-stock trees. Thus removals are substantially less than total harvested volume.

Removals for timber products include both the volume processed in mills and logging residue—the volume harvested or killed but not utilized. Tables 10, 11, and 12 show removals by product, species, and ownership group in cubic feet for growing-stock removals, and board feet International ¼-inch and Scribner log rules for removals from the sawlog portion of sawtimber trees.

About 5.4 million cubic feet of wood, exclusive of land clearing volume and changes in land use, were removed from growing-stock on Utah's non-reserved timberland during 2002. Nearly 95 percent of the volume was for wood products, and 5 percent was not utilized and was left in the woods as logging residue. Sawlogs were the largest component of removals from growing-stock followed by fiber logs.

National Forests supplied 43 percent of the volume removed from growing-stock. Other public landowners, including the Bureau of Land Management and the State of Utah, provided slightly less than 4 percent, while private and tribal landowners supplied the majority (53 percent).

Removals from the sawlog portion of sawtimber included 18.8 million board feet Scribner log rule, or 21.1 million board feet expressed in International ¼-inch log rule. Logs harvested to produce lumber (sawlogs) dominated products harvested from sawtimber, accounting for 88 percent of sawtimber removals. Logging residues accounted for just 1.7 percent of total sawtimber removals.

Spruce was the leading species harvested, accounting for 36 percent of growing-stock removals and 42 percent of sawtimber removals. Hardwoods, primarily aspen and cottonwood, accounted for 25 percent of growing-stock removals and almost 17 percent of sawtimber removals. Lodgepole pine, ponderosa pine, Douglas-fir, true fir, and other pine species accounted for the remaining removals.

Forest Industry (Revised from Morgan and others 2006)

Utah's primary forest products industry consisted of 49 active manufacturers operating in 20 counties during 2002 (table 13). The sawmill sector, manufacturing lumber and other sawn products, was the largest sector, operating 23 mills during 2002; 14 facilities produced house logs and log homes. There were 10 log furniture producers, one post and pole firm, and a decorative bark producer also operating in 2002. Changes in Utah's industry structure over the past 10 years were similar to those experienced throughout the Interior West, with the number of sawmills decreasing and the number and diversity of other manufacturers increasing.

USDA Forest Service Resour. Bull. RMRS-RB-10. 2010

79

Table 10--Removals from nonreserved timberland by species and product, Utah, 2002, from RPA-TPO data calculated by BBER from FIDACS data.

Thousand cubic feet--growing stock removals

	Sawlogs	Fiber logs	Fuelwood	Post, pole, piling	Other products*	All products	Logging residue	Total removals
Douglas-fir	455.778	10.587	-	-	1.870	468.234	25.864	494.098
True fir	92.277	10.105	-	-	0.890	103.272	5.704	108.977
Lodgepole pine	485.846	-	-	259.466	30.695	776.006	42.865	818.871
Ponderosa pine	631.687	-	-	2.887	3.811	638.384	35.263	673.647
Other pine	2.730	-	-	-	-	2.730	0.151	2.881
Spruce	1,722.737	-	-	115.537	23.643	1,861.918	102.847	1,964.765
Hardwoods	347.157	923.432	13.807	-	-	1,284.396	70.184	1,354.580
Total species	**3,738.212**	**944.124**	**13.807**	**377.890**	**60.909**	**5,134.942**	**282.878**	**5,417.820**

Thousand board feet (International 1/4")--sawlog removals from sawtimber trees

	Sawlogs	Fiber logs	Fuelwood	Post, pole, piling	Other products*	All products	Logging residue	Total removals
Douglas-fir	2,271.541	19.956	-	-	9.445	2,300.943	40.637	2,341.580
True fir	459.896	19.049	-	-	4.498	483.443	8.538	491.981
Lodgepole pine	2,421.393	-	-	0.553	155.069	2,577.016	45.513	2,622.528
Ponderosa pine	3,148.246	-	-	0.006	19.251	3,167.503	55.941	3,223.444
Other pine	13.606	-	-	-	-	13.606	0.240	13.847
Spruce	8,585.904	-	-	0.246	119.445	8,705.594	153.749	8,859.344
Hardwoods	1,730.188	1,740.711	19.321	-	-	3,490.220	61.300	3,551.520
Total species	**18,630.775**	**1,779.716**	**19.321**	**0.806**	**307.708**	**20,738.325**	**365.918**	**21,104.243**

Thousand board feet (Scribner)--sawlog removals from sawtimber trees

	Sawlogs	Fiber logs	Fuelwood	Post, pole, piling	Other products*	All products	Logging residue	Total removals
Douglas-fir	2,028.162	17.818	-	-	8.433	2,054.413	36.283	2,090.696
True fir	410.621	17.008	-	-	4.016	431.645	7.623	439.269
Lodgepole pine	2,161.958	-	-	0.494	138.455	2,300.907	40.636	2,341.543
Ponderosa pine	2,810.934	-	-	0.005	17.188	2,828.128	49.948	2,878.075
Other pine	12.149	-	-	-	-	12.149	0.215	12.363
Spruce	7,665.985	-	-	0.220	106.647	7,772.852	137.276	7,910.129
Hardwoods	1,544.811	1,554.206	17.251	-	-	3,116.268	54.732	3,171.000
Total species	**16,634.620**	**1,589.032**	**17.251**	**0.719**	**274.739**	**18,516.362**	**326.713**	**18,843.074**

*Other products include house logs and log furniture logs.

Table 11--Removals from nonreserved timberland by species and product, Utah, 2002, from RPA-TPO data calculated by BBER from FIDACS data.

	Thousand cubic feet--growing stock removals			
	National Forest	Other public	Private	All owners
Douglas-fir	61.287	0.960	431.852	494.098
True fir	42.964	0.691	65.321	108.977
Lodgepole pine	510.931	1.344	306.596	818.871
Ponderosa pine	223.726	174.812	275.109	673.647
Other pine	-	-	2.881	2.881
Spruce	1,395.953	2.065	566.747	1,964.765
Hardwoods	91.305	19.206	1,244.069	1,354.580
Total species	**2,326.166**	**199.078**	**2,892.575**	**5,417.820**
	Thousand board feet (International 1/4")--sawlog removals from sawtimber trees			
	National Forest	Other public	Private	All owners
Douglas-fir	294.623	4.616	2,042.341	2,341.580
True fir	206.558	3.323	282.099	491.981
Lodgepole pine	1,257.628	6.460	1,358.440	2,622.528
Ponderosa pine	1,060.897	840.217	1,322.330	3,223.444
Other pine	-	-	13.847	13.847
Spruce	6,125.037	9.953	2,724.354	8,859.344
Hardwoods	438.848	92.311	3,020.361	3,551.520
Total species	**9,383.591**	**956.880**	**10,763.772**	**21,104.243**
	Thousand board feet (Scribner)--sawlog removals from sawtimber trees			
	National Forest	Other public	Private	All owners
Douglas-fir	263.056	4.121	1,823.519	2,090.696
True fir	184.427	2.967	251.874	439.269
Lodgepole pine	1,122.882	5.768	1,212.893	2,341.543
Ponderosa pine	947.230	750.194	1,180.652	2,878.075
Other pine	-	-	12.363	12.363
Spruce	5,468.783	8.886	2,432.459	7,910.129
Hardwoods	391.828	82.421	2,696.751	3,171.000
Total species	**8,378.206**	**854.357**	**9,610.511**	**18,843.074**

Sales from Utah's primary wood products industry during 2002 totaled nearly $36.6 million, including finished products and mill residues. House logs and log homes accounted for 50 percent of total sales; lumber, mine timbers, and other sawn products accounted for about 32 percent; while other products and mill residues accounted for 18 percent. Utah was the leading market area for lumber, log homes, posts, poles, and log furniture, with in-State sales accounting for almost 46 percent of total sales. The other Four Corners States (Arizona, Colorado, and New Mexico) accounted for about 22 percent of total sales, with log homes accounting for 45 percent of sales in the region.

Timber processors in Utah received 32.5 million board feet (MMBF) Scribner of timber in 2002 (table 14), including 2.8 MMBF that was harvested outside the State. Private and tribal timberlands provided 9.2 MMBF (28 percent) of the timber delivered to Utah mills during 2002. National Forests provided 67 percent (21.9 MMBF) of timber receipts, with 29 of Utah's timber processors receiving timber cut from National Forests. State lands provided less than 5 percent of the timber received by mills in Utah.

Table 12--Removals from nonreserved timberland by species and product, Utah, 2002, from RPA-TPO data calculated by BBER from FIDACS data.

	Thousand cubic feet--growing stock removals			
	National Forest	Other public	Private	All owners
Sawlogs	1,805.695	188.230	1,744.286	3,738.212
Fiber logs	-	-	944.124	944.124
Fuelwood	-	-	13.807	13.807
Post, pole, piling	355.033	-	22.857	377.890
Other products*	43.673	0.427	16.809	60.909
Total products	2,204.401	188.657	2,741.883	5,134.942
Logging residue	121.765	10.421	150.692	282.878
Total removals	**2,326.166**	**199.078**	**2,892.575**	**5,417.820**

	Thousand board feet (International 1/4")--sawlog removals from sawtimber trees			
	National Forest	Other public	Private	All owners
Sawlogs	8,999.356	938.115	8,693.303	18,630.775
Fiber logs	-	-	1,779.716	1,779.716
Fuelwood	-	-	19.321	19.321
Post, pole, piling	0.757	-	0.049	0.806
Other products*	220.630	2.159	84.919	307.708
Total products	9,220.744	940.274	10,577.307	20,738.325
Logging residue	162.848	16.606	186.465	365.918
Total removals	**9,383.591**	**956.880**	**10,763.772**	**21,104.243**

	Thousand board feet (Scribner)--sawlog removals from sawtimber trees			
	National Forest	Other public	Private	All owners
Sawlogs	8,035.140	837.603	7,761.878	16,634.620
Fiber logs	-	-	1,589.032	1,589.032
Fuelwood	-	-	17.251	17.251
Post, pole, piling	0.676	-	0.044	0.719
Other products*	196.991	1.928	75.820	274.739
Total products	8,232.807	839.530	9,444.024	18,516.362
Logging residue	145.400	14.827	166.486	326.713
Total removals	**8,378.206**	**854.357**	**9,610.511**	**18,843.074**

*Other products include house logs and log furniture logs.

Table 13--Active Utah primary wood products facilities by county and product, 2002.

County	Lumber	Log homes and house logs	Log furniture and other products[a]	Total
Beaver	1		1	2
Cache	3		1	4
Davis	1			1
Duchesne	2	2		4
Emery	1			1
Garfield	1	1	1	3
Iron	1		1	2
Millard			1	1
Morgan	1			1
Piute			1	1
Salt Lake	1	1	2	4
San Juan	1			1
Sanpete		1	1	2
Sevier	1			1
Summit	3	1		4
Uintah	1	4	1	6
Utah			2	2
Wasatch	2	2		4
Wayne	2	1		3
Weber	1	1		2
2002 Total	**23**	**14**	**12**	**49**
1992 Total	34	13	4	51

[a]Other products include posts, poles, and bark products.

Table 14--Timber received by Utah forest products industry by ownership class and product, 2002.

Ownership class	Sawlogs	House logs	Other products[a]	All products
	---------------Thousand board feet, Scribner------------			
Private and tribal timberland	7,630	951	661	9,241
Public timberland	12,571	8,918	1,755	23,245
National Forest	11,571	8,618	1,709	21,898
State lands	1,000	300	46	1,346
Other owners[b]	-	-	33	33
All owners	**20,201**	**9,869**	**2,448**	**32,518**

[a]Other products include furniture logs, fiber logs, posts, and poles.

[b]Other owners include the BLM and Canada.

Utah's sawmill sector has been in decline for several decades. Lumber production in 2002 was 58 percent lower than in 1992 and 63 percent lower than in 1966. Most of the production loss was among the State's larger mills, while the greatest loss of actual milling facilities was among the small mills. Average annual lumber production among the State's six largest mills was about 3.8 MMBF lumber tally in 2002. The remaining 17 small mills had an average lumber production of 204 MBF in 2002. On average, Utah sawmills produced approximately 1.28 board feet of lumber for every board foot Scribner of timber processed, resulting in an average overrun of 28 percent in 2002.

Sales value from Utah's log home sector increased substantially over the past 10 years even though only one more house log manufacturer was identified in 2002 than in 1992. During 2002, Utah's 14 log home manufacturers processed 11.0 MMBF of timber, produced about 3.0 million lineal feet of house logs, and generated about $18.5 million in product sales. By sales value, Utah's log home sector is the fourth largest in the western United States, behind Montana, Idaho, and Colorado.

Across all industry sectors, total timber-processing capacity was 78.5 MMBF Scribner. A total of 32.6 MMBF Scribner was processed by Utah firms in 2002, making capacity utilization about 42 percent. Utah timber processors produced 41,106 bone dry tons (BDT) of mill residue, with 89 percent utilized. Sawmills were the main residue producers in Utah, producing 31,294 BDT of residue, or 1.176 BDT of residue per MBF of lumber, during 2002.

VIII. Summary and Conclusions

Changes in definitions and other factors have affected direct comparisons of past periodic to present annual inventories. These changes represent a continual improvement process within the FIA program, so there is some trade-off between inventory consistency and improvement. The same holds true for the FIA annual inventory system, which is, and will be, continually updated and improved. Utah's 19.5 million acres of forest and other wooded lands are constantly changing. As a full inventory cycle is completed and remeasurement begins in 2010, direct plot-to-plot and tree-to-tree measurements will reflect real change in another 10 percent of the plots each year. Forest resource trends of area, number of trees, volume, biomass, growth, mortality, and other attributes will be linked directly to permanent plots that can be tracked both temporally and spatially.

Even though there have been definitional changes, the annual inventory showed more forest area (especially in woodland types) and more live trees (especially in Gambel oak) than the previous periodic inventory of Utah (O'Brien 1999); there was little difference in total volume from the past. However, at the species level there were some noticeable differences. Aspen, Utah juniper, and lodgepole pine had the largest increases in volume, while Douglas-fir and Engelmann spruce had the largest decreases in volume. Based on the annual inventory, aspen, subalpine fir, and Douglas-fir had the largest gross growth. Engelmann spruce had the highest mortality followed by subalpine fir, common pinyon, and Douglas-fir. Aspen area and volume increased from the past, while the total number of trees decreased, with fewer small-diameter and greater large-diameter trees.

"Other wooded land," a new land type classification, may prove useful for future assessments of change, especially in States like Utah where there is a significant amount of forest with sparse tree crown cover, like pinyon and juniper. Although they are a relatively long-lived species, the expansion of pinyon and juniper woodlands since Euro-American settlement of the West and the recent drought-related pinyon mortality in the southwestern United States are evidence that they are not immune to rapid change events.

In recent years there has been concern about the future of aspen on the landscape, primarily due to the characteristics of aspen and how they relate to changes in disturbance regimes. According to FIA's current annual data, aspen appears to be fairly stable in Utah. However, conifer species, such as Engelmann spruce, have shown substantial recent mortality due to beetle attack. Excluding the impacts of fire, which can affect all species, other common conifers in Utah such as Douglas-fir, subalpine fir, lodgepole pine, and ponderosa pine are particularly susceptible to forest insect outbreaks, which can have widespread affects. The long-term outlook for these species will depend on the composition and structure of the current stands, weather and climate conditions, and insect population trends. In addition, this selective mortality, which often occurs in older trees, can alter the tree age distribution of stands. This can affect the balance of structural stand-size distributions on the landscape for long-term sustainability, and important stand structures like "old forest."

Although noxious plant species can have many negative effects on forest communities, in Utah they are not prevalent in the pinyon-juniper forest type group; whereas the oak, aspen, and other western hardwood types are more susceptible to invasion. This may be due to one or more factors, including soil conditions, accessibility to livestock grazing, road and foot traffic, and/or high frequency of both natural and human-induced disturbance. On the other hand, cheatgrass which is most common in the pinyon-juniper forest type group in Utah, can present a threat to western ecosystems.

Standing dead trees (snags) provide important habitat for many species in the forested ecosystems of Utah including cavity-nesting birds, silver-haired bats, and black bears. In general, Engelmann spruce contributes the most snags for all three wildlife

USDA Forest Service Resour. Bull. RMRS-RB-10. 2010

85

species combined, with aspen and subalpine fir available in abundance for both bats and cavity-nesting birds. Douglas-fir and lodgepole pine also contribute significantly to the needs of birds and bats while ponderosa pine provides the bulk of the remaining potential den sites for black bear.

FIA's Phase 3 indicators are useful for monitoring forest health issues such as tree crown conditions, lichen community composition, understory vegetation, down woody materials, and soil attributes at the regional or national scale. In addition, this data can often be used as a flag for events that may guide to information needs at a much finer scale.

Although more recently there has been a downturn in Utah's Forest Industry, in 2002 Utah's primary forest products industry consisted of 49 active manufacturers operating in 20 counties. Sales from Utah's primary wood products industry during 2002 totaled nearly $36.6 million, including finished products and mill residues. The industrial timber harvest was 41.3 million board feet Scribner, and dead trees accounted for nearly 17.6 million board feet (43 percent) of the harvest. About 5.4 million cubic feet of wood, exclusive of land clearing volume and changes in land use, were removed from growing-stock on Utah's non-reserved timberland during 2002. Spruce was the leading species harvested, accounting for 36 percent of growing-stock removals and 42 percent of sawtimber removals.

At the national level, there are many discussions about how to coordinate assessments of forest and other lands in a more seamless manner. One way FIA plans to facilitate this is by collecting land use and tree crown cover on all Phase 2 plots, regardless of whether they meet FIA's definition of forest land. In the near future, this information can be used for initial assessments as a broad scoping tool for all lands. As FIA maintains its role as the Nations continuous forest census, it will be necessary to adapt to the continually changing needs and expectations of users.

86

USDA Forest Service Resour. Bull. RMRS-RB-10. 2010

IX. Standard Forest Inventory and Analysis Terminology

Average annual mortality—The average annual volume of trees 5.0 inches d.b.h./d.r.c. and larger that died from natural causes.

Average net annual growth—Average annual net change in volume of trees 5.0 inches d.b.h./d.r.c. and larger in the absence of cutting (average annual gross growth minus average annual mortality).

Basal area (BA)—The cross-sectional area of a tree stem/bole (trunk) at the point where diameter is measured, inclusive of bark. BA is calculated for trees 1.0 inch and larger in diameter, and is expressed in square feet. The calculation is based on diameter at breast height (d.b.h.) for timber species; for woodland species, it is based on diameter at root collar (d.r.c.).

Biomass—The quantity of wood fiber, for trees 1.0-inch d.b.h./d.r.c. and larger, expressed in terms of oven-dry weight. Includes above-ground portions of trees: bole/ stem (trunk), bark, and branches. Biomass estimates can be computed for live and/ or dead trees.

Board-foot volume— A board-foot is a unit of measure indicating the amount of wood contained in an unfinished board 1-foot wide, 1-foot long, and 1-inch thick. Board-foot volume is computed for the sawlog portion of a sawtimber-size tree; the sawlog portion includes the part of the bole on sawtimber-size tree from a 1-foot stump to a minimum sawlog top of 7-inches d.o.b. for softwoods, or 9-inches d.o.b. for hardwoods. **Net board-foot volume** is calculated as the gross board-foot volume in the sawlog portion of a sawtimber-size tree, less deductions for cull (note: board-foot cull deductions are limited to rotten/missing material and form defect – referred to as the **merchantability factor —board-foot**). Board-foot volume estimates are computed in both Scribner and International ¼-inch rule, and can be calculated for live and/or dead (standing or down) trees.

Census water—Streams, sloughs, estuaries, canals, and other moving bodies of water 200 feet wide and greater, and lakes, reservoirs, ponds, and other permanent bodies of water 4.5 acres in area and greater.

Coarse woody debris—Down pieces of wood leaning more than 45 degrees from vertical with a diameter of at least 3.0 inches and length of at least 3.0 feet.

Condition class—The combination of discrete landscape and forest attributes that identify, define, and stratify the area associated with a plot. Examples of such attributes include condition status, forest type, stand origin, stand size, owner group, and stand density.

Crown class—A classification of trees based on dominance in relation to adjacent trees in the stand as indicated by crown development and amount of sunlight received from above and the sides.

Crown cover (Canopy cover)—The percentage of the ground surface area covered by a vertical projection of plant crowns. Tree crown cover for a sample site includes the combined cover of timber and woodland trees 1.0-inch d.b.h./d.r.c. and larger. Maximum crown cover for a site is 100 percent; overlapping cover is not double counted.

USDA Forest Service Resour. Bull. RMRS-RB-10. 2010

87

Cubic-foot volume (merchantable)—A cubic-foot is a unit of measure indicating the amount of wood contained in a cube 1x1x1 foot. Cubic-foot volume is computed for the merchantable portion of timber and woodland species; the merchantable portion for timber species includes that part of a bole from a 1-foot stump to a minimum 4-inch top d.o.b, or above the place(s) of diameter measurement for any woodland tree with a single 5.0-inch stem or larger or a cumulative (calculated) d.r.c. of at least 5.0 inches to the 1.5-inch ends of all branches. **Net cubic-foot volume** is calculated as the gross cubic-foot volume in the merchantable portion of a tree, less deductions for cull.

Diameter at breast height (d.b.h.)—The diameter of a tree bole/stem (trunk) measured at breast height (4.5 feet above ground), measured outside the bark. The point of diameter measurement may vary for abnormally formed trees.

Diameter at root collar (d.r.c.)—The diameter of a tree stem(s) measured at root collar or at the point nearest the ground line (whichever is higher) that represents the basal area of the tree, measured outside the bark. For multistemmed trees, d.r.c. is calculated from an equation that incorporates the individual stem diameter measurements. The point of diameter measurement may vary for woodland trees with stems that are abnormally formed. With the exception of seedlings, woodland stems qualifying for measurement must be at least 1.0 inch diameter or larger and at least 1.0-foot in length.

Diameter class—A grouping of tree diameters (d.b.h. or d.r.c.) into classes of a specified range. For some diameter classes, the number referenced (e.g., 4-inch, 6-inch, 8-inch) is designated as the midpoint of an individual class range. For example, if 2-inch classes are specified (the range for an individual class) and even numbers are referenced, the 6-inch class would include trees 5.0- to 6.9-inches in diameter.

Diameter outside bark (d.o.b.)—Tree diameter measurement inclusive of the outside perimeter of the tree bark. d.o.b. may be taken at various points on a tree (e.g., breast height, tree top) or log, and is sometimes estimated.

Field plot/location—A reference to the sample site or plot; an area containing the field location center (LC) and all sample points. A field location consists of four subplots and four microplots.
- **Subplot**—A 1/24-acre fixed-radius area (24-foot horizontal radius) used to sample trees 5.0-inches d.b.h./d.r.c. and larger and understory vegetation.
- **Microplot**—A 1/300-acre fixed-radius plot (6.8-foot radius), located at the center of each subplot, used to inventory seedlings and saplings.

Fixed-radius plot—A circular sample plot of a specified horizontal radius: 1/300 acre = 6.8-foot radius (microplot); 1/24 acre = 24.0-foot radius (subplot).

Forest industry land—Land owned by a company or an individual(s) operating a primary wood-processing plant.

Forest land—Land that has at least 10 percent cover of live tally tree species of any size, or land formerly having such tree cover, and not currently developed for a nonforest use. The minimum area for classification as forest land is 1 acre. Roadside, stream-side, and shelterbelt strips of trees must be at least 120 feet wide to qualify as forest land. Unimproved roads and trails, streams and other bodies of water, or natural clearings in forested areas are classified as forest, if less than 120 feet wide or 1 acre in size. Grazed woodlands, reverting fields, and pastures that are not actively maintained are included if above qualifications are satisfied.

Forest type—A classification of forest land based on the species forming a plurality of live-tree stocking.
- Timber type—Forest types based on species that are measured at d.b.h.
- Woodland type—Forest types based on species that are measured at d.r.c.

Gross growth—The annual increase in volume of trees 5.0 inches d.b.h. and larger in absence of cutting and mortality. Gross growth includes survivor growth, ingrowth, growth on ingrowth, growth on removals before removal, and growth on mortality prior to death.

Growing-stock trees— A live timber species 5.0-inches d.b.h. or larger with less than $^2/_3$ (67 percent) of the merchantable volume cull, and containing at least one solid 8-foot section, now or prospectively, reasonably free of form defect, on the merchantable portion of the tree.

Growing-stock volume—the cubic-foot volume of sound wood in growing-stock trees at least 5.0 inches d.b.h. from a 1-foot stump to a minimum 4-inch top d.o.b. to the central stem.

Hardwoods—Dicotyledonous trees, usually broadleaf and deciduous.

Hexagonal grid (Hex)—A hexagonal grid formed from equilateral triangles for the purpose of tessellating the FIA inventory sample. Each hexagon in the base grid has an area of 5,937 acres (2,403.6 ha) and contains one inventory plot. The base grid can be subdivided into smaller hexagons to intensify the sample.

Indian Trust lands—American Indian lands held in fee, or trust, by the Federal Government, but administered for tribal groups or as individual trust allotments.

Land use—The classification of a land condition by use or type.

Litter—The uppermost layer of organic debris on a forest floor; that is, essentially the freshly fallen, or only slightly decomposed material, mainly foliage, but also bark fragments, twigs, flowers, fruits, and so forth. Duff is the organic layer, unrecognizable as to origin, immediately beneath the litter layer from which it is derived.

Logging residue/products—
- **Bolt**—A short piece of pulpwood; a short log.
- **Industrial wood**—All commercial roundwood products, excluding fuelwood.
- **Logging residue**—The unused sections within the merchantable portions of sound (growing-stock) trees cut or killed during logging operations.
- **Mill or plant residue**—Wood material from mills or other primary manufacturing plants that is not utilized for the mill's or plant's primary products. Mill or plant residue includes bark, slabs, edgings, trimmings, miscuts, sawdust, and shavings. Much of the mill and plant residue is used as fuel and as the raw material for such products as pulp, palletized fuel, fiberwood, mulch, and animal bedding.
- **Coarse residue**—Wood material suitable for chipping, such as slabs, edgings, and trim.
- **Fine residue**—Wood material unsuitable for chipping, such as sawdust and shavings.
- **Primary wood-processing plants**—An industrial plant that processes roundwood products, such as sawlogs, pulpwood bolts, or veneer logs.
- **Pulpwood**—Roundwood, whole-tree chips, or wood residues that are used for the production of wood pulp.
- **Roundwood**—Logs, bolts, or other round sections cut from trees.

USDA Forest Service Resour. Bull. RMRS-RB-10. 2010

89

Mapped-plot design — A sampling technique that identifies (maps) and separately classifies distinct "conditions" on the field location sample area. Each condition must meet minimum size requirements. At the most basic level, condition class delineations include forest land, nonforest land, and water. Forest land conditions can be further subdivided into separate condition classes if there are distinct variations in forest type, stand-size class, stand origin, and stand density, given that each distinct area meets minimum size requirements.

Merchantable portion — For trees measured at d.b.h. and 5.0-inches d.b.h. and larger, the merchantable portion (or "merchantable bole") includes the part of the tree bole from a 1-foot stump to a 4.0-inch top (d.o.b.). For trees measured at d.r.c., the merchantable portion includes all qualifying segments above the place(s) of diameter measurement for any tree with a single 5.0-inch stem or larger or a cumulative (calculated) d.r.c. of at least 5.0 inches to the 1.5-inch ends of all branches; sections below the place(s) of diameter measurement are not included. Qualifying segments are stems or branches that are a minimum of 1 foot in length and at least 1.0 inch diameter; portions of stems or branches smaller than 1.0 inch diameter, such as branch tips, are not included in the merchantable portion of the tree.

Miscellaneous Federal lands — Public lands administered by Federal agencies other than the Forest Service, U.S. Department of Agriculture, or the Bureau of Land Management, U.S. Department of the Interior.

Mortality tree — All standing or down dead trees 5.0-inches d.b.h./d.r.c. and larger that were alive within the previous 5 years.

National Forest System (NFS) lands — Public lands administered by the Forest Service, U.S. Department of Agriculture, such as National Forests, National Grasslands, and some National Recreation Areas.

National Park lands — Public lands administered by the Park Service, U.S. Department of the Interior, such as National Parks, National Monuments, National Historic Sites (such as National Memorials and National Battlefields), and some National Recreation Areas.

Noncensus water — Portions of rivers, streams, sloughs, estuaries, and canals that are 30 to 200 feet wide and at least 1 acre in size; and lakes, reservoirs, and ponds 1 to 4.5 acres in size. Portions of rivers and streams not meeting the criteria for census water, but at least 30 feet wide and 1 acre in size, are considered noncensus water. Portions of braided streams not meeting the criteria for census water, but at least 30 feet in width and 1 acre in size, and more than 50 percent water at normal high-water level are also considered noncensus water.

Nonforest land — Land that does not support, or has never supported, forests, and lands formerly forested where tree regeneration is precluded by development for other uses. Includes areas used for crops, improved pasture, residential areas, city parks, improved roads of any width and adjoining rights-of-way, power line clearings of any width, and noncensus water. If intermingled in forest areas, unimproved roads and nonforest strips must be more than 120 feet wide, and clearings, etc., more than 1 acre in size, to qualify as nonforest land.

Nonindustrial private lands — Privately owned land excluding forest industry land.

Nonreserved forest land — Forest land not withdrawn from management for production of wood products through statute or administrative designation.

Other private lands—Privately owned lands other than forest industry or Indian Trust.

Other public lands—Public lands administered by agencies other than the Forest Service, U.S. Department of Agriculture. Includes lands administered by other Federal, State, county, and local government agencies, including lands leased by these agencies for more than 50 years.

Other wooded land—Land that has 5-10 percent cover of live tally tree species of any size, or from 40 to 199 seedlings per acre; or land formerly having such tree cover, and not currently developed for a nonforest use. The minimum area for classification as forest land is 1 acre. Roadside, stream-side, and shelterbelt strips of trees must be at least 120 feet wide to qualify as forest land. Unimproved roads and trails, streams and other bodies of water, or natural clearings in forested areas are classified as forest, if less than 120 feet wide or 1 acre in size. Grazed woodlands, reverting fields, and pastures that are not actively maintained are included if above qualifications are satisfied.

Poletimber-size trees—For trees measured at d.b.h, softwoods 5.0 to 8.9 inches d.b.h. and hardwoods 5.0 to 10.9 inches d.b.h. For trees measured at d.r.c., all live trees 5.0 to 8.9 inches d.r.c.

Productivity—The potential yield capability of a stand calculated as a function of site index (expressed in terms of cubic-foot growth per acre per year at age of culmination of MAI). Productivity values for forest land provide an indication of biological potential. Timberland stands are classified by the potential net annual growth attainable in fully stocked natural stands. For FIA reporting, Productivity Class is a variable that groups stand productivity values into categories of a specified range. Productivity is sometimes referred to as "Yield" or "Mean annual increment (MAI)."

Removals—The net volume of sound (growing-stock) trees removed from the inventory by harvesting or other cultural operations (such as timber-stand improvement), by land clearing, or by changes in land use (such as a shift to wilderness).

Reserved land—Land withdrawn from management for production of wood products through statute or administrative designation. Examples include Wilderness areas and National Parks and Monuments.

Sampling error—A statistical term used to describe the accuracy of the inventory estimates. Expressed on a percentage basis in order to enable comparisons between the precision of different estimates, sampling errors are computed by dividing the estimate into the square root of its variance.

Sapling—A live tree 1.0-4.9-inches d.b.h./d.r.c.

Sawlog portion—The part of the bole of sawtimber-size trees between a 1-foot stump and the sawlog top.

Sawlog top—The point on the bole of sawtimber-size trees above which a sawlog cannot be produced. The minimum sawlog top is 7 inches d.o.b. for softwoods, and 9 inches d.o.b. for hardwoods.

Sawtimber-size trees—Softwoods 9.0 inches d.b.h. and larger and hardwoods 11.0 inches and larger.

Sawtimber volume—The growing-stock volume in the saw-log portion of sawtimber-size trees in board feet.

Seedlings— Live trees less than 1.0 inch d.b.h./d.r.c.

USDA Forest Service Resour. Bull. RMRS-RB-10. 2010

91

Site index—A measure of forest productivity for a timberland tree/stand. Expressed in terms of the expected height (in feet) of trees on the site at an index age of 50 (or 80 years for aspen and cottonwood). Calculated from height-to-age equations.

Site tree—A tree used to provide an index of site quality. Timber species selected for site index calculations must meet specified criteria with regards to age, diameter, crown class, and damage.

Snag—A standing-dead tree.

Softwood trees—Coniferous trees, usually evergreen, having needle- or scale-like leaves.

Stand—A community of trees that can be distinguished from adjacent communities due to similarities and uniformity in tree and site characteristics, such as age-class distribution, species composition, spatial arrangement, structure, etc.

Stand density—A relative measure that quantifies the relationship between trees per acre, stand basal area, average stand diameter, and stocking of a forested stand.

Stand density index (SDI)—A widely used measure developed by Reineke (1933), SDI is an index that expresses relative stand density based on a comparison of measured stand values with some standard condition; **relative stand density** is the ratio, proportion, or percent of absolute stand density to a reference level defined by some standard level of competition. For FIA reporting, the SDI for a site is usually presented as a percentage of the maximum SDI for the forest type. Site SDI values are sometimes grouped into SDI classes of a specified percentage range. Maximum SDI values vary by species and region.

Standing tree—To qualify as a standing dead tally tree, dead trees must be at least 5.0 inches in diameter, have a bole that has an unbroken actual length of at least 4.5 feet, and lean less than 45 degrees from vertical as measured from the base of the tree to 4.5 feet. Portions of boles on dead trees that are separated greater than 50 percent (either above or below 4.5 feet), are considered severed and are included in Down Woody Material (DWM) if they otherwise meet DWM tally criteria. For western woodland species with multiple stems, a tree is considered down if more than 2/3 of the volume is no longer attached or upright; do not consider cut and removed volume. For western woodland species with single stems to qualify as a standing dead tally tree, dead trees must be at least 5.0 inches in diameter, be at least 1.0 foot in unbroken actual length, and lean less than 45 degrees from vertical.

Stand-size class—A classification of forest land based on the predominant diameter size of live trees presently forming the plurality of live-tree stocking. Classes are defined as follows:
- **Sawtimber stand (Large-tree stand**—A stand at least 10 percent stocked with live trees, in which half or more of the total stocking is from live trees 5.0-inches or larger in diameter, and with sawtimber (large tree) stocking equal to or greater than poletimber (medium tree) stocking.
- **Poletimber stand (Medium-tree stand)**—A stand at least 10 percent stocked with live trees, in which half or more of the total stocking is from live trees 5.0 inches or larger in diameter, and with poletimber (medium tree) stocking exceeding sawtimber (large tree) stocking.
- **Sapling/seedling stand**—A stand at least 10 percent stocked with live trees, in which half or more of the total stocking is from live trees less than 5.0 inches in diameter.

- **Nonstocked stand**—A formerly stocked stand that currently has less than 10 percent stocking, but has the potential to again become 10 percent stocked. For example, recently harvested, burned, or windthrow-damaged areas.

Stockability (Stockability factor)—An estimate of the stocking potential of a given site; for example, a stockability factor of 0.8 for a given site indicates that the site is capable of supporting only about 80 percent of "normal" stocking as indicated by yield tables Stockability factors (maximum site value of 1.0) are assigned to sites based on habitat type/plant associations.

Stocking—An expression of the extent to which growing space is effectively utilized by live trees.

Timber species—Tally tree species traditionally used for industrial wood products. These include all species of conifers, except pinyon and juniper. Timber species are measured at d.b.h.

Timber stand improvement—A term comprising all intermediate cuttings or treatments, such as thinning, pruning, release cutting, girdling, weeding, or poisoning, made to improve the composition, health, and growth of the remaining trees in the stand.

Timberland—Nonreserved forest land capable of producing 20 cubic feet of industrial wood per acre per year.

Wilderness area—An area of undeveloped land currently included in the Wilderness System, managed to preserve its natural conditions and retain its primeval character and influence.

Woodland species—Tally tree species that are not usually converted into industrial wood products. Common uses of woodland trees are fuelwood, fenceposts, and Christmas trees. These species include pinyon, juniper (except Western juniper), mesquite, locust, mountain-mahogany (*Cercocarpus* spp.), Rocky Mountain maple, bigtooth maple, desert ironwood, and most oaks (note: Bur oak and Chinkapin oak are classified as timber species). Because most woodland trees are extremely variable in form, diameter is measured at d.r.c.

Note: For the FIA national glossary please go to:
http://socrates.lv-hrc.nevada.edu/fia/ab/issues/pending/glossary.html

USDA Forest Service Resour. Bull. RMRS-RB-10. 2010

93

94

USDA Forest Service Resour. Bull. RMRS-RB-10. 2010

X. References

Aplet, G.H.; Laven, R.D.; Smith, F.W. 1988. Patterns of community dynamics in Colorado Engelmann spruce-subalpine fir forests. Ecology 69: 312-319.

Bailey, Robert G. 1978. Description of the ecoregions of the United States. Ogden, UT: U.S. Department of Agriculture, Forest Service, Intermountain Region. 77 p.

Baker, W.L.; Shinneman, D.J. 2004. Fire and restoration of piñon-juniper woodlands in the western United States: a review. Forest Ecology and Management 189: 1-21.

Bartos, Dale L.; Campbell, Robert B. 1998. Decline of quaking aspen in the Interior West—examples from Utah. Rangelands 20(1): 15-22.

Bechtold, William A.; Patterson, Paul L., eds. 2005. The enhanced Forest
Inventory and Analysis program—national sampling design and estimation
procedures. Gen. Tech. Rep. SRS-80. Asheville, NC: U.S. Department of
Agriculture, Forest Service, Southern Research Station. 85 p.

Bentz, B.J., Munson, A.S., 2000. Spruce beetle population suppression in northern Utah. Western Journal of Applied Forestry 15: 122-128.

Bottomley, T.; Menlove, J.M. 2006. BLM forest lands report—2006: Status and condition. BLM/ST/ST -07/001+5000. Denver, CO: U.S. Department of the Interior, Bureau of Land Management. 111 p.

Breshears, D.D.; Cobb, N.S.; Rich, P.M.; and others. 2005. Regional vegetation die-off in response to global-change-type drought. Proceedings of the National Academy of Sciences 102: 15144-15148.

Brickell, James E 1970. Equations and computer subroutines for estimating site quality of eight Rocky Mountain Species. Res. Pap. INT-75. Ogden, UT: U.S. Department of Agriculture, Forest Service, Intermountain Forest and Range Experiment Station.

Burkhardt, J.W.; Tisdale, E.W. 1976. Causes of juniper invasion in southwestern Idaho. Ecology 57: 472-484.

Campbell, L.A.; Hallett, J.G.; O'Connell, M.A. 1996. Conservation of bats in managed forests: Use of roosts by *Lasionycteris noctivagans*. Journal of Mammalogy 77: 976-984.

Caratti, J.F. 2006. FIREMON Database. In: Lutes, D.C.; Keane, R.E.; Caratti, J.F.; and others. FIREMON: Fire effects monitoring and inventory system. Gen. Tech. Rep. RMRS-GTR-164-CD. Fort Collins, CO: U.S. Department of Agriculture, Forest Service, Rocky Mountain Research Station: DB-1-38.

Chojnacky, D.C. 1985. Pinyon-juniper volume equations for the central Rocky Mountain States. Res. Note INT-339. Ogden, UT: U.S. Department of Agriculture, Forest Service, Intermountain Forest and Range Experiment Station.

Chojnacky, D.C. 1994. Volume equations for New Mexico pinyon-juniper dryland forests. Res. Note INT-471. Ogden, UT: U.S. Department of Agriculture, Forest Service, Intermountain Research Station.

Chojnacky, David C. 1984. Volume and biomass for curlleaf *cercocarpus* in Nevada. Res. Pap. INT-332. Ogden, UT: U.S. Department of Agriculture, Forest Service, Intermountain Forest and Range Experiment Station. 8 p.

Chojnacky, David C. 1992. Estimating volume and biomass for dryland oak species. In: Ecology and management of oak and associated woodlands: Perspectives in the southwestern United States and northern Mexico; 1992 April 27-30; Sierra Vista, AZ. Gen. Tech. Rep. GTR-RM-218. Fort Collins, CO: U.S. Department of Agriculture, Forest Service, Rocky Mountain Forest and Range Experiment Station: 155-161.

Chojnacky, David C.; Moisen, Gretchen. G. 1993. Converting wood volume to biomass for pinyon and juniper. Res. Note INT-411. Ogden, UT: U.S. Department of Agriculture, Forest Service, Intermountain Research Station. 5 p.

Covington, W.W.; Moore, M.M. 1994. Southwestern ponderosa forest structure and resource conditions: Changes since Euro-American settlement. Journal of Forestry 92: 39-47.

DeRose, R.J.; Long, J.N. 2007. Disturbance, structure, and composition: Spruce beetle and Engelmann spruce forests on the Markagunt Plateau, Utah. Forest Ecology and Management 244: 16–23.

DeRose, R.J.; Long, J.N. 2009. Wildfire and spruce beetle outbreak: Simulation of interacting disturbances in the central Rocky Mountains. Ecoscience 16: 28-38.

DeRose, R.J.; Long, J.N.; Shaw, J.D. 2008. Relationships between forest structure, composition, site, and spruce beetle occurrence in the Intermountain West. In: McWilliams, Will; Moisen, Gretchen; Czaplewski, Ray, comps. 2008. Forest Inventory and Analysis (FIA) symposium 2008; October 21-23, 2008; Park City, UT. Proc. RMRS-P-56CD. Fort Collins, CO: U.S. Department of Agriculture, Forest Service, Rocky Mountain Research Station. 1 CD.

Di Orio, Aaron P.; Callasa, Richard; Schaefer, Robert J. 2005. Forty-eight year decline and fragmentation of aspen (*Populus tremuloides*) in the South Warner Mountains of California. Forest Ecology and Management 206(1-3): 307-313.

USDA Forest Service Resour. Bull. RMRS-RB-10. 2010

95

Dymerski, A.D.; Anhold, J.A.; Munson, A.S. 2001. Spruce beetle *Dendroctonus rufipennis* outbreak in Engelmann spruce *Picea engelmannii* in central Utah, 1986-1998. Western North American Naturalist 61: 19-24.

Edminster, C.B.; Beeson, R.T.; Metcalf, G.E. 1980. Volume tables and point-sampling factors for ponderosa pine in the Colorado Front Range. Res. Note RM-218. Fort Collins, CO: U.S. Department of Agriculture, Forest Service, Rocky Mountain Forest and Range Experiment Station.

Edminster, C.B.; Mowrer, H.T.; Hinds, T.E. 1982. Volume tables and point-sampling factors for aspen in Colorado. Res. Note RM-232. Fort Collins, CO: U.S. Department of Agriculture, Forest Service, Rocky Mountain Forest and Range Experiment Station.

Edminster, C.B.; Mowrer, H. T.; Sheppard, W. D. 1985. Site index curves for aspen in the central Rocky Mountains. Res. Note: RM-453. Fort Collins, CO: U.S. Department of Agriculture, Forest Service, Rocky Mountain Forest and Range Experiment Station. 4 p.

Gillespie, A.J.R. 1999. Rationale for a national annual forest inventory program. Journal of Forestry 97(12): 16-20.

Gingrich, S.F. 1967. Measuring and evaluating stocking and stand density in upland hardwood forests in the Central States. Forest Science 13: 38-53.

Hann, D.W.; Bare, B.B. 1978. Comprehensive tree volume equations for major species of New Mexico and Arizona: I. Results and Methodology. Res. Note INT-209. Ogden, UT: U.S. Department of Agriculture, Forest Service, Intermountain Forest and Range Experiment Station.

Hansen, E.M.; Bentz, B.J.; Turner, D.L. 2001. Physiological basis for flexible voltinism in the spruce beetle (Coleoptera: Scolytidae). The Canadian Entomologist 133: 805-817.

Harestad, A.S.; Keisker, D.G. 1989. Nest tree use by primary cavity-nesting birds in south-central British Columbia. Canadian Journal of Zoology 67: 1067-1073.

Hessl, Amy E.; Graumlich, Lisa J. 2002. Interactive effects of human activities, herbivory and fire on quaking aspen (*Populus tremuloides*) age structures in western Wyoming. Journal of Biogeography 29: 889-902.

Holsten, E.H.; Their, R.W.; Munson, A.S.; Gibson, K.E. 1999. The spruce beetle. Forest Insect and Disease Leaflet 127. U.S. Department of Agriculture, Forest Service. 12 p.

Jenny, H. 1994. Factors of soil formation—a system of quantitative pedology. Dover Edition. New York: Dover Publications. 191 p.

Johnson, M. 1994. Changes in southwestern forests: Stewardship implications. Journal of Forestry 92:16-19.

Kay, C.E. 1997. Is aspen doomed? Journal of Forestry 95(5):4–11.

Kearns, H.S.J., Jacobi, W.R. and Johnson, D.W. 2005. Persistence of pinyon pine snags and logs in southwestern Colorado. Western Journal of Applied Forestry 20(4):247-252.

Kemp, P.D., 1956. Region I Volume Tables for ADP Cruise Computations. Timber Cruising Handbook, R1-2430-31.

Kolenosky, G.B.; Strathearn, S.M. 1987. Black bear. In: Novak, M.; Baker, J.A.; Obbard, M.E.; Malloch, B., eds. Wildlife furbearer management and conservation in North America. Toronto, ON; Ontario Ministry of Natural Resources; North Bay ON: Ontario Trappers' Association: 443-454.

Kulakowski, D.; Veblen, T.T.; Drinkwater, S. 2004. The persistence of quaking aspen (*Populus tremuloides*) in the Grand Mesa area, Colorado. Ecological Applications 14 (5): 1603-1614.

Lawler, J.J. 1999. Modeling habitat attributes of cavity-nesting birds in the Uinta Mountains, Utah: A hierarchical approach. Logan, UT. Utah State University. Ph.D. Dissertation.

Lilieholm, R.J.; Long, J.N.; Patla, S. 1994. Assessing goshawk nest stand habitat using stand density index. Cooper Ornithological Society. Studies in Avian Biology 16: 18-24.

Logan, J.A.; Bentz, B.J. 1999. Model analysis of mountain pine beetle (Coleoptera: Scolytidae) seasonality. Environmental Entomology 28: 924-934.

Long, J.N. 1985. A practical approach to density management. Forest Chronicle 61:23-37.

Long, J.N.; Daniel, T.W. 1990. Assessment of growing stock in uneven-aged stands. Western Journal of Applied Forestry 5: 93-96.

Long, J.N.; Shaw, J.D. 2005. A density management diagram for even-aged ponderosa pine stands. Western Journal of Applied Forestry 20: 205-215.

Lund, H. Gyde. 2004. (Revised 6 May 2005). Considerations for developing U.S. standard definitions of forest and rangeland. Report prepared for Meridian Institute, Contract No. 0045-A. Project No. 9147.8 - Process to Develop a Definition of Forest and Rangeland. Gainesville, VA: Forest Information Services. 108 p.

McClelland, B. R. 1977. Relationship between hole-nesting birds, forest snags, and decay in western larch-Douglas-fir forests of the Northern Rocky Mountains. Missoula, MT. University of Montana. Ph.D. Dissertation.

Miller, R.F.; Wigand, P.E. 1994. Holocene changes in semiarid pinyon-juniper woodlands. Bioscience 44: 465-474.

Miller, Richard F.; Tausch, Robin J.; McArthur, E. Durant; Johnson, Dustin D.; Sanderson, Stewart C. 2008. Age structure and expansion of piñon-juniper woodlands: A regional perspective in the Intermountain West. Res. Pap. RMRS-RP-69. Fort Collins, CO: U.S. Department of Agriculture, Forest Service, Rocky Mountain Research Station. 15 p.

Morgan, Todd A.; Dillon, Thale; Keegan, Charles E., III; Chase, Alfred L.; Thompson, Mike T. 2006. Four Corners timber harvest and forest products industry, 2002. Resour. Bull. RMRS-RB-7. Fort Collins, CO: United States Department of Agriculture, Forest Service, Rocky Mountain Research Station. 64 p.

Mueller, R.C.; Scudder, C.M.; Porter, M.E.; Trotter, R.T., III; Gehring, C.A.; Whitham, T.G. 2005. Differential tree mortality in response to severe drought: Evidence for long-term vegetation shifts. Journal of Ecology 93: 1085-1093.

Myers, C.A. 1964. Volume table and point sampling factors for lodgepole pine in Colorado and Wyoming. Res. Note RM-6. Fort Collins, CO: U.S. Department of Agriculture, Forest Service, Rocky Mountain Forest and Range Experiment Station.

Myers, C.A.; Edminster, C.B. 1972. Volume Table and point sampling factors for Engelmann spruce in Colorado and Wyoming. Res. Note RM-95. Fort Collins, CO: U.S. Department of Agriculture, Forest Service, Rocky Mountain Forest and Range Experiment Station.

National Climatic Data Center. 1994. Time bias corrected divisional Temperature-Precipitation-Drought Index. Documentation for dataset TD-9640. Available from DBMB, NCDC, NOAA, Federal Building, 37 Battery Park Ave. Asheville, NC 28801-2733. 12 p.

Neitlich, P.N.; Will-Wolf, S.; McCune, B. 2001. FIA and FHM lichen community indicator. Development of regional gradient models: Methods and priorities. Draft report. Washington, DC: U.S. Department of Agriculture, Forest Service, Forest Inventory and Analysis Program.

O'Brien, Renee A. 1999. Comprehensive inventory of Utah's forest resources, 1993. Resour. Bull. RMRS-RB-1. Ogden UT: U.S. Department of Agriculture, Forest Service, Rocky Mountain Research Station. 105 p.

Oli, M.K.; Jacobson, H.A.; Leopold, B.D. 1997. Denning ecology of black bears in the White River National Wildlife Refuge, Arkansas. Journal of Wildlife Management 61: 700–706.

Pfister, Robert D.; Kovalchik, Bernard L.; Arno, Stephen F.; Presby, Richard C. 1977. Forest habitat types of Montana. Gen. Tech. Rep. INT-34, Ogden, UT: U.S. Department of Agriculture, Forest Service, Intermountain Forest and Range Experiment Station. 174 p.

Pollard, James E.; Westfall, James A.; Patterson, Paul L.; Gartner, David L.; Hansen, Mark; Kuegler, Olaf. 2006. Forest inventory and analysis national data quality assessment report 2000 to 2003. Gen. Tech. Rep. RMRS-GTR-181. Fort Collins, CO: U.S. Department of Agriculture, Forest Service, Rocky Mountain Research Station. 43 p.

Reineke, L. H. 1933. Perfecting a stand density index for even-aged forests. Journal of Agricultural Research 46(7):627-638.

Reynolds, R.T.; and others. 1992. Management recommendations for the northern goshawk in the southwestern United States. Gen. Tech. Rep. RM-217. Fort Collins, CO: U.S. Department of Agriculture, Forest Service, Rocky Mountain Forest and Range Experiment Station. 90 p.

Rogers, P.C.; Ryel, R.J. 2008. Lichen community change in response to succession in aspen forests of the southern Rocky Mountains. Forest Ecology and Management 256: 1760-1770.

Romme W.H.; Allen C.D.; Bailey J.D.; and others. 2007. Historical and modern disturbance regimes of pinon-juniper vegetation in the Western U.S. Fort Collins, CO: Colorado State University, Colorado Forest Restoration Institute. 35 p.

Romme, W.H.; Craig, D.A.; Bailey, J.D.; and others. 2009. Historical and modern disturbance regimes, stand structures, and landscape dynamics in piñon-juniper vegetation of the western United States. Rangeland Ecology and Management 62: 203-222.

Romme, W.H.; Floyd-Hanna, L.; Hanna, D.D. 2003. Ancient piñon-juniper forests of Mesa Verde and the West: A cautionary note for forest restoration programs. In: Omi, P.N.; Joyce, L.A., tech. eds. Fire, fuel treatments, and ecological restoration: Conference proceedings; 2002 16-18 April; Fort Collins CO. Proc. RMRS-P-29. Fort Collins CO: U.S. Department of Agriculture, Forest Service, Rocky Mountain Research Station: 335-350.

Schmid, J.M. 1981. Spruce beetles in blowdown. Res. Note RM-141, U.S. Department of Agriculture, Forest Service, Rocky Mountain Forest and Range Experiment Station. 4 p.

Schmid, J.M.; Frye, R.H.1976. Stand ratings for spruce beetles. Res. Note RM-309. U.S. Department of Agriculture, Forest Service, Rocky Mountain Forest and Range Experiment Station. 4 p.

Scott, J.H.; Burgan, R.E. 2005. Standard fire behavior fuel models: A comprehensive set for use with Rothermel's surface fire spread model. Gen. Tech. Rep. RMRS-GTR-153. Fort Collins, CO: U.S. Department of Agriculture, Forest Service, Rocky Mountain Research Station. 72 p.

Shaw, J.D. 2000. Application of stand density index to irregularly structured stands, Western Journal of Applied Forestry 15: 40-42.

Shaw, John D. 2006. Drought-related mortality in pinyon-juniper woodlands: A test case for the FIA annual inventory system. In: McRoberts, R. E.; and others, eds. Proceedings of the sixth annual Forest Inventory and Analysis symposium; September 21-24, 2004; Denver, CO. Gen. Tech. Rep. WO-GTR-70. Washington, DC: U.S. Department of Agriculture, Forest Service: 71-76.

Shaw, John D.; Steed, Brytten E.; DeBlander, Larry T. 2005. Forest Inventory and Analysis (FIA) annual inventory answers the question: What is happening to pinyon-juniper woodlands? Journal of Forestry 103(6): 280-285.

Shaw, J.D.; Long, J.N. [In preparation]. Consistent definition and use of stand density index.

Smith, F.W.; Long, J.N. 1987. Elk hiding and thermal cover guidelines in the context of lodgepole pine stand density. Western Journal of Applied Forestry 2: 6-10.

Smith, W. Brad, tech. coord.; Miles, Patrick D., data coord.; Perry, Charles H., map coord.; Pugh, Scott A., data CD coord. 2009. Forest resources of the United States, 2007. Gen. Tech. Rep. WO-78. Washington, DC: U.S. Department of Agriculture, Forest Service. 336 p.

Society of American Foresters. 2004. Western US drought outlook improves. The Forestry Source 9(12):1,5. Bethesda, MD: Society of American Foresters.

Stage, A.R. 1966. Simultaneous derivation of site-curve and productivity rating procedures. Society of American Foresters Proceedings 1966: 134-136. [Original equations were reformulated by John Shaw; documentation on file at U.S. Department of Agriculture, Forest Service, Rocky Mountain Research Station, Ogden, UT.]

Stage, A.R. 1969. Computing procedure for grand fir site evaluation and productivity estimation. Res. Note INT-98. Ogden, UT: U.S. Department of Agriculture, Forest Service, Intermountain Forest and Range Experiment Station.

St. Clair, L.L. 2000. Establishment of a lichen air quality biomonitoring program and baseline for selected sites in the Manti-LaSal National Forest, Utah. Final report submitted to the Manti-LaSal National Forest, USDA Forest Service. 57 p. Available online: http://gis.nacse.org/lichenair/doc/Manti_Sal_NF.pdf.

St. Clair, L.L.; Newberry, C. 1994. Establishment of a lichen biomonitoring program and baseline at selected sites in the High Uintas Wilderness Area, Wasatch-Cache National Forest. Final report submitted to the Wasatch-Cache National Forest, USDA Forest Service. 70 p. Available online: http://gis.nacse.org/lichenair/doc/High_Uintas_NF.pdf.

Steele, Robert; Cooper, Stephen V.; Ondov, David M.; Roberts, David W; Pfister, Robert 1983. Forest habitat types of Eastern Idaho-Western Wyoming. Gen. Tech. Rep. Int-144. Ogden, UT: U.S. Department of Agriculture, Forest Service, Intermountain Forest and Range Experiment Station. 122 p.

Tausch, R.J.; Hood, S. 2007. Chapter 4—Pinyon/juniper woodlands. In: Hood, Sharon M.; Miller, Melanie, eds. Fire ecology and management of the major ecosystems of southern Utah. Gen. Tech. Rep. RMRS-GTR-202. Fort Collins, CO: U.S. Department of Agriculture, Forest Service, Rocky Mountain Research Station: 57-71.

Thompson, M.T. 2009. Analysis of conifer mortality in Colorado using Forest Inventory and Analysis's annual forest inventory. Western Journal of Applied Forestry 24(4): 193-197.

U.S. Department of Agriculture, Forest Service, 1958. Timber resources for America's future. Forest Resource Report No. 14. Washington, DC: U. S Department of Agriculture, Forest Service. 713 p.

U.S. Department of Agriculture, Forest Service. 1996. Properly functioning condition process. Report on file at: U.S. Department of Agriculture, Forest Service, Intermountain Region, Ogden, UT. 76 p.

U.S. Department of Agriculture, Forest Service. 2005. Analysis for the North Slope of the Uinta Mountains, Wasatch-Cache National Forest. Report on file at: U.S. Department of Agriculture, Forest Service, Rocky Mountain Research Station, Forestry Sciences Laboratory, Interior West Forest Inventory and Analysis Program, Ogden, UT.

U.S. Department of Agriculture, Forest Service. 2000-2005a. Forest survey field procedures. Unpublished field guide on file at: U.S. Department of Agriculture, Forest Service, Rocky Mountain Research Station, Forestry Sciences Laboratory, Interior West Forest Inventory and Analysis Program, Ogden, UT. Available online at: http://fsweb.ogden.rmrs.fs.fed.us/manual/manual.html.

U.S. Department of Agriculture, Forest Service. 2000-2005b. Phase 3 field procedures. Unpublished field guide on file at: U.S. Department of Agriculture, Forest Service, Rocky Mountain Research Station, Forestry Sciences Laboratory, Interior West Forest Inventory and Analysis Program, Ogden, UT. Available online at: http://fsweb.ogden.rmrs.fs.fed.us/manual/manual.html.

Van Hooser, Dwane D. 1981. [Letter to Gyde Lund]. October 30. 3 leaves. On file at: U.S. Department of Agriculture, Forest Service, Rocky Mountain Research Station, Forestry Sciences Laboratory, Interior West Forest Inventory and Analysis Program, Ogden, UT.

Van Hooser, Dwane D. 1983. [Letter to Frank G. Sadowski]. December 9. 2 leaves. On file at: U.S. Department of Agriculture, Forest Service, Rocky Mountain Research Station, Forestry Sciences Laboratory, Interior West Forest Inventory and Analysis Program, Ogden, UT.

Van Hooser, Dwane D.; Chojnacky, David C. 1983. Whole tree volume estimates for the Rocky Mountain States. Resour. Bull. RB-INT-29. Ogden, UT: U.S. Department of Agriculture, Forest Service, Intermountain Forest and Range Experiment Station. 7 p.

Veblen, T.T.; Hadley, K.S.; Nel, E.M.; Kitzberger, T.; Reid, M.; Villalba, R. 1994. Disturbance regime and disturbance interactions in a Rocky Mountain subalpine forest. Journal of Ecology 82: 125-135.

Weisberg, P.J.; Ko, D.; Py, C.; Bauer, J.M. 2008. Modeling fire and landform influences on the distribution of old-growth pinyon-juniper woodland. Landscape Ecology 23: 931-943.

Weisberg, Peter J.; Lingua, E.; Pillai, R.B. 2007. Spatial patterns of pinyon-juniper woodland expansion in central Nevada. Rangeland Ecology and Management 60: 115-124.

Will-Wolf, S. 2010. Analyzing lichen indicator data in the Forest Inventory and Analysis Program. Gen. Tech. Rep. PNW-GTR-818. Portland, OR: U.S. Department of Agriculture, Forest Service, Pacific Northwest Research Station. 62 p.

Williams, Clinton K. 2009. Properly Functioning Conditions. U.S. Department of Agriculture, Forest Service, Intermountain Region, Vegetation Management, Ecology. [Online]. Available only on U.S. Forest Service Intranet site: http://fsweb.r4.fs.fed.us/unit/vm/ecology/ecology_temp.html.

Woodall, C.W.; Williams, M.S. 2005. Sampling protocol, estimation, and analysis procedures for down woody materials indicator of the FIA program. Gen. Tech. Rep. NC-256. St. Paul, MN: U.S. Department of Agriculture, Forest Service, North Central Research Station. 47 p.

Woodall, Christopher W.; Monleon, Vicente J. 2008. Sampling protocol, estimation, and analysis procedures for the down woody materials indicator of the FIA program. Gen. Tech. Rep. NRS-22. Newtown Square, PA: U.S. Department of Agriculture, Forest Service, Northern Research Station. 68 p.

Worrall, James J.; Egeland, Leanne; Eager, Thomas; and others. 2008. Rapid mortality of Populus tremuloides in southwestern Colorado, USA. Forest Ecology and Management 255(3-4): 686-696.

USDA Forest Service Resour. Bull. RMRS-RB-10. 2010

99

XI. Appendices

Appendix A—Inventory History and "New Proposed Land Class"

FIA has historically used variables such as stocking, crown cover, land use, wood product use, and tree form to help define forest land. In terms of the relationships between stocking and crown cover, the minimum stocking threshold of 10 percent for defining forest land in the Interior West has remained constant since the 1950s for both periodic and annual inventories (USDA Forest Service 1958). However, the surrogate for evaluating 10 percent stocking, based primarily on field estimates of tree crown cover, has changed over the years (Van Hooser 1981). This was mainly due to concerns that some arid timber species (e.g. ponderosa pine) and many woodland species (e.g. pinyon and juniper) that lacked distinct stocking equations may exhibit minimum stocking thresholds at lower crown cover densities (Lund 2004). In addition, due to concerns in "negative bias in sampling for forest land," IWFIA first implemented a 5 percent crown cover surrogate for 10 percent minimum stocking as early as 1982 (Van Hooser 1981, 1983).

By the time annual inventories commenced in 2000 in Utah, IWFIA had adopted a minimum 5 percent crown cover timber/woodland species surrogate for 10 percent stocking. Although crown cover was the most significant factor in terms of definitional differences from past periodic inventories, other important factors that still confound direct trend comparisons include tree form, species, field plot imagery, and changing forest type algorithms.

In preparation for the 2007 Resource Planning Act (RPA) report, there was an expressed concern whether 5 percent crown cover was a legitimate surrogate for 10 percent stocking. In 2006, IWFIA implemented a retroactive process called *plot-filtering* (see below) on its previous annual inventory data to assess the definitional change in crown cover by classifying plots that had 5 to 9 percent cover. By identifying and separating this unique and potentially useful land class (other wooded land), forest land could now be more comparable to the past and still meet current national standards.

Changes From Past Definitions

Stocking vs. Crown Cover—The minimum surrogate threshold used for 10 percent stocking for forest land in the 1978 periodic inventory of Utah was 10 percent crown cover (timber and woodland species combined). By the 1993 periodic inventory of Utah, this changed to 5 percent cover for timber species and 10 percent for woodland. Stands with combinations of both species required a minimum 10 percent cover, if timber species were still less than 5 percent. As a result, considering differences in crown cover alone from 1993 to 2006 and without excluding other wooded land, a definitional increase in total forest land area would be expected (see "Area Discussion" in Section IV for more details).

Tree Form—Tree form is another factor that has complicated trend comparisons. Prior to 1985 in the Interior West, the variability in form of a tree species was irrelevant to its forest land potential. In contrast, due to concerns about the low potential of trees on some poor sites to obtain tree form, the 1993 inventory of Utah excluded woodland tree species on sites that did not meet specified tree-form requirements (the capacity to produce at least one stem 3 inches or larger in diameter at root collar, and 8 feet or more in length to a minimum branch diameter of 1.5 inches). However, field crews often had difficulty agreeing on the "potential" of a site. Consequently, by 2000, when annual inventories commenced in Utah, this was again reversed. Species, not form,

USDA Forest Service Resour. Bull. RMRS-RB-10. 2010

101

determined whether or not individual trees contributed to stocking and crown cover. Qualifying species were based solely on regional FIA tally species lists (USDA Forest Service 2000-2005a). In essence, the overall tree-form potential of a species within the entire Interior West was built into the species list decision.

As a result, an increase in forest land due to the tree-form criteria would be expected between 1993 and 2006. For example, the current apparent increase in the deciduous oak woodland type (see Section IV), a species that is often shrub form, is probably caused by eliminating the tree-form criteria. In addition, since tree form is often internationally considered an important part of forest land definitions (e.g. Kyoto protocols), and given the marginal sites that many woodland species occupy in the Interior West, IWFIA is currently collecting a regional tree-form variable. This could potentially serve as a combined climatic and edaphic indicator for woodland site productivity and other stress-related influences.

Species—As mentioned above, past definitions considered *form* within a species to be a constituent of forest land potential; whereas, annual inventories now reference tree *species* lists, regardless of form. Some species previously considered as forest trees (Rocky Mountain maple and true mountain mahogany) are no longer considered valid forest tree species in the Interior West. In addition, other species previously not considered (mesquite) are now included on IWFIA's tree species list. The net effect of this on forest land is probably minimal since these species are somewhat infrequently encountered in Utah. However, this explains why some species may or may not be included in a particular inventory.

Other Factors—In addition, other factors may have had significant influences on trend comparisons. Since it is impractical to physically field visit every hex-grid plot in the Interior West, our prefield protocols have long depended on remotely sensed imagery for distinguishing non-visit plots from potential forest land plots. Past inventories were often constrained to using low-quality imagery for identification of potential forest land, possibly causing marginally forested or nonstocked lands to get missed during the prefield examination. The expected result would be a potential increase in forest land in subsequent inventories as better imagery became available statewide.

Another factor affecting comparisons to the past are shifts in area between forest types due to changing forest type algorithms. Most IWFIA periodic inventories used a 5 percent cover threshold for timber types regardless of the amount of woodland species cover; whereas, annual inventories use the plurality of stocking to distinguish between timber and woodland forest types. This has a tendency to shift some area from timber types to woodland types when comparing periodic to annual inventories (see Appendix C for periodic to annual forest type crosswalk lists).

Plot-Filtering and the Definition of Forest and Other Wooded Lands

Other than land use, the three main factors that influence FIA's definition of forest land are cover/stocking, past disturbance, and regeneration—meaning that the sample acre either currently, formerly, or will in the future meet the definition of forest land. Observations or measurements are made by IWFIA field crews to determine whether thresholds for any of these three factors are met on the ground, based on the condition sample acre. In the past, generally, if any of the three factors met the appropriate threshold the condition was classified as forest land. However, other than the decision to measure the plot, it was unknown which of the factors, or combination of factors, were the definitive reason for classifying plots as forest land, since these factors were not documented.

As previously mentioned, plot-filtering was a retroactive process that classified all annual IWFIA plots according to current live tree crown cover, missing crown cover (disturbance), and seedlings per acre. Subsequently, these three regional variables were used to separate forest from other wooded land. These three variables were designed to address the above factors that influence FIA's definition of forest land and are currently collected at the condition level on all IWFIA field plots. All three variables are recorded as whole numbers, allowing any definitional threshold to be applied for more flexible analysis.

Under this paradigm, forest land is filtered in the IWFIA database as conditions with live plus missing crown cover greater than or equal to 10 percent, or greater than or equal to 200 seedlings per acre. Other wooded land is filtered in the IWFIA database as conditions with 5 to 9 percent live plus missing crown cover, or 40 to 199 seedlings per acre. Although other wooded land does not meet FIA's national standards for forest land, it is an important ecotone between forest and nonforest land that continues to be measured by IWFIA (see Sections IV and V).

Appendix B—Common Name, Scientific Name, and Timber (T) or Woodland (W) Designation for Trees

Aspen (*Populus tremuloides*) T

Bigtooth maple (*Acer grandidentatum*) W

Blue spruce (*Picea pungens*) T

Common or twoneedle pinyon (*Pinus edulis*) W

Curlleaf mountain-mahogany (*Cercocarpus ledifolius*) W

Douglas-fir (*Pseudotsuga menziesii*) T

Engelmann spruce (*Picea engelmannii*) T

Fremont cottonwood *(Populus fremontii)* T

Gambel oak (*Quercus gambelii*) W

Great Basin bristlecone pine *(Pinus longaeva)* T

Limber pine (*Pinus flexilis*) T

Lodgepole pine (*Pinus contorta*) T

Narrowleaf cottonwood *(Populus angustifolia)* T

Ponderosa pine (*Pinus ponderosa*) T

Rocky Mountain juniper (*Juniperus scopulorum*) W

Singleleaf pinyon (*Pinus monophylla*) W

Subalpine fir (*Abies lasiocarpa*) T

Utah juniper (*Juniperus osteosperma*) W

White fir *(Abies concolor)* T

Appendix C—Forest Type Groups, Forest Type Names—Annual and (Periodic), and Timber (T) or Woodland (W) Designation for Forest Type

Aspen-birch group
Aspen (Aspen) T

Douglas-fir group
Douglas-fir (Douglas-fir) T

Elm-ash-cottonwood group
Cottonwood (Cottonwood) T

Fir-spruce-mountain hemlock group
Blue spruce (Blue spruce) T
Engelmann spruce (Engelmann spruce) T
Engelmann spruce-subalpine fir (Spruce-fir) T
Subalpine fir (Spruce-fir) T
White fir (White fir) T

Lodgepole pine group
Lodgepole pine (Lodgepole pine) T

Nonstocked
Nonstocked (only as stand-size class) T or W

Other western hardwoods group
Cercocarpus woodland (Mountain mahogany) W
Intermountain maple woodland (Maple woodland) W

Other western softwoods group
Foxtail pine-bristlecone pine (grouped with spruce-fir) T
Limber pine (Limber pine) T

Pinyon-juniper group
Juniper woodland (Juniper) W
Pinyon-juniper woodland (Pinyon-juniper) W
Rocky Mountain juniper (Juniper) W

Ponderosa pine group
Ponderosa pine (Ponderosa pine) T

Western oak group
Deciduous oak woodland (Oak) W

USDA Forest Service Resour. Bull. RMRS-RB-10. 2010

105

Appendix D—Volume, Biomass, and Site Index Equation Sources

Volume

Chojnacky (1985) was used for bigtooth maple, curlleaf mountain-mahogany, gamble oak, and singleleaf pinyon pine volume estimation.

Chojnacky (1994) was used for common or twoneedle pinyon pine, Rocky Mountain juniper, and Utah juniper volume estimation.

Edminster and others (1980) was used for ponderosa pine volume estimation in northeastern Utah.

Edminister and others (1982) was used for aspen volume estimation in northeastern Utah.

Hann and Bare (1978) was used for aspen, blue spruce, Douglas-fir, Engelmann spruce, Great Basin bristlecone pine, limber pine, lodgepole pine, ponderosa pine, subalpine fir, and white fir volume estimation in southwestern Utah.

Kemp (1956) was used for Fremont and narrowleaf cottonwood volume estimation.

Myers (1964) was used for limber and lodgepole pine volume estimation in northeastern Utah.

Myers and Edminister (1972) was used for blue spruce, Douglas-fir, Engelmann spruce, subalpine fir, and white fir volume estimation in northeastern Utah.

Biomass

Chojnacky (1984) was used for curlleaf mountain mahogany biomass estimation.

Chojnacky (1992). was used for bigtooth maple and gamble oak biomass estimation.

Chojnacky and Moisen (1993) was used for all juniper and pinyon species biomass estimation.

Van Hooser and Chojnacky (1983) was used for all timber (T) species biomass estimation.

Site Index

Brickell (1970) was used for blue spruce, Douglas-fir, Engelmann spruce, Great Basin bristlecone pine, limber pine, lodgepole pine, ponderosa pine, and subalpine fir site index estimation.

Edminster and others (1985) was used for aspen, and Fremont and narrowleaf cottonwood site index estimation.

Stage (1966, 1969) was used for white fir site index estimation. [Original equations were reformulated by John Shaw; documentation on file at U.S. Department of Agriculture, Forest Service, Rocky Mountain Research Station, Ogden, UT.]

Appendix E—List of Tables and Appendix E Tables

Table 9—Area of timberland by forest type group and stand-size class, Utah, cycle 2, 2000-2005.

Table 10—Number of live trees on forest land by species group and diameter class, Utah, cycle 2, 2000-2005.

Table 11—Number of growing stock trees on timberland by species group and diameter class, Utah, cycle 2, 2000-2005.

Table 12—Net volume of all live trees by owner class and forest land status, Utah, cycle 2, 2000-2005.

Table 13—Net volume of all live trees on forest land by forest type group and stand-size class, Utah, cycle 2, 2000-2005.

Table 14—Net volume of all live trees on forest land by species group and ownership group, Utah, cycle 2, 2000-2005.

Table 15—Net volume of all live trees on forest land by species group and diameter class, Utah, cycle 2, 2000-2005.

Table 16—Net volume of all live trees on forest land by forest type group and stand origin, Utah, cycle 2, 2000-2005.

Table 17—Net volume of growing stock trees on timberland by species group and diameter class, Utah, cycle 2, 2000-2005.

Table 18—Net volume of growing stock trees on timberland by species group and ownership group, Utah, cycle 2, 2000-2005.

Table 19—Net volume of sawtimber trees (International 1/4 inch rule) on timberland by species group and diameter class, Utah, cycle 2, 2000-2005.

Table 20—Net volume of sawtimber trees on timberland by species group and ownership group, Utah, cycle 2, 2000-2005.

Table 21—Average annual net growth of all live trees by owner class and forest land status, Utah, cycle 2, 2000-2005.

Table 22—Average annual net growth of all live trees on forest land by forest type group and stand-size class, Utah, cycle 2, 2000-2005.

Table 23—Average annual net growth of all live trees on forest land by species group and ownership group, Utah, cycle 2, 2000-2005.

Table 24—Average annual net growth of growing stock trees on timberland by species group and ownership group, Utah, cycle 2, 2000-2005.

Table 25—Average annual mortality of all live trees by owner class and forest land status, Utah, cycle 2, 2000-2005.

Table 26—Average annual mortality of all live trees on forest land by forest type group and stand-size class, Utah, cycle 2, 2000-2005.

Table 27—Average annual mortality of all live trees on forest land by species group and ownership group, Utah, cycle 2, 2000-2005.

Table 28—Average annual mortality of growing stock trees on timberland by species group and ownership group, Utah, cycle 2, 2000-2005.

Table 29—Aboveground dry weight of all live trees by owner class and forest land status, Utah, cycle 2, 2000-2005.

Table 30—Aboveground dry weight of all live trees on forest land by species group and diameter class, Utah, cycle 2, 2000-2005.

List of Appendix F Tables:

Appendix E tables

Table 1--Percentage of area by land status, Utah, cycle 2, 2000-2005.

Land status	Percentage of area
Accessible forest land	
Unreserved forest land	
Timberland	6.9
Unproductive	21.1
Total unreserved forest land	28.0
Reserved forest land	
Productive	0.8
Unproductive	2.5
Total reserved forest land	3.3
All accessible forest land	31.3
Nonforest and other land	
Nonforest and other-wooded land	62.2
Water	
Census	3.3
Non-Census	0.1
All nonforest and other land	65.6
Nonsampled land	
Access denied	1.0
Hazardous conditions	1.7
Other	0.3
All land	100.0

Total area (thousands of acres)	54,335

All table cells without observations in the inventory sample are indicated by --. Table value of 0.0 indicates the percentage rounds to less than 0.1 percent. Columns and rows may not add to their totals due to rounding.

Table 2--Area of accessible forest land by owner class and forest land status, Utah, cycle 2, 2000-2005.

(In thousand acres)

Owner class	Unreserved forests			Reserved forests			All forest land
	Timberland	Unproductive	Total	Productive	Unproductive	Total	
Forest Service							
National Forest	2,995.2	2,736.6	5,731.8	398.8	120.9	519.7	6,251.5
Other National Forest	--	--	--	--	7.4	7.4	7.4
Other federal							
National Park Service	--	--	--	64.9	280.3	345.2	345.2
Bureau of Land Management	140.6	5,740.0	5,880.6	10.2	909.0	919.2	6,799.8
Fish and Wildlife Service	--	--	--	--	10.9	10.9	10.9
Department of Defense or Energy	--	10.0	10.0	--	--	--	10.0
State and local government							
State	154.2	1,261.0	1,415.2	--	98.5	98.5	1,513.7
Local (county, municipal, etc.)	11.3	--	11.3	--	--	--	11.3
Private							
Undifferentiated private	690.5	2,319.0	3,009.6	--	3.1	3.1	3,012.7
All owners	3,991.8	12,066.6	16,058.3	473.9	1,430.2	1,904.1	17,962.5

All table cells without observations in the inventory sample are indicated by --. Table value of 0.0 indicates the acres round to less than 0.1 thousand acres. Columns and rows may not add to their totals due to rounding.

Table 3--Area of accessible forest land by forest type group and productivity class, Utah, cycle 2, 2000-2005.

(In thousand acres)

Forest type group	Site productivity class (cubic feet/acre/year)							All classes
	0-19	20-49	50-84	85-119	120-164	165-224	225+	
Pinyon-juniper group	10,210.5	--	--	--	--	--	--	10,210.5
Douglas-fir group	9.2	472.1	145.7	23.4	--	--	--	650.5
Ponderosa pine group	--	338.6	49.8	--	--	--	--	388.4
Fir-spruce-mountain hemlock group	14.7	890.2	484.0	34.6	--	--	--	1,423.4
Lodgepole pine group	--	393.2	--	--	--	--	--	393.2
Other western softwoods group	7.1	40.1	--	--	--	--	--	47.2
Elm-ash-cottonwood group	10.1	19.1	2.3	--	--	--	--	31.6
Aspen-birch group	140.2	1,158.5	341.7	--	--	--	--	1,640.3
Western oak group	1,986.9	--	--	--	--	--	--	1,986.9
Other western hardwoods group	654.8	--	--	--	--	--	--	654.8
Nonstocked	463.3	61.6	10.9	--	--	--	--	535.7
All forest type groups	13,496.8	3,373.3	1,034.4	58.0	--	--	--	17,962.5

All table cells without observations in the inventory sample are indicated by --. Table value of 0.0 indicates the acres round to less than 0.1 thousand acres. Columns and rows may not add to their totals due to rounding.

Table 4--Area of accessible forest land by forest type group, ownership group, and land status, Utah, cycle 2, 2000-2005.

(In thousand acres)

Forest type group	Forest Service		Other federal		State and local government		Undifferentiated private		All forest land
	Timber-land	Other forest land	Timber-land	Other forest land	Timber-land	Other forest land	Timber-land	Other forest land	
Pinyon-juniper group	--	1,553.2	--	6,215.8	--	1,125.9	--	1,315.6	10,210.5
Douglas-fir group	348.9	49.9	69.4	9.2	48.7	--	124.4	--	650.5
Ponderosa pine group	255.8	8.3	30.8	50.5	9.4	--	33.7	--	388.4
Fir-spruce-mountain hemlock group	1,082.0	217.6	8.3	9.6	18.6	--	87.3	--	1,423.4
Lodgepole pine group	298.1	81.8	--	--	--	--	13.3	--	393.2
Other western softwoods group	31.7	7.1	--	5.8	--	--	2.7	--	47.2
Elm-ash-cottonwood group	3.0	--	6.3	10.1	--	--	12.2	--	31.6
Aspen-birch group	933.2	130.4	10.9	--	88.6	--	412.0	65.1	1,640.3
Western oak group	--	789.2	--	340.9	--	167.1	--	689.7	1,986.9
Other western hardwoods group	--	310.9	--	143.3	--	33.6	--	167.1	654.8
Nonstocked	42.6	115.3	15.0	240.1	--	33.0	5.0	84.7	535.7
All forest type groups	2,995.2	3,263.7	140.6	7,025.2	165.4	1,359.5	690.5	2,322.2	17,962.5

All table cells without observations in the inventory sample are indicated by --. Table value of 0.0 indicates the acres round to less than 0.1 thousand acres. Columns and rows may not add to their totals due to rounding.

Table 5--Area of accessible forest land by forest type group and stand-size class, Utah, cycle 2, 2000-2005.

(In thousand acres)

Forest type group	Stand-size class					All size classes
	Large diameter	Medium diameter	Small diameter	Chaparral	Non stocked	
Pinyon-juniper group	9,694.5	219.3	296.7	--	--	10,210.5
Douglas-fir group	547.4	53.5	49.6	--	--	650.5
Ponderosa pine group	369.9	9.2	9.2	--	--	388.4
Fir-spruce-mountain hemlock group	1,117.3	150.6	155.6	--	--	1,423.4
Lodgepole pine group	157.8	173.2	62.2	--	--	393.2
Other western softwoods group	39.1	8.1	--	--	--	47.2
Elm-ash-cottonwood group	20.7	1.3	9.5	--	--	31.6
Aspen-birch group	315.9	1,014.3	310.1	--	--	1,640.3
Western oak group	20.5	146.0	1,820.4	--	--	1,986.9
Other western hardwoods group	344.3	116.4	194.2	--	--	654.8
Nonstocked	--	--	--	--	535.7	535.7
All forest type groups	12,627.3	1,892.0	2,907.5	--	535.7	17,962.5

All table cells without observations in the inventory sample are indicated by --. Table value of 0.0 indicates the acres round to less than 0.1 thousand acres. Columns and rows may not add to their totals due to rounding.

112

USDA Forest Service Resour. Bull. RMRS-RB-10. 2010

Table 6—Area of accessible forest land by forest type group and stand-age class, Utah, cycle 2, 2000-2005.

(In thousand acres)

Forest type group	Non stocked	Stand-age class (years)											All classes
		1-20	21-40	41-60	61-80	81-100	101-120	121-140	141-160	161-180	181-200	201+	
Pinyon-juniper group	--	181.8	122.4	377.4	802.1	1,064.7	1,211.8	1,348.5	1,032.2	818.3	1,029.1	2,221.9	10,210.5
Douglas-fir group	--	42.5	7.1	10.6	74.8	162.5	134.9	93.9	66.4	35.9	--	21.8	650.5
Ponderosa pine group	--	--	9.2	9.2	104.3	69.8	47.9	38.7	30.0	5.9	10.2	63.2	388.4
Fir-spruce-mountain hemlock group	--	60.9	79.6	55.7	80.9	168.1	322.5	129.0	253.5	91.9	85.8	95.6	1,423.4
Lodgepole pine group	--	32.1	10.1	8.0	29.8	83.4	87.7	50.5	20.4	30.3	--	40.9	393.2
Other western softwoods group	--	--	--	--	--	8.1	--	14.6	--	--	7.1	17.4	47.2
Elm-ash-cottonwood group	--	--	1.3	--	2.3	8.3	10.1	--	--	--	--	--	31.6
Aspen-birch group	--	163.3	122.7	100.7	556.9	420.3	171.8	73.5	31.2	--	--	--	1,640.3
Western oak group	--	1,560.5	218.9	34.2	50.1	74.1	23.2	16.3	9.6	--	--	--	1,986.9
Other western hardwoods group	--	165.5	34.3	35.7	31.9	82.2	50.2	134.7	61.0	51.6	7.9	--	654.8
Nonstocked	535.7												535.7
All forest type groups	535.7	2,216.0	605.7	631.5	1,733.1	2,141.5	2,060.2	1,899.7	1,504.4	1,033.9	1,140.1	2,460.8	17,962.5

All table cells without observations in the inventory sample are indicated by --. Table value of 0.0 indicates the acres round to less than 0.1 thousand acres. Columns and rows may not add to their totals due to rounding.

Table 7—Area of accessible forest land by forest type group and stand origin, Utah, cycle 2, 2000-2005.

(In thousand acres)

Forest type group	Stand origin		All forest land
	Natural stands	Artificial regeneration	
Pinyon-juniper group	10,210.5	--	10,210.5
Douglas-fir group	650.5	--	650.5
Ponderosa pine group	379.2	9.2	388.4
Fir-spruce-mountain hemlock group	1,423.4	--	1,423.4
Lodgepole pine group	393.2	--	393.2
Other western softwoods group	47.2	--	47.2
Elm-ash-cottonwood group	31.6	--	31.6
Aspen-birch group	1,640.3	--	1,640.3
Western oak group	1,986.9	--	1,986.9
Other western hardwoods group	654.8	--	654.8
Nonstocked	535.7	--	535.7
All forest type groups	17,953.2	9.2	17,962.5

All table cells without observations in the inventory sample are indicated by --. Table value of 0.0 indicates the acres round to less than 0.1 thousand acres. Columns and rows may not add to their totals due to rounding.

Table 8--Area of forest land by forest type group and primary disturbance class, Utah, cycle 2, 2000-2005.

(In thousand acres)

Forest type group	None	Insects	Disease	Weather	Fire	Domestic animals	Wild animals	Human	Other	All forest land
Pinyon-juniper group	9,667.4	205.1	73.6	92.3	47.8	101.3	--	11.1	11.9	10,210.5
Douglas-fir group	556.2	15.6	40.2	9.2	7.1	10.1	11.9	--	--	650.5
Ponderosa pine group	367.0	--	--	--	21.4	--	--	--	--	388.4
Fir-spruce-mountain hemlock group	1,155.2	106.1	59.5	70.2	10.2	--	--	--	22.2	1,423.4
Lodgepole pine group	332.8	31.1	20.7	--	--	--	--	8.5	--	393.2
Other western softwoods group	47.2	--	--	--	--	--	--	--	--	47.2
Elm-ash-cottonwood group	27.0	--	--	1.3	--	--	3.2	--	--	31.6
Aspen-birch group	1,473.3	21.7	72.2	12.5	28.9	31.6	0.2	--	--	1,640.3
Western oak group	1,805.7	10.2	2.4	10.2	78.2	80.1	--	--	--	1,986.9
Other western hardwoods group	628.3	--	--	--	10.3	16.3	--	--	--	654.8
Nonstocked	337.6	--	--	--	182.6	15.4	--	--	--	535.7
All forest type groups	16,397.7	389.8	268.7	195.8	386.6	254.8	15.3	19.6	34.1	17,962.5

All table cells without observations in the inventory sample are indicated by --. Table value of 0.0 indicates the acres round to less than 0.1 thousand acres. Columns and rows may not add to their totals due to rounding.

Table 9--Area of timberland by forest type group and stand-size class, Utah, cycle 2, 2000-2005.

(In thousand acres)

Forest type group	Large diameter	Medium diameter	Small diameter	Chaparral	Non stocked	All size classes
Douglas-fir group	497.5	53.5	40.4	--	--	591.4
Ponderosa pine group	311.2	9.2	9.2	--	--	329.6
Fir-spruce-mountain hemlock group	927.8	148.4	120.1	--	--	1,196.3
Lodgepole pine group	76.0	173.2	62.2	--	--	311.4
Other western softwoods group	26.2	8.1	--	--	--	34.3
Elm-ash-cottonwood group	10.6	1.3	9.5	--	--	21.4
Aspen-birch group	299.5	925.5	219.7	--	--	1,444.8
Nonstocked	--	--	--	--	62.6	62.6
All forest type groups	2,148.8	1,319.3	461.1	--	62.6	3,991.8

All table cells without observations in the inventory sample are indicated by --. Table value of 0.0 indicates the acres round to less than 0.1 thousand acres. Columns and rows may not add to their totals due to rounding.

Table 10–Number of live trees on forest land by species group and diameter class, Utah, cycle 2, 2000-2005.

(In thousand trees)

Species group	Diameter class (inches)															All classes
	1.0-2.9	3.0-4.9	5.0-6.9	7.0-8.9	9.0-10.9	11.0-12.9	13.0-14.9	15.0-16.9	17.0-18.9	19.0-20.9	21.0-24.9	25.0-28.9	29.0-32.9	33.0-36.9	37.0+	
Softwood species groups																
Western softwood species groups																
Douglas-fir	79,960	40,745	24,035	21,642	14,154	10,604	9,290	7,845	3,559	2,216	2,637	609	283	72	57	217,706
Ponderosa and Jeffrey pines	9,381	9,564	6,416	5,848	4,162	3,756	3,097	2,388	1,638	1,195	1,723	370	294	168	76	50,077
True fir	330,109	99,400	58,244	37,777	22,853	16,852	9,412	6,007	3,748	2,185	2,433	785	201	228	84	590,316
Engelmann and other spruces	63,703	43,362	25,371	18,046	13,029	9,755	8,047	6,344	3,318	2,622	3,063	1,026	233	114	--	198,032
Lodgepole pine	114,608	83,786	64,895	33,087	15,246	9,462	4,935	2,076	1,076	539	182	--	--	--	--	329,892
Western woodland softwoods	581,513	348,286	246,892	198,173	165,238	129,791	104,202	75,812	51,322	36,885	40,053	17,793	7,301	2,101	1,050	2,006,411
Other western softwoods	7,104	5,092	2,330	1,684	1,591	1,364	474	405	386	220	310	72	--	--	72	21,104
All softwoods	1,186,378	630,234	428,183	316,257	236,274	181,583	139,457	100,877	65,047	45,862	50,402	20,654	8,311	2,682	1,338	3,413,538
Hardwood species groups																
Western hardwood species groups																
Cottonwood and aspen	276,237	177,241	121,944	83,644	41,895	20,229	10,393	3,602	1,798	1,228	408	--	--	--	--	738,619
Western woodland hardwoods	3,451,036	533,359	130,587	51,529	22,368	12,590	5,255	2,174	1,982	383	453	123	--	--	--	4,211,837
All hardwoods	3,727,274	710,599	252,531	135,173	64,262	32,819	15,648	5,775	3,780	1,610	862	123	--	--	--	4,950,456
All species groups	4,913,651	1,340,833	680,713	451,430	300,537	214,401	155,105	106,653	68,827	47,472	51,263	20,777	8,311	2,682	1,338	8,363,995

All table cells without observations in the inventory sample are indicated by --. Table value of 0 indicates the number of trees rounds to less than 1 thousand trees. Columns and rows may not add to their totals due to rounding.

Table 11–Number of growing stock trees on timberland by species group and diameter class, Utah, cycle 2, 2000-2005.

(In thousand trees)

Species group	Diameter class (inches)														All classes
	5.0-6.9	7.0-8.9	9.0-10.9	11.0-12.9	13.0-14.9	15.0-16.9	17.0-18.9	19.0-20.9	21.0-24.9	25.0-28.9	29.0-32.9	33.0-36.9	37.0+	
Softwood species groups															
Western softwood species groups															
Douglas-fir	18,907	16,575	11,352	8,958	7,059	6,064	2,427	1,809	1,717	374	211	72	--	75,526
Ponderosa and Jeffrey pines	4,713	4,662	3,286	3,098	2,622	1,926	1,208	721	1,052	198	172	112	76	23,847
True fir	50,049	33,133	19,796	15,091	8,095	5,043	3,283	1,710	2,078	671	143	228	84	139,404
Engelmann and other spruces	17,934	12,699	9,562	7,227	5,864	4,394	2,491	2,191	2,391	905	169	56	--	65,883
Lodgepole pine	58,872	27,622	11,244	4,496	2,524	954	583	115	64	--	--	--	--	106,473
Other western softwoods	1,468	1,228	1,018	789	362	222	271	55	248	72	--	--	72	5,804
All softwoods	151,943	95,918	56,258	39,659	26,526	18,604	10,263	6,602	7,549	2,220	696	467	232	416,936
Hardwood species groups															
Western hardwood species groups															
Cottonwood and aspen	94,121	68,921	35,505	18,209	9,825	3,352	1,478	1,084	281	--	--	--	--	232,777
All hardwoods	94,121	68,921	35,505	18,209	9,825	3,352	1,478	1,084	281	--	--	--	--	232,777
All species groups	246,064	164,838	91,763	57,868	36,351	21,955	11,742	7,687	7,830	2,220	696	467	232	649,713

All table cells without observations in the inventory sample are indicated by --. Table value of 0 indicates the number of trees rounds to less than 1 thousand trees. Columns and rows may not add to their totals due to rounding.

USDA Forest Service Resour. Bull. RMRS-RB-10. 2010

115

Table 12--Net volume of all live trees 5.0" diameter and greater by owner class and forest land status, Utah, cycle 2, 2000-2005.

(In million cubic feet)

Owner class	Unreserved forests Timberland	Unreserved forests Unproductive	Unreserved forests Total	Reserved forests Productive	Reserved forests Unproductive	Reserved forests Total	All forest land
Forest Service							
National Forest	5,758.2	1,440.9	7,199.1	1,070.1	55.3	1,125.4	8,324.5
Other National Forest	- -	- -	- -	- -	2.8	2.8	2.8
Other federal							
National Park Service	- -	- -	- -	85.7	147.8	233.4	233.4
Bureau of Land Management	142.5	3,221.5	3,364.0	2.8	539.2	542.1	3,906.1
Fish and Wildlife Service	- -	- -	- -	- -	14.6	14.6	14.6
Department of Defense or Energy	- -	1.1	1.1	- -	- -	- -	1.1
State and local government							
State	256.2	683.4	939.6	- -	56.9	56.9	996.5
Local (county, municipal, etc.)	23.4	- -	23.4	- -	- -	- -	23.4
Private							
Undifferentiated private	1,057.0	1,117.6	2,174.7	- -	- -	- -	2,174.7
All owners	7,237.2	6,464.6	13,701.8	1,158.6	816.6	1,975.2	15,677.0

All table cells without observations in the inventory sample are indicated by --. Table value of 0.0 indicates the volume rounds to less than 0.1 million cubic feet. Columns and rows may not add to their totals due to rounding.

Table 13--Net volume of all live trees 5.0" diameter and greater on forest land by forest type group and stand-size class, Utah, cycle 2, 2000-2005.

(In million cubic feet)

Forest type group	Stand-size class Large diameter	Stand-size class Medium diameter	Stand-size class Small diameter	Stand-size class Chaparral	Stand-size class Non stocked	All size classes
Pinyon-juniper group	6,434.0	66.1	29.6	- -	- -	6,529.7
Douglas-fir group	1,141.3	49.6	10.6	- -	- -	1,201.4
Ponderosa pine group	542.7	3.6	3.2	- -	- -	549.5
Fir-spruce-mountain hemlock group	2,936.9	170.9	39.4	- -	- -	3,147.2
Lodgepole pine group	484.2	367.7	50.4	- -	- -	902.2
Other western softwoods group	51.1	12.6	- -	- -	- -	63.7
Elm-ash-cottonwood group	18.9	0.4	2.0	- -	- -	21.3
Aspen-birch group	1,012.7	1,484.5	79.9	- -	- -	2,577.1
Western oak group	43.4	104.0	194.8	- -	- -	342.3
Other western hardwoods group	192.7	76.5	54.2	- -	- -	323.4
Nonstocked	- -	- -	- -	- -	19.3	19.3
All forest type groups	12,857.9	2,335.7	464.1	- -	19.3	15,677.0

All table cells without observations in the inventory sample are indicated by --. Table value of 0.0 indicates the volume rounds to less than 0.1 million cubic feet. Columns and rows may not add to their totals due to rounding.

USDA Forest Service Resour. Bull. RMRS-RB-10. 2010

Table 14—Net volume of all live trees 5.0" diameter and greater on forest land by species group and ownership group, Utah, cycle 2, 2000-2005.

(In million cubic feet)

Species group	Ownership group				
	Forest Service	Other federal	State and local government	Undifferentiated private	All owners
Softwood species groups					
Western softwood species groups					
Douglas-fir	962.4	154.0	111.0	235.9	1,463.3
Ponderosa and Jeffrey pines	435.9	107.7	22.3	44.2	610.1
True fir	1,449.6	41.3	39.3	231.2	1,761.5
Engelmann and other spruces	1,604.9	0.5	- -	29.9	1,635.2
Lodgepole pine	1,058.2	- -	- -	81.1	1,139.4
Western woodland softwoods	1,200.5	3,737.6	683.2	846.5	6,467.7
Other western softwoods	87.4	5.7	- -	3.8	96.9
All softwoods	6,799.0	4,046.7	855.7	1,472.6	13,174.0
Hardwood species groups					
Western hardwood species groups					
Cottonwood and aspen	1,343.0	15.0	130.6	492.5	1,981.1
Western woodland hardwoods	185.2	93.5	33.5	209.6	521.9
All hardwoods	1,528.3	108.5	164.1	702.1	2,503.0
All species groups	8,327.3	4,155.2	1,019.9	2,174.7	15,677.0

All table cells without observations in the inventory sample are indicated by --. Table value of 0.0 indicates the volume rounds to less than 0.1 million cubic feet. Columns and rows may not add to their totals due to rounding.

Table 15.--Net volume of all live trees on forest land by species group and diameter class, Utah, cycle 2, 2000-2005.

(In million cubic feet)

Species group	Diameter class (inches)													All classes
	5.0-6.9	7.0-8.9	9.0-10.9	11.0-12.9	13.0-14.9	15.0-16.9	17.0-18.9	19.0-20.9	21.0-24.9	25.0-28.9	29.0-32.9	33.0-36.9	37.0+	
Softwood species groups														
Western softwood species groups														
Douglas-fir	40	99	124	159	209	243	147	118	196	53	50	9	16	1,463
Ponderosa and Jeffrey pines	8	21	28	46	62	63	63	56	120	43	45	35	20	610
True fir	98	176	209	260	211	191	166	120	164	78	30	41	16	1,761
Engelmann and other spruces	43	92	131	163	204	234	162	155	270	125	28	27	- -	1,635
Lodgepole pine	189	236	203	190	143	79	53	31	14	- -	- -	- -	- -	1,139
Western woodland softwoods	239	411	598	733	787	756	638	571	777	495	270	106	87	6,468
Other western softwoods	3	6	11	14	8	8	12	5	15	4	- -	- -	11	97
All softwoods	621	1,042	1,305	1,565	1,623	1,575	1,242	1,056	1,557	797	424	218	150	13,174
Hardwood species groups														
Western hardwood species groups														
Cottonwood and aspen	236	424	413	341	255	126	79	77	30	- -	- -	- -	- -	1,981
Western woodland hardwoods	165	128	87	59	30	19	19	5	7	3	- -	- -	- -	522
All hardwoods	401	552	500	400	285	145	99	82	37	3	- -	- -	- -	2,503
All species groups	1,022	1,593	1,805	1,964	1,908	1,719	1,340	1,138	1,594	801	424	218	150	15,677

All table cells without observations in the inventory sample are indicated by ---. Table value of 0 indicates the volume rounds to less than 1 million cubic feet. Columns and rows may not add to their totals due to rounding.

Table 16--Net volume of all live trees 5.0" diameter and greater on forest land by forest type group and stand origin, Utah, cycle 2, 2000-2005.

(In million cubic feet)

Forest type group	Stand origin		All forest land
	Natural stands	Artificial regeneration	
Pinyon-juniper group	6,529.7	--	6,529.7
Douglas-fir group	1,201.4	--	1,201.4
Ponderosa pine group	546.3	3.2	549.5
Fir-spruce-mountain hemlock group	3,147.2	--	3,147.2
Lodgepole pine group	902.2	--	902.2
Other western softwoods group	63.7	--	63.7
Elm-ash-cottonwood group	21.3	--	21.3
Aspen-birch group	2,577.1	--	2,577.1
Western oak group	342.3	--	342.3
Other western hardwoods group	323.4	--	323.4
Nonstocked	19.3	--	19.3
All forest type groups	15,673.7	3.2	15,677.0

All table cells without observations in the inventory sample are indicated by --. Table value of 0.0 indicates the volume rounds to less than 0.1 million cubic feet. Columns and rows may not add to their totals due to rounding.

Table 17--Net volume of growing-stock trees on timberland by species group and diameter class, Utah, cycle 2, 2000-2005.

(In million cubic feet)

Species group	Diameter class (inches)													All classes
	5.0-6.9	7.0-8.9	9.0-10.9	11.0-12.9	13.0-14.9	15.0-16.9	17.0-18.9	19.0-20.9	21.0-24.9	25.0-28.9	29.0-32.9	33.0-36.9	37.0+	
Softwood species groups														
Western softwood species groups														
Douglas-fir	32	80	104	136	167	193	104	100	128	36	39	9	--	1,127
Ponderosa and Jeffrey pines	7	17	23	39	55	53	47	35	75	22	25	24	20	442
True fir	85	156	185	234	181	162	152	98	142	65	25	41	16	1,543
Engelmann and other spruces	32	66	100	124	153	168	128	135	216	109	22	14	--	1,268
Lodgepole pine	174	201	152	95	77	41	32	8	7	--	--	--	--	787
Other western softwoods	3	5	8	8	6	4	7	2	13	4	--	--	11	71
All softwoods	333	525	572	636	638	622	471	378	581	237	111	89	46	5,239
Hardwood species groups														
Western hardwood species groups														
Cottonwood and aspen	197	368	365	311	246	119	66	71	23	--	--	--	--	1,765
All hardwoods	197	368	365	311	246	119	66	71	23	--	--	--	--	1,765
All species groups	529	893	937	948	884	741	537	449	604	237	111	89	46	7,004

All table cells without observations in the inventory sample are indicated by --. Table value of 0 indicates the volume rounds to less than 1 million cubic feet. Columns and rows may not add to their totals due to rounding.

Table 18—Net volume of growing-stock trees on timberland by species group and ownership group, Utah, cycle 2, 2000-2005.

(In million cubic feet)

Species group	Forest Service	Other federal	State and local government	Undifferentiated private	All owners
Softwood species groups					
Western softwood species groups					
Douglas-fir	751.9	83.5	92.0	199.7	1,127.1
Ponderosa and Jeffrey pines	357.6	27.0	18.4	39.3	442.3
True fir	1,272.3	12.3	38.7	220.0	1,543.3
Engelmann and other spruces	1,237.6	0.5	- -	29.9	1,267.9
Lodgepole pine	707.1	- -	- -	80.0	787.1
Other western softwoods	68.1	0.1	- -	2.9	71.1
All softwoods	4,394.6	123.3	149.2	571.7	5,238.7
Hardwood species groups					
Western hardwood species groups					
Cottonwood and aspen	1,206.6	4.9	117.9	436.1	1,765.4
All hardwoods	1,206.6	4.9	117.9	436.1	1,765.4
All species groups	5,601.1	128.2	267.1	1,007.8	7,004.2

All table cells wi hout observations in the inventory sample are indicated by --. Table value of 0.0 indicates he volume round to less than 0.1 million cubic feet. Columns and rows may not add to heir totals due to rounding.

Table 19—Net volume of sawtimber trees (International 1/4 inch rule) on timberland by species group and diameter class, Utah, cycle 2, 2000-2005.

(In million board feet) [1]

Species group	Diameter class (inches)											All classes
	9.0-10.9	11.0-12.9	13.0-14.9	15.0-16.9	17.0-18.9	19.0-20.9	21.0-24.9	25.0-28.9	29.0-32.9	33.0-36.9	37.0+	
Softwood species groups												
Western softwood species groups												
Douglas-fir	364	586	784	991	558	542	722	186	241	21	- -	4,995
Ponderosa and Jeffrey pines	77	176	287	296	277	209	456	142	167	156	135	2,379
True fir	734	1,086	896	838	806	505	735	360	121	227	95	6,404
Engelmann and other spruces	411	603	809	929	713	743	1,241	629	127	84	- -	6,289
Lodgepole pine	556	410	370	214	177	46	40	- -	- -	- -	- -	1,813
Other western softwoods	25	28	26	20	36	10	66	23	- -	- -	70	304
All softwoods	2,168	2,888	3,172	3,288	2,568	2,056	3,261	1,340	655	488	299	22,184
Hardwood species groups												
Western hardwood species groups												
Cottonwood and aspen	- -	1,533	1,276	654	383	402	120	- -	- -	- -	- -	4,368
All hardwoods	- -	1,533	1,276	654	383	402	120	- -	- -	- -	- -	4,368
All species groups	2,168	4,421	4,448	3,941	2,951	2,458	3,381	1,340	655	488	299	26,552

All table cells wi hout observations in he inventory sample are indicated by --. Table value of 0 indicates the volume rounds to less han 1 million board feet. Columns and rows may not add to their totals due to rounding.
[1] International 1/4 inch rule.

Table 20—Net volume of saw timber trees on timberland by species group and ownership group, Utah, cycle 2, 2000-2005.

(In million cubic feet)

Species group	Forest Service	Other federal	State and local government	Undifferentiated private	All owners
Softwood species groups					
Western softwood species groups					
Douglas-fir	617.8	70.8	79.1	166.3	934.0
Ponderosa and Jeffrey pines	322.9	25.6	17.0	37.0	402.5
True fir	982.7	10.3	27.0	180.3	1,200.3
Engelmann and other spruces	1,069.1	--	--	27.0	1,096.2
Lodgepole pine	304.7	--	--	71.9	376.5
Other western softwoods	59.4	--	--	2.2	61.6
All softwoods	3,356.5	106.7	123.0	484.8	4,071.0
Hardwood species groups					
Western hardwood species groups					
Cottonwood and aspen	485.0	3.0	57.8	148.5	694.3
All hardwoods	485.0	3.0	57.8	148.5	694.3
All species groups	3,841.5	109.7	180.8	633.3	4,765.4

All table cells without observations in he inventory sample are indicated by --. Table value of 0.0 indicates the volume rounds to less than 0.1 million cubic feet. Columns and rows may not add to their totals due to rounding.

Table 21—Average annual net growth of all live trees 5.0" diameter and greater by owner class and forest land status. Utah, cycle 2, 2000-2005

(In million cubic feet)

Owner class	Unreserved forests				Reserved forests				All forest land
	Timberland	Unproductive	Total		Productive	Unproductive	Total		
Forest Service									
National Forest	38.6	8.2	46.8		5.4	-7.9	-2.5		44.3
Other National Forest	- -	- -	- -		- -	0.0	0.0		0.0
Other federal									
National Park Service	- -	- -	- -		-2.1	-2.7	-4.9		-4.9
Bureau of Land Management	-1.7	9.2	7.5		0.0	1.4	1.5		8.9
Fish and Wildlife Service	- -	- -	- -		- -	0.0	0.0		0.0
Department of Defense or Energy	- -	0.0	0.0		- -	- -	- -		0.0
State and local government									
State	0.1	2.5	2.6		- -	-0.1	-0.1		2.6
Local (county, municipal, etc.)	0.5	- -	0.5		- -	- -	- -		0.5
Private									
Undifferentiated private	14.6	11.4	26.0		- -	- -	- -		26.0
All owners	52.1	31.4	83.5		3.3	-9.2	-5.9		77.6

All table cells without observations in the inventory sample are indicated by --. Table value of 0.0 indicates the volume rounds to less than 0.1 million cubic feet. Columns and rows may not add to their totals due to rounding.

Table 22–Average annual net growth of all live trees 5.0" diameter and greater on forest land by forest type group and stand-size class, Utah, cycle 2, 2000-2005.

(In million cubic feet)

Forest type group	Large diameter	Medium diameter	Small diameter	Chaparral	Non stocked	All size classes
Pinyon-juniper group	31.2	1.8	0.4	--	--	33.3
Douglas-fir group	10.1	0.1	0.4	--	--	10.6
Ponderosa pine group	9.5	-0.1	0.0	--	--	9.4
Fir-spruce-mountain hemlock group	13.6	-14.9	-9.5	--	--	-10.8
Lodgepole pine group	4.4	10.4	0.6	--	--	15.4
Other western softwoods group	0.6	0.3	--	--	--	0.8
Elm-ash-cottonwood group	0.5	0.0	0.0	--	--	0.5
Aspen-birch group	12.7	30.0	-5.3	--	--	37.4
Western oak group	0.7	2.9	-13.2	--	--	-9.5
Other western hardwoods group	2.3	2.0	2.1	--	--	6.4
Nonstocked	--	--	--	--	-15.9	-15.9
All forest type groups	85.4	32.5	-24.5	--	-15.9	77.6

All table cells without observations in he inventory sample are indicated by --. Table value of 0.0 indicates the volume rounds to less than 0.1 million cubic feet. Columns and rows may not add to their totals due to rounding.

Table 23–Average annual net grow h of all live trees 5.0" diameter and greater on forest land by species group and ownership group, Utah, cycle 2, 20

(In million cubic feet)

Species group	Forest Service	Other federal	State and local government	Undifferentiated private	All owners
Softwood species groups					
Western softwood species groups					
Douglas-fir	9.2	-1.0	-0.1	4.5	12.5
Ponderosa and Jeffrey pines	2.1	-1.7	-0.5	0.8	0.7
True fir	0.9	-4.3	1.1	-1.9	-4.3
Engelmann and other spruces	-14.6	0.0	--	0.3	-14.3
Lodgepole pine	15.5	--	--	0.4	15.9
Western woodland softwoods	3.8	11.9	1.1	3.2	20.0
Other western softwoods	0.0	0.1	--	0.1	0.2
All softwoods	16.9	4.9	1.5	7.4	30.8
Hardwood species groups					
Western hardwood species groups					
Cottonwood and aspen	22.7	0.3	0.6	12.2	35.8
Western woodland hardwoods	4.6	-1.1	0.9	6.4	10.9
All hardwoods	27.4	-0.7	1.5	18.6	46.8
All species groups	44.3	4.1	3.1	26.0	77.6

All table cells without observations in he inventory sample are indicated by --. Table value of 0.0 indicates the volume rounds to less than 0.1 million cubic feet. Columns and rows may not add to their totals due to rounding.

124

USDA Forest Service Resour. Bull. RMRS-RB-10. 2010

Table 24—Average annual net growth of growing-stock trees on timberland by species group and ownership group. Utah, cycle 2, 2000-2005.

(In million cubic feet)

Species group	Ownership group				
	Forest Service	Other federal	State and local government	Undifferentiated private	All owners
Softwood species groups					
Western softwood species groups					
Douglas-fir	7.6	-0.4	-0.6	3.7	10.4
Ponderosa and Jeffrey pines	6.4	0.2	-0.5	0.6	6.7
True fir	4.7	-1.8	1.0	-2.1	1.9
Engelmann and other spruces	-16.8	0.0	--	0.3	-16.5
Lodgepole pine	13.6	--	--	0.4	14.0
Western woodland softwoods	--	--	--	--	--
Other western softwoods	0.2	0.0	--	0.0	0.2
All softwoods	15.8	-2.0	-0.1	2.9	16.7
Hardwood species groups					
Western hardwood species groups					
Cottonwood and aspen	19.8	0.1	0.3	10.3	30.5
Western woodland hardwoods	--	--	--	--	--
All hardwoods	19.8	0.1	0.3	10.3	30.5
All species groups	35.6	-1.9	0.2	13.2	47.2

All table cells without observations in the inventory sample are indicated by --. Table value of 0.0 indicates he volume rounds to less than 0.1 million cubic feet. Columns and rows may not add to their totals due to rounding.

Table 25—Average annual mortality of all live trees 5.0" diameter and greater by owner class and forest land status. Utah, cycle 2, 2000-2005.

(In million cubic feet)

Owner class	Unreserved forests			Reserved forests			All forest land
	Timberland	Unproductive	Total	Productive	Unproductive	Total	
Forest Service							
National Forest	88.0	10.3	98.4	9.5	8.9	18.4	116.8
Other National Forest	--	--	--	--	--	--	--
Other federal							
National Park Service	--	--	--	3.2	3.9	7.2	7.2
Bureau of Land Management	4.0	17.7	21.7	--	1.8	1.8	23.4
Fish and Wildlife Service	--	--	--	--	--	--	--
Department of Defense or Energy	--	--	--	--	--	--	--
State and local government							
State	4.8	4.0	8.8	--	0.4	0.4	9.2
Local (county, municipal, etc.)	0.1	--	0.1	--	--	--	0.1
Private							
Undifferentiated private	13.4	5.0	18.3	--	--	--	18.3
All owners	110.3	37.0	147.2	12.7	15.1	27.8	175.0

All table cells wi hout observations in the inventory sample are indicated by --. Table value of 0.0 indicates the volume rounds to less than 0.1 million cubic feet. Columns and rows may not add to their totals due to rounding.

Table 26—Average annual mortality of all live trees 5.0" diameter and greater on forest land by forest type group and stand-size class, Utah, cycle 2, 2000-2005.

(In million cubic feet)

Forest type group	Stand-size class					All size classes
	Large diameter	Medium diameter	Small diameter	Chaparral	Non stocked	
Pinyon-juniper group	20.1	0.1	0.4	- -	- -	20.6
Douglas-fir group	10.3	1.2	- -	- -	- -	11.5
Ponderosa pine group	0.2	0.3	- -	- -	- -	0.5
Fir-spruce-mountain hemlock group	36.0	20.4	10.9	- -	- -	67.2
Lodgepole pine group	2.3	0.8	2.1	- -	- -	5.2
Aspen-birch group	9.3	15.8	8.3	- -	- -	33.4
Western oak group	- -	0.1	19.7	- -	- -	19.8
Other western hardwoods group	0.4	0.0	0.2	- -	- -	0.6
Nonstocked	- -	- -	- -	- -	16.2	16.2
All forest type groups	78.7	38.6	41.5	- -	16.2	175.0

All table cells without observations in the inventory sample are indicated by --. Table value of 0.0 indicates the volume rounds to less than 0.1 million cubic feet. Columns and rows may not add to their totals due to rounding.

Table 27—Average annual mortality of all live trees 5.0" diameter and greater on forest land by species group and ownership group, Utah, cycle 2, 2000-2005.

(In million cubic feet)

Species group	Ownership group				All owners
	Forest Service	Other federal	State and local government	Undifferentiated private	
Softwood species groups					
Western softwood species groups					
Douglas-fir	8.4	3.9	2.5	1.3	16.0
Ponderosa and Jeffrey pines	5.7	3.2	0.8	- -	9.7
True fir	35.6	5.1	0.5	8.2	49.3
Engelmann and other spruces	39.3	- -	- -	0.1	39.4
Lodgepole pine	8.4	- -	- -	0.8	9.1
Western woodland softwoods	7.6	15.5	4.4	4.4	31.8
Other western softwoods	1.1	- -	- -	- -	1.1
All softwoods	106.1	27.6	8.1	14.7	156.5
Hardwood species groups					
Western hardwood species groups					
Cottonwood and aspen	10.0	- -	1.2	3.2	14.4
Western woodland hardwoods	0.7	3.0	0.0	0.4	4.0
All hardwoods	10.7	3.0	1.2	3.6	18.5
All species groups	116.8	30.6	9.3	18.3	175.0

All table cells without observations in the inventory sample are indicated by --. Table value of 0.0 indicates the volume rounds to less than 0.1 million cubic feet. Columns and rows may not add to their totals due to rounding.

126

USDA Forest Service Resour. Bull. RMRS-RB-10. 2010

Table 28—Average annual mortality of growing-stock trees on timberland by species group and ownership group. Utah, cycle 2, 2000-2005.

(In million cubic feet)

Species group	Forest Service	Other federal	State and local government	Undifferentiated private	All owners
Softwood species groups					
Western softwood species groups					
Douglas-fir	6.8	1.9	2.4	1.3	12.5
Ponderosa and Jeffrey pines	0.3	0.1	0.8	--	1.2
True fir	27.3	2.0	0.5	8.2	38.0
Engelmann and other spruces	36.8	--	--	0.1	36.9
Lodgepole pine	5.9	--	--	0.8	6.7
Western woodland softwoods	--	--	--	--	--
Other western softwoods	0.8	--	--	--	0.8
All softwoods	78.0	4.0	3.7	10.4	96.1
Hardwood species groups					
Western hardwood species groups					
Cottonwood and aspen	8.9	--	1.1	2.9	12.9
Western woodland hardwoods	--	--	--	--	--
All hardwoods	8.9	4.0	1.1	2.9	12.9
All species groups	86.9	4.0	4.8	13.2	108.9

All table cells without observations in the inventory sample are indicated by --. Table value of 0.0 indicates the volume rounds to less than 0.1 million cubic feet. Columns and rows may not add to their totals due to rounding.

Table 29—Aboveground dry weight of all live trees 1.0" diameter and greater by owner class and forest land status, Utah, cycle 2, 2000-2005.

(In thousand dry tons)

Owner class	Unreserved forests Timberland	Unproductive	Total	Reserved forests Productive	Unproductive	Total	All forest land
Forest Service							
National Forest	106,521	33,847	140,368	18,515	1,516	20,031	160,399
Other National Forest	--	--	--	--	43	43	43
Other federal							
National Park Service	--	--	--	1,807	3,012	4,819	4,819
Bureau of Land Management	3,110	62,247	65,357	71	9,816	9,887	75,245
Fish and Wildlife Service	--	--	--	--	245	245	245
Department of Defense or Energy	--	28	28	--	--	--	28
State and local government							
State	5,184	14,090	19,274	--	1,032	1,032	20,307
Local (county, municipal, etc.)	475	--	475	--	--	--	475
Private							
Undifferentiated private	20,197	27,373	47,569	--	9	9	47,579
All owners	135,487	137,585	273,071	20,393	15,674	36,067	309,138

All table cells without observations in the inventory sample are indicated by --. Table value of 0 indicates the aboveground tree biomass rounds to less than 1 thousand dry tons. Columns and rows may not add to their totals due to rounding.

Table 30—Aboveground dry weight of all live trees on forest land by species group and diameter class, Utah, cycle 2, 2000-2005.

(In thousand dry tons)

Species group	1.0-2.9	3.0-4.9	5.0-6.9	7.0-8.9	9.0-10.9	11.0-12.9	13.0-14.9	15.0-16.9	17.0-18.9	19.0-20.9	21.0-22.9	23.0-24.9	25.0-26.9	27.0-28.9	29.0+	All classes
Softwood species groups																
Western softwood species groups																
Douglas-fir	440	998	1,055	2,185	2,553	3,130	4,004	4,584	2,795	2,185	1,917	1,693	954	65	1,338	29,896
Ponderosa and Jeffrey pines	47	191	265	436	552	884	1,197	1,246	1,247	1,150	1,598	629	470	380	2,006	12,498
True fir	1,789	2,137	2,236	3,252	3,547	4,160	3,391	3,014	2,618	1,934	1,462	1,231	910	332	1,444	33,457
Engelmann and other spruces	382	932	975	1,629	2,111	2,511	3,039	3,397	2,331	2,281	2,208	1,567	1,098	682	809	25,953
Lodgepole pine	573	1,676	3,978	3,823	3,166	3,014	2,278	1,252	824	492	129	102	--	--	--	21,308
Western woodland softwoods	1,066	2,636	4,959	7,793	10,754	12,832	13,730	13,188	11,146	9,929	7,741	5,833	5,168	3,150	7,682	117,588
Other western softwoods	36	102	100	121	201	269	141	143	203	116	125	130	72	--	188	1,946
All softwoods	4,332	8,672	13,567	19,239	22,885	26,801	27,782	26,804	21,164	18,087	15,180	11,385	8,672	4,609	13,467	242,647
Hardwood species groups																
Western hardwood species groups																
Cottonwood and aspen	552	1,684	4,083	7,262	7,142	5,884	4,488	2,172	1,377	1,328	239	254	--	--	--	36,464
Western woodland hardwoods	5,481	5,607	5,562	4,210	2,968	2,264	1,319	784	977	253	285	122	82	113	--	30,027
All hardwoods	6,033	7,291	9,646	11,472	10,110	8,148	5,807	2,955	2,354	1,581	524	376	82	113	--	66,491
All species groups	10,366	15,963	23,213	30,711	32,995	34,949	33,589	29,759	23,518	19,668	15,705	11,761	8,754	4,722	13,467	309,138

All table cells without observations in the inventory sample are indicated by --. Table value of 0 indicates the aboveground tree biomass rounds to less than 1 thousand dry tons. Columns and rows may not add to their totals due to rounding.

Table 31—Area of accessible forest land by Forest Survey Unit, county and forest land status, Utah, cycle 2, 2000-2005.

(In thousand acres)

Forest Survey Unit and county	Unreserved forests			Reserved forests			All forest land
	Timberland	Unproductive	Total	Productive	Unproductive	Total	
Northern							
Box Elder	8.3	327.6	336.0	7.0	--	7.0	342.9
Cache	129.4	130.8	260.2	35.3	15.4	50.7	310.9
Davis	11.3	11.3	22.5	--	--	--	22.5
Morgan	93.2	113.7	206.8	--	--	--	206.8
Rich	69.7	14.5	84.2	--	--	--	84.2
Salt Lake	37.1	74.1	111.2	24.0	17.5	41.5	152.7
Summit	425.9	210.9	636.8	97.8	10.6	108.4	745.2
Tooele	12.2	381.5	393.6	10.0	8.8	18.8	412.4
Utah	197.7	506.9	704.6	8.9	11.9	20.8	725.4
Wasatch	345.8	147.3	493.1	--	--	--	493.1
Weber	48.2	103.3	151.5	--	--	--	151.5
Total	1,378.8	2,021.7	3,400.5	182.9	64.2	247.1	3,647.5
Uinta							
Daggett	194.7	111.6	306.3	--	--	--	306.3
Duchesne	356.7	566.0	922.7	176.6	2.6	179.2	1,101.9
Uintah	209.9	675.3	885.2	--	36.7	36.7	921.9
Total	761.3	1,352.9	2,114.2	176.6	39.4	215.9	2,330.1
Central							
Juab	14.3	409.1	423.3	9.5	9.5	19.0	442.3
Millard	54.4	607.8	662.1	--	7.4	7.4	669.5
Piute	89.2	160.2	249.4	--	--	--	249.4
Sanpete	169.6	361.6	531.2	--	--	--	531.2
Sevier	205.5	487.6	693.1	--	--	--	693.1
Wayne	61.1	173.3	234.3	--	69.4	69.4	303.7
Total	594.0	2,199.4	2,793.4	9.5	86.3	95.8	2,889.2
Eastern							
Carbon	147.2	354.7	501.8	--	--	--	501.8
Emery	106.8	614.3	721.1	--	--	--	721.1
Grand	109.5	737.6	847.1	--	3.1	3.1	850.2
San Juan	142.3	1,476.9	1,619.2	5.9	85.4	91.3	1,710.5
Total	505.8	3,183.4	3,689.2	5.9	88.6	94.5	3,783.7
Southwestern							
Beaver	42.9	699.8	742.7	--	--	--	742.7
Garfield	424.8	710.0	1,134.7	25.8	376.4	402.2	1,536.9
Iron	124.6	764.0	888.5	11.9	7.2	19.1	907.6
Kane	130.5	528.9	659.5	20.4	698.4	718.8	1,378.3
Washington	29.3	606.4	635.7	40.9	69.8	110.7	746.4
Total	752.0	3,309.1	4,061.1	99.0	1,151.8	1,250.8	5,311.9

(Table 31 continued)

Forest Survey Unit and county	Unreserved forests			Reserved forests			All forest land
	Timberland	Unproductive	Total	Productive	Unproductive	Total	
All counties	3,991.8	12,066.6	16,058.3	473.9	1,430.2	1,904.1	17,962.5

All table cells without observations in the inventory sample are indicated by --. Table value of 0.0 indicates the acres round to less than 0.1 thousand acres. Columns and rows may not add to their totals due to rounding.

Table 32—Area of accessible forest land by Forest Survey Unit, county, ownership group and forest land status, Utah, cycle 2, 2000-2005.

(In thousand acres)

Forest Survey Unit and county	Forest Service		Other federal			State and local government		Undifferentiated private		All forest land
	Timber-land	Other forest land	Timber-land	Other forest land	Total	Timber-land	Other forest land	Timber-land	Other forest land	
Northern										
Box Elder	8.3	27.7	--	102.6	102.6	--	32.4	--	171.8	342.9
Cache	110.9	114.5	--	--	--	--	--	18.5	66.9	310.9
Davis	--	11.3	--	--	--	11.3	--	--	--	22.5
Morgan	28.1	--	--	--	--	--	8.8	65.1	104.8	206.8
Rich	34.0	--	--	12.9	12.9	2.4	--	33.3	1.6	84.2
Salt Lake	19.7	68.2	--	--	--	--	--	17.5	47.4	152.7
Summit	306.4	119.0	--	10.6	10.6	10.6	10.6	108.9	179.0	745.2
Tooele	2.2	49.0	--	285.2	285.2	--	29.9	10.0	36.2	412.4
Utah	185.8	345.7	--	32.7	32.7	--	36.5	11.9	112.7	725.4
Wasatch	253.4	61.0	--	--	--	8.9	29.8	83.4	56.5	493.1
Weber	9.7	42.7	--	--	--	9.7	--	28.8	60.5	151.5
Total	958.5	839.1	--	444.0	444.0	42.9	148.0	377.3	837.6	3,647.5
Uinta										
Daggett	192.1	35.3	--	32.6	32.6	--	43.8	2.5	--	306.3
Duchesne	268.2	228.3	--	77.7	77.7	27.0	71.9	61.4	367.3	1,101.9
Uintah	170.5	29.9	11.9	394.4	406.3	10.9	99.8	16.6	187.9	921.9
Total	630.9	293.6	11.9	504.7	516.6	37.9	215.4	80.5	555.2	2,330.1
Central										
Juab	7.1	99.1	7.1	210.5	217.6	--	28.5	--	90.0	442.3
Millard	54.4	286.0	--	256.8	256.8	--	40.8	--	31.7	669.5
Piute	87.2	63.4	--	82.6	82.6	2.0	14.2	--	--	249.4
Sanpete	159.3	65.1	--	104.5	104.5	--	51.6	10.3	140.4	531.2
Sevier	198.8	337.3	--	88.0	88.0	--	26.7	6.7	35.6	693.1
Wayne	53.4	51.2	6.3	154.5	160.8	--	25.2	1.3	11.8	303.7
Total	560.2	902.1	13.4	896.8	910.2	2.0	186.9	18.3	309.5	2,889.2
Eastern										
Carbon	19.3	2.8	35.7	212.2	247.9	22.0	66.1	70.2	73.6	501.8
Emery	85.9	66.1	2.3	418.3	420.6	--	120.6	18.6	9.3	721.1
Grand	30.9	48.7	25.1	424.9	450.0	40.9	206.8	12.6	60.4	850.2
San Juan	108.9	278.6	--	1,014.3	1,014.3	10.1	91.1	23.3	184.2	1,710.5
Total	244.9	396.1	63.2	2,069.7	2,132.9	73.0	484.6	124.7	327.5	3,783.7

(Table 32 continued on next page)

(Table 32 continued)

Forest Survey Unit and county	Forest Service		Other federal		State and local government		Undifferentiated private		All forest land
	Timber-land	Other forest land	Timber-land	Other forest land	Timber-land	Other forest land	Timber-land	Other forest land	
Southwestern									
Beaver	26.4	76.2	16.5	538.2	--	68.9	--	16.5	742.7
Garfield	420.1	300.3	4.6	677.9	--	115.6	--	18.4	1,536.9
Iron	64.5	86.0	--	555.6	9.6	82.6	50.5	58.9	907.6
Kane	86.4	20.4	11.0	1,022.2	--	47.8	33.2	157.4	1,378.3
Washington	3.3	350.0	20.1	316.2	--	9.6	5.9	41.3	746.4
Total	600.7	832.9	52.1	3,110.0	9.6	324.6	89.7	292.4	5,311.9
All counties	2,995.2	3,263.7	140.6	7,025.2	165.4	1,359.5	690.5	2,322.2	17,962.5

All table cells without observations in the inventory sample are indicated by --. Table value of 0.0 indicates the acres round to less than 0.1 thousand acres. Columns and rows may not add to their totals due to rounding.

USDA Forest Service Resour. Bull. RMRS-RB-10. 2010

131

Table 33—Area of timberland by Forest Survey Unit, county and stand-size class, Utah, cycle 2, 2000-2005.

(In thousand acres)

Forest Survey Unit and county	Large diameter	Medium diameter	Small diameter	Chaparral	Nonstocked	All size classes
Northern						
Box Elder	7.6	- -	0.7	- -	- -	8.3
Cache	42.0	59.2	21.2	- -	7.1	129.4
Davis	11.3	- -	- -	- -	- -	11.3
Morgan	56.1	37.1	- -	- -	- -	93.2
Rich	40.4	26.9	2.4	- -	- -	69.7
Salt Lake	17.5	17.5	2.2	- -	- -	37.1
Summit	161.1	193.8	71.0	- -	- -	425.9
Tooele	12.2	- -	- -	- -	- -	12.2
Utah	114.8	79.9	- -	- -	3.0	197.7
Wasatch	171.8	110.3	63.7	- -	- -	345.8
Weber	9.3	19.5	19.5	- -	- -	48.2
Total	644.1	544.0	180.6	- -	10.0	1,378.8
Uinta						
Daggett	80.9	83.4	30.3	- -	- -	194.7
Duchesne	152.0	152.3	52.4	- -	- -	356.7
Uintah	99.5	67.1	25.0	- -	18.4	209.9
Total	332.4	302.9	107.7	- -	18.4	761.3
Central						
Juab	7.1	- -	7.1	- -	- -	14.3
Millard	43.5	10.9	- -	- -	- -	54.4
Piute	38.5	32.4	18.2	- -	- -	89.2
Sanpete	59.9	76.8	32.9	- -	- -	169.6
Sevier	116.4	69.0	17.8	- -	2.2	205.5
Wayne	28.3	13.9	18.9	- -	- -	61.1
Total	293.8	203.1	94.9	- -	2.2	594.0
Eastern						
Carbon	101.8	34.4	11.0	- -	- -	147.2
Emery	83.5	23.3	- -	- -	- -	106.8
Grand	82.7	12.6	14.2	- -	- -	109.5
San Juan	124.6	12.6	5.0	- -	- -	142.3
Total	392.7	82.9	30.2	- -	- -	505.8

(Table 33 continued on next page)

(Table 33 continued)

Forest Survey Unit and county	Stand-size class					All size classes
	Large diameter	Medium diameter	Small diameter	Chaparral	Nonstocked	
Southwestern						
Beaver	16.5	17.0	9.4	--	--	42.9
Garfield	262.5	127.7	18.4	--	16.1	424.8
Iron	79.2	35.8	9.6	--	--	124.6
Kane	117.8	--	10.2	--	2.6	130.5
Washington	10.0	5.9	--	--	13.3	29.3
Total	485.9	186.5	47.6	--	32.0	752.0
All counties	2,148.8	1,319.3	461.1	--	62.6	3,991.8

All table cells without observations in the inventory sample are indicated by --. Table value of 0.0 indicates the acres round to less than 0.1 thousand acres. Columns and rows may not add to their totals due to rounding.

Table 34—Area of timberland by Forest Survey Unit, county and stocking class, Utah, cycle 2, 2000-2005.

(In thousand acres)

Forest Survey Unit and county	Stocking class of growing-stock trees					All classes
	Nonstocked	Poorly stocked	Moderately stocked	Fully stocked	Over-stocked	
Northern						
Box Elder	--	7.6	--	0.7	--	8.3
Cache	16.5	61.2	49.4	--	2.4	129.4
Davis	--	11.3	--	--	--	11.3
Morgan	--	40.4	28.1	24.5	0.2	93.2
Rich	2.4	13.8	25.5	28.0	--	69.7
Salt Lake	--	19.7	--	8.7	8.7	37.1
Summit	2.7	71.4	244.0	107.8	--	425.9
Tooele	--	--	12.2	--	--	12.2
Utah	3.0	71.3	109.6	13.8	--	197.7
Wasatch	--	32.6	176.2	110.3	26.8	345.8
Weber	--	19.5	19.0	9.7	--	48.2
Total	24.5	348.7	663.9	303.6	38.1	1,378.8
Uinta						
Daggett	--	103.7	50.6	40.4	--	194.7
Duchesne	--	89.0	119.5	127.8	20.4	356.7
Uintah	18.4	38.6	64.1	86.2	2.7	209.9
Total	18.4	231.3	234.1	254.4	23.1	761.3
Central						
Juab	--	--	7.1	7.1	--	14.3
Millard	--	2.7	19.0	32.6	--	54.4
Piute	--	22.3	16.2	16.2	34.5	89.2
Sanpete	--	63.3	35.5	60.3	10.4	169.6
Sevier	11.1	49.2	65.1	69.0	11.1	205.5
Wayne	--	13.9	34.6	12.6	--	61.1
Total	11.1	151.4	177.5	197.9	56.0	594.0
Eastern						
Carbon	--	27.4	75.7	44.1	--	147.2
Emery	--	25.6	32.6	48.6	--	106.8
Grand	--	23.0	47.1	25.1	14.2	109.5
San Juan	--	56.3	43.0	27.8	15.2	142.3
Total	--	132.3	198.5	145.6	29.3	505.8

(Table 34 continued on next page)

(Table 34 continued)

Forest Survey Unit and county	Stocking class of growing-stock trees					All classes
	Nonstocked	Poorly stocked	Moderately stocked	Fully stocked	Over-stocked	
Southwestern						
Beaver	--	--	33.5	9.4	--	42.9
Garfield	16.1	146.1	88.5	151.0	23.0	424.8
Iron	--	9.6	35.8	69.6	9.6	124.6
Kane	2.6	84.6	23.0	20.4	--	130.5
Washington	23.3	--	--	5.9	--	29.3
Total	42.0	240.2	180.8	256.4	32.6	752.0
All counties	96.0	1,103.9	1,454.9	1,157.8	179.2	3,991.8

All table cells without observations in the inventory sample are indicated by --. Table value of 0.0 indicates the acres round to less than 0.1 thousand acres. Columns and rows may not add to their totals due to rounding.

USDA Forest Service Resour. Bull. RMRS-RB-10. 2010

135

Table 35—Net volume of growing stock and sawtimber (International 1/4 inch rule) on timberland by Forest Survey Unit, county, and major species group, Utah, cycle 2, 2000-2005.

Forest Survey Unit and county	Growing stock					Sawtimber				
	Major species group					Major species group				
	Pine	Other softwoods	Soft hardwoods	Hard hardwoods	All species	Pine	Other softwoods	Soft hardwoods	Hard hardwoods	All species
	(In million cubic feet)					(In million board feet)[1]				
Northern										
Box Elder	- -	3.0	- -	- -	3.0	- -	6.9	- -	- -	6.9
Cache	- -	116.2	24.6	- -	140.8	- -	551.1	40.9	- -	592.0
Davis	- -	21.0	- -	- -	21.0	- -	106.6	- -	- -	106.6
Morgan	- -	160.1	40.5	- -	200.6	- -	817.8	98.5	- -	916.3
Rich	63.0	60.7	55.7	- -	179.4	317.7	290.3	135.6	- -	743.6
Salt Lake	- -	8.3	47.7	- -	56.0	- -	36.3	127.6	- -	164.0
Summit	329.1	253.5	124.2	- -	706.7	865.4	1,101.1	180.8	- -	2,147.3
Tooele	- -	22.9	- -	- -	22.9	- -	103.7	- -	- -	103.7
Utah	1.7	337.8	45.8	- -	385.3	3.4	1,525.8	61.8	- -	1,591.0
Wasatch	30.9	262.6	235.6	- -	529.2	158.1	1,125.3	594.9	- -	1,878.3
Weber	- -	44.6	13.0	- -	57.6	- -	236.4	7.0	- -	243.4
Total	424.8	1,290.7	587.0	- -	2,302.4	1,344.7	5,901.3	1,247.1	- -	8,493.0
Uinta										
Daggett	114.2	100.9	4.8	- -	219.9	117.6	428.1	1.4	- -	547.1
Duchesne	201.7	305.1	63.8	- -	570.5	477.0	1,334.8	45.9	- -	1,857.7
Uintah	113.2	201.2	76.9	0.5	391.7	194.3	872.3	81.8	2.3	1,150.6
Total	429.1	607.1	145.4	0.5	1,182.1	788.8	2,635.2	129.1	2.3	3,555.4
Central										
Juab	0.1	19.6	0.5	- -	20.2	- -	64.7	- -	- -	64.7
Millard	- -	82.7	36.5	- -	119.1	- -	323.5	128.3	- -	451.8
Piute	6.5	129.6	89.7	- -	225.9	27.7	604.3	241.6	- -	873.6
Sanpete	- -	177.8	91.3	- -	269.1	- -	772.2	209.4	- -	981.7
Sevier	4.2	219.7	148.6	- -	372.5	14.8	982.5	454.3	- -	1,451.6
Wayne	20.9	29.9	5.2	2.4	58.4	137.1	120.5	13.9	6.5	278.0
Total	31.8	659.4	371.7	2.4	1,065.2	179.6	2,867.7	1,047.5	6.5	4,101.3
Eastern										
Carbon	2.1	241.1	62.2	- -	305.4	5.6	1,112.7	102.6	- -	1,221.0
Emery	9.2	303.0	44.1	- -	356.2	38.4	1,582.2	123.0	- -	1,743.6
Grand	18.4	96.2	93.8	- -	208.4	104.8	394.3	379.9	- -	879.0
San Juan	148.5	84.3	78.3	- -	311.1	802.0	394.0	279.3	- -	1,475.3
Total	178.2	724.5	278.4	- -	1,181.1	950.7	3,483.3	884.8	- -	5,318.8

(Table 35 continued on next page)

(Table 35 continued)

	Growing stock					Sawtimber				
	Major species group					Major species group				
	(In million cubic feet)					(In million board feet)[1]				
Forest Survey Unit and county	Pine	Other softwoods	Soft hardwoods	Hard hardwoods	All species	Pine	Other softwoods	Soft hardwoods	Hard hardwoods	All species
Southwestern										
Beaver	21.8	23.6	17.2	--	62.7	131.5	95.2	--	--	226.7
Garfield	150.7	434.0	140.3	--	725.0	770.1	1,927.9	123.5	--	2,821.5
Iron	3.7	119.6	189.8	--	313.1	20.7	446.1	820.3	--	1,287.2
Kane	59.6	79.4	23.8	--	162.7	307.4	330.9	85.3	--	723.6
Washington	0.9	--	9.0	--	9.9	2.7	--	21.7	--	24.3
Total	236.7	656.6	380.1	--	1,273.4	1,232.4	2,800.1	1,050.8	--	5,083.3
All counties	1,300.4	3,938.3	1,762.6	2.8	7,004.2	4,496.3	17,687.7	4,359.2	8.7	26,551.9

All table cells without observations in he inventory sample are indicated by --. Table value of 0.0 indicates the volume rounds to less han 0.1 million cubic or board feet. Columns and rows may not add to their totals due to rounding.
[1] International 1/4 inch rule.

Table 36—Average annual net growth of growing stock and sawtimber (International 1/4 inch rule) on timberland by Forest Survey Unit, county, and major species group, Utah, cycle 2, 2000-2005.

Forest Survey Unit and county	Growing stock					Sawtimber				
	Major species group					Major species group				
	Pine	Other softwoods	Soft hardwoods	Hard hardwoods	All species	Pine	Other softwoods	Soft hardwoods	Hard hardwoods	All species
	(In million cubic feet)					(In million board feet)[1]				
Northern										
Box Elder	--	0.1	--	--	0.1	--	0.3	--	--	0.3
Cache	--	1.9	-0.5	--	1.4	--	12.5	-2.3	--	10.2
Davis	--	0.3	--	--	0.3	--	2.4	--	--	2.4
Morgan	--	2.5	1.2	--	3.8	--	14.7	1.6	--	16.3
Rich	0.2	1.7	0.0	--	2.0	1.5	10.4	1.5	--	13.4
Salt Lake	--	0.3	1.5	--	1.8	--	2.6	4.0	--	6.7
Summit	5.9	-0.9	2.7	--	7.7	13.4	2.2	2.6	--	18.2
Tooele	--	-0.5	--	--	-0.5	--	-2.7	--	--	-2.7
Utah	-0.1	5.3	0.1	--	5.3	-0.5	26.6	-3.0	--	23.2
Wasatch	0.6	4.1	5.0	--	9.8	1.7	26.0	39.4	--	67.0
Weber	--	0.8	0.7	--	1.5	--	7.4	0.3	--	7.7
Total	6.5	15.8	10.8	--	33.2	16.2	102.4	44.1	--	162.7
Uinta										
Daggett	4.2	-1.2	0.2	--	3.2	8.7	-6.1	0.0	--	2.6
Duchesne	3.2	5.1	1.5	--	9.7	6.8	25.5	0.8	--	33.1
Uintah	1.1	0.1	1.7	0.0	2.8	0.9	1.0	0.8	0.0	2.7
Total	8.4	4.0	3.4	0.0	15.8	16.4	20.4	1.6	0.0	38.4
Central										
Juab	0.0	0.2	0.0	--	0.2	--	0.5	--	--	0.5
Millard	--	2.1	0.9	--	3.0	--	12.1	2.3	--	14.5
Piute	0.0	2.1	1.8	--	4.0	0.6	12.1	13.4	--	26.1
Sanpete	--	-26.5	1.9	--	-24.6	0.0	-127.4	21.9	--	-105.5
Sevier	0.1	0.9	2.7	--	3.7	0.4	10.2	18.8	--	29.4
Wayne	0.2	0.1	0.0	0.1	0.4	1.1	-0.8	0.1	0.0	0.4
Total	0.3	-21.1	7.4	0.1	-13.4	2.1	-93.2	56.4	0.0	-34.6
Eastern										
Carbon	0.1	-0.3	1.0	--	0.7	1.2	4.9	1.6	--	7.7
Emery	0.1	4.3	0.9	--	5.3	0.3	24.1	14.3	--	38.7
Grand	-0.5	0.4	0.2	--	0.0	-2.8	2.9	9.3	--	9.5
San Juan	3.2	0.4	0.9	--	4.5	19.7	4.3	8.7	--	32.7
Total	2.7	4.8	3.0	--	10.5	18.4	36.2	34.0	--	88.6

(Table 36 continued on next page)

138

USDA Forest Service Resour. Bull. RMRS-RB-10. 2010

(Table 36 continued)

Forest Survey Unit and county	Growing stock					Sawtimber				
	Major species group					Major species group				
	Pine	Other softwoods	Soft hardwoods	Hard hardwoods	All species	Pine	Other softwoods	Soft hardwoods	Hard hardwoods	All species
	(In million cubic feet)					(In million board feet) [1]				
Southwestern										
Beaver	0.2	-2.0	0.2	- -	-1.7	0.9	-9.5	- -	- -	-8.6
Garfield	2.0	-1.0	2.9	- -	3.9	14.6	7.3	6.2	- -	28.0
Iron	0.0	-4.7	2.5	- -	-2.2	0.2	-24.8	11.0	- -	-13.6
Kane	0.8	0.0	0.1	- -	0.8	3.9	2.8	0.7	- -	7.3
Washington	0.0	- -	0.2	- -	0.2	0.1	- -	0.3	- -	0.4
Total	2.9	-7.7	5.8	- -	1.0	19.6	-24.2	18.2	- -	13.6
All counties	20.9	-4.3	30.5	0.1	47.2	72.7	41.6	154.3	0.1	268.6

All table cells without observations in the inventory sample are indicated by --. Table value of 0.0 indicates the volume rounds to less than 0.1 million cubic or board feet. Columns and rows may not add to their totals due to rounding.
[1] International 1/4 inch rule.

Table 37—Sampling errors by Forest Survey Unit and county for area of timberland, volume, average annual net growth, average annual removals, and average annual mortality on timberland, Utah, cycle 2, 2000-2005.

(Sampling error in percent)

Forest Survey Unit and county	Forest area	Timberland area	Growing stock				Sawtimber			
			Volume	Average annual net growth	Average annual removals	Average annual mortality	Volume	Average annual net growth	Average annual removals	Average annual mortality
Northern										
Box Elder	13.16	90.88	99.31	99.31	--	--	99.31	99.31	--	--
Cache	9.55	21.77	34.03	100.00	--	54.76	39.52	83.54	--	60.29
Davis	66.78	95.83	95.83	95.83	--	95.83	95.83	95.83	--	--
Morgan	9.86	25.88	34.59	29.14	--	64.48	38.19	37.00	--	86.99
Rich	18.19	23.26	36.83	66.18	--	60.65	45.69	53.48	--	76.92
Salt Lake	11.48	46.34	68.38	70.48	--	--	73.20	80.85	--	--
Summit	5.31	10.75	15.23	36.08	--	32.17	19.61	68.29	--	38.49
Tooele	11.07	84.84	90.36	100.00	--	100.00	94.19	100.00	--	100.00
Utah	4.78	19.00	22.62	24.14	--	43.93	25.20	28.95	--	42.93
Wasatch	6.41	10.85	16.41	19.18	--	30.98	18.96	35.95	--	56.91
Weber	15.44	42.30	68.25	61.03	--	100.00	82.22	93.44	--	--
Total	2.81	6.30	8.91	13.77	--	18.41	10.74	19.78	--	22.85
Uinta										
Daggett	8.68	13.18	19.24	98.75	--	71.61	31.67	100.00	--	85.09
Duchesne	4.26	14.30	18.93	19.91	--	42.94	22.62	26.71	--	55.14
Uintah	5.71	19.32	25.34	100.00	--	53.44	31.50	100.00	--	53.92
Total	3.23	9.20	12.91	31.65	--	36.49	16.35	53.86	--	42.07
Central										
Juab	8.43	73.34	90.28	78.40	--	100.00	100.00	100.00	--	100.00
Millard	7.73	39.03	40.61	43.92	--	73.46	39.45	45.40	--	97.94
Piute	8.37	26.30	40.42	45.96	--	76.13	49.10	51.05	--	100.00
Sanpete	6.15	20.64	24.95	57.61	--	45.49	26.83	67.11	--	47.17
Sevier	5.68	18.60	26.13	80.46	--	58.12	29.09	65.71	--	62.29
Wayne	11.77	34.51	46.88	100.00	--	90.39	53.70	100.00	--	100.00
Total	3.17	10.96	15.06	100.00	--	38.86	17.07	100.00	--	40.72
Eastern										
Carbon	5.47	22.15	29.10	100.00	--	53.75	31.42	100.00	--	51.81
Emery	7.39	26.29	37.68	36.24	--	68.87	41.06	44.83	--	82.58
Grand	5.61	27.83	43.04	100.00	--	78.99	42.46	100.00	--	77.86
San Juan	4.22	24.95	31.29	33.90	--	62.70	30.47	36.63	--	74.60
Total	2.78	12.57	17.65	54.16	--	38.54	18.81	33.85	--	38.57

(Table 37 continued on next page)

(Table 37 continued)

Forest Survey Unit and county	Forest area	Timberland area	Growing stock				Sawtimber			
			Volume	Average annual net growth	Average annual removals	Average annual mortality	Volume	Average annual net growth	Average annual removals	Average annual mortality
Southwestern										
Beaver	5.27	46.11	58.42	100.00	--	92.33	64.17	100.00	--	95.55
Garfield	4.10	13.07	17.07	93.62	--	29.22	18.45	56.19	--	36.93
Iron	4.19	26.41	33.24	100.00	--	55.99	37.29	100.00	--	63.42
Kane	4.63	26.20	31.46	100.00	--	67.69	30.72	90.05	--	74.05
Washington	6.32	54.05	95.63	90.28	--	--	93.98	90.65	--	--
Total	2.17	10.28	13.65	100.00	--	25.82	14.88	100.00	--	31.21
All counties	1.23	4.09	5.79	38.96	--	16.25	6.77	35.27	--	19.15

Sampling errors that exceed 100% are reported as 100%. The sampling error is not calculated when the estimated value is equal to 0 and is indicated by --.

Appendix F—Tables of Mean Soil Properties

Table 1—Mean properties of forest floor by forest type, Utah, cycle 2, 2000-2004.

Forest type	Number of plots	% Water pontent[1] (Oven dry basis)	% Organic carbon[2]	% Total nitrogen[2]	C/N ratio[2]
Rocky Mountain juniper	3	28.94	33.76 a	0.815 ab	49.8 abc
Juniper woodland	23	5.86	32.14 a	0.761 ab	44.0 ab
Pinyon-juniper woodland	88	10.61	28.87 a	0.624 b	48.6 a
Douglas fir	11	14.43	30.83 a	0.987 a	32.4 abc
Ponderosa pine	5	29.14	31.95 a	0.777 ab	42.6 abc
White fir	4	21.81	28.83 a	0.901 ab	32.8 abc
Engelmann spruce	5	41.10	28.06 a	0.917 ab	32.0 abc
Engelmann spruce-subalpine fir	1	113.83	41.28 a	0.890 ab	46.0 abc
Subalpine fir	7	22.23	30.08 a	0.830 ab	42.5 abc
Lodgepole pine	3	195.83	48.74 a	1.081 ab	46.3 abc
Aspen	19	42.16	33.24 a	1.143 a	29.8 bc
Deciduous oak woodland	14	23.09	29.64 a	0.979 a	28.0 c
Cercocarpus woodland	3	8.64	33.40 a	0.902 ab	37.0 abc

[1] Arithmetic mean
[2] Estimated Tukey-Kramer means. Means not followed by the same letter are significantly different (p < 0.01).

Table 2—Mean physical properties of soil cores by forest type, Utah, cycle 2, 2000-2004.

Forest type	Number of samples	% Water content[1] (Oven dry basis)	SQI[2,3] %	Bulk density[2] g/cm³	% Coarse fragments[2]
		0 – 10 cm soil cores			
Rocky Mountain juniper	3	14.22	65 ab	1.06 ab	19.69 a
Juniper woodland	16	3.60	58 b	1.27 ab	13.75 a
Pinyon-juniper woodland	78	4.11	59 b	1.34 a	10.31 a
Douglas fir	12	10.25	74 a	0.95 ab	28.57 a
Ponderosa pine	4	10.16	69 ab	1.39 ab	6.74 a
White fir	3	7.19	72 ab	1.07 ab	28.71 a
Engelmann spruce	4	9.61	69 ab	0.90 ab	19.58 a
Engelmann spruce-subalpine fir	1	19.93	80 ab		1.26 a
Subalpine fir	6	14.69	68 ab	1.14 ab	28.15 a
Lodgepole pine	2	15.59	62 ab	0.98 ab	36.92 a
Aspen	15	18.08	73 a	0.90 b	23.41 a
Deciduous oak woodland	14	10.14	74 a	0.97 ab	16.84 a
Cercocarpus woodland	3	7.68	61 ab	1.18 ab	31.31 a
		10 – 20 cm soil cores			
Rocky Mountain juniper	3	9.77	62 ab	1.16 ab	34.12 a
Juniper woodland	15	5.82	54 b	1.35 ab	11.17 a
Pinyon-juniper woodland	64	5.45	57 b	1.40 a	13.62 a
Douglas fir	12	10.65	68 ab	1.07 ab	33.21 a
Ponderosa pine	4	9.03	64 ab	1.48 ab	15.58 a
White fir	3	5.72	65 ab	1.21 ab	40.23 a
Engelmann spruce	4	6.09	58 ab	1.05 ab	27.63 a
Engelmann spruce-subalpine fir	1	19.17	75 ab	1.09 ab	6.35 a
Subalpine fir	6	11.31	59 ab	1.24 ab	37.91 a
Lodgepole pine	2	13.80	57 ab	1.36 ab	31.43 a
Aspen	14	13.55	72 a	0.90 b	20.96 a
Deciduous oak woodland	14	9.90	70 a	1.20 ab	13.93 a
Cercocarpus woodland	1	3.65	70 ab	1.36 ab	51.08 a

[1] Arithmetic mean
[2] Estimated Tukey-Kramer means. Means not followed by the same letter are significantly different (p < 0.01).
[3] Soil Quality Index

Table 3—Mean chemical properties of soil cores by forest type, Utah, cycle 2, 2000-2004.

Forest type	Number of samples	pH H₂O	pH CaCl₂	Organic carbon %	Inorganic carbon %	Total nitrogen %	Bray 1 extractable phosphorus mg/kg	Olsen extractable phosphorus Mg/kg
				0 – 10 cm soil cores				
Rocky Mountain juniper	3	7.91 ab	7.34 ab	2.19 ab	0.64 a	0.151 ab	6.6 a	8.7 abc
Juniper woodland	16	8.04 a	7.47 a	0.88 b	0.77 a	0.080 b	5.8 a	4.1 bc
Pinyon-juniper woodland	78	7.78 a	7.21 ac	1.19 b	0.60 a	0.084 b	5.4 a	5.3 c
Douglas fir	12	7.08 bc	6.74 abd	3.70 a	0.38 a	0.229 ab	7.8 a	14.1 abc
Ponderosa pine	4	6.56 bcd	6.10 bcde	2.35 ab	0.17 a	0.129 ab	7.7 a	6.0 abc
White fir	3	6.80 abcd	6.56 abde	4.48 ab	0.19 a	0.185 ab	159.2 a	9.6 abc
Engelmann spruce	4	5.84 d	5.37 e	8.17 a	0.25 a	0.265 ab	23.8 a	15.9 abc
Engelmann spruce-subalpine fir	1	5.96 abcd	5.84 abde	15.12 ab		0.384 ab	53.8 a	
Subalpine fir	6	6.28 cd	5.69 de	2.98 ab	0.20 a	0.129 ab	23.3 a	5.8 abc
Lodgepole pine	2	5.53 cd	4.94 e	1.75 ab	0.12 a	0.053 ab	10.1 a	5.8 abc
Aspen	15	6.32 cd	5.83 e	4.19 a	0.25 a	0.299 a	24.3 a	17.1 a
Deciduous oak woodland	14	6.86 bcd	6.32 bde	3.99 a	0.26 a	0.301 a	14.5 a	17.4 ab
Cercocarpus woodland	3	7.14 abcd	6.59 abde	1.40 ab	0.80 a	0.123 ab	24.0 a	6.0 abc
				10 – 20 cm soil cores				
Rocky Mountain juniper	3	7.86 abc	7.38 abc	1.43 abc	0.65 a	0.119 a	6.1 a	4.7 abc
Juniper woodland	15	8.26 a	7.64 a	0.72 c	0.97 a	0.078 a	1.7 a	1.2 c
Pinyon-juniper woodland	64	7.75 ab	7.21 a	1.03 bc	0.62 a	0.073 a	2.4 a	2.1 bc
Douglas fir	12	7.27 bcd	6.85 ab	2.38 ab	0.58 a	0.163 a	14.6 a	7.7 abc
Ponderosa pine	4	6.45 cde	5.90 bcd	1.03 abc	0.15 a	0.061 a	2.6 a	2.7 abc
White fir	3	6.97 abcde	6.64 abcd	3.04 abc	0.14 a	0.125 a		12.1 abc
Engelmann spruce	4	5.80 e	5.36 d	3.34 abc	0.23 a	0.128 a	15.6 a	15.3 abc
Engelmann spruce-subalpine fir	1	5.74 bcde	5.36 abcd	1.96 abc		0.082 a	39.8 a	
Subalpine fir	6	6.20 de	5.57 d	1.79 abc	0.17 a	0.052 a	8.4 a	4.6 abc
Lodgepole pine	2	5.30 e	4.74 d	1.76 abc	0.11 a	0.053 a	6.5 a	2.0 abc
Aspen	14	6.58 cde	5.91 cd	2.87 a	0.22 a	0.218 a	19.1 a	14.3 a
Deciduous oak woodland	14	6.96 cde	6.49 bcd	2.35 ab	0.24 a	0.182 a	15.7 a	9.3 ab
Cercocarpus woodland	1	5.80 bcde	5.76 abcd	1.94 abc		0.146 a	6.4 a	

Table 4—Mean chemical properties of soil cores by forest type, Utah, cycle 2, 2000-2004 (continuation of table 3 with additional chemicals).

Forest type	Number of samples	1 M NH₄Cl Exchangeable cations (mg/kg)					ECEC (cmolc/kg)	Mn	1 M NH₄Cl Extractable (mg/kg)						S
		Na	K	Mg	Ca	Al			Fe	Ni	Cu	Zn	Cd	Pb	
0 – 10 cm soil cores															
Rocky Mountain juniper	3	5 a	462 a	435 a	5438 a	0 a	32.22 a	0.8 abc	0.0	0.1 a	0.0	0.1 a	0.0 a	0.6 a	1.8 a
Juniper woodland	16	16 a	263 a	295 a	3716 a	1 a	22.35 a	0.6 c	0.1 a	0.1 a	0.0	0.1 a	0.0 a	0.2 a	5.2 a
Pinyon-juniper woodland	78	9 a	163 a	213 a	3088 a	1 a	18.08 a	1.4 bc	0.4 a	0.1 a	0.0	0.1 a	0.0 a	0.2 a	5.6 a
Douglas fir	12	7 a	339 a	374 a	3995 a	2 a	24.24 a	3.0 abc	0.6 a	0.4 a	0.0	0.0	0.0 a	0.7 a	15.4 a
Ponderosa pine	4	11 a	257 a	219 a	2130 a	1 a	13.44 a	6.7 abc	0.1 a	0.1 a	0.0	0.2 a	0.0 a	0.0	11.0 a
White fir	3	8 a	192 a	224 a	4356 a	3 a	24.73 a	5.5 abc	0.4 a	0.0 a	0.0	0.0	0.0 a	0.0	19.9 a
Engelmann spruce	4	10 a	166 a	275 a	3596 a	9 a	23.95 a	20.6 a	0.0	0.0	0.0	0.0 a	0.1 a	0.4 a	23.7 a
Engelmann spruce-subalpine fir	1	9 a	330 a	215 a	3427 a	3 a	19.79 a	73.0 ab							40.6 a
Subalpine fir	6	25 a	169 a	183 a	1839 a	1 a	11.39 a	10.5 a	0.1 a	0.2 a	0.0	0.3 a	0.1 a	0.1 a	4.6 a
Lodgepole pine	2	14 a	63 a	157 a	1146 a	2 a	7.29 a	6.1 abc	4.4 a	0.2 a	0.0	0.0	0.0 a	0.0	5.9 a
Aspen	15	8 a	301 a	256 a	2667 a	2 a	16.43 a	9.6 a	0.7 a	0.2 a	0.0	0.4 a	0.1 a	0.2 a	6.1 a
Deciduous oak woodland	14	12 a	329 a	290 a	3896 a	1 a	23.12 a	5.7 a	0.1 a	0.1 a	0.0	0.0	0.1 a	0.2 a	8.2 a
Cercocarpus woodland	3	7 a	189 a	158 a	2590 a	2 a	14.97 a	8.7 abc	0.0	0.0	0.0	0.0	0.0 a	0.5 a	4.8 a
10 – 20 cm soil cores															
Rocky Mountain juniper	3	15 a	434 a	363 a	4018 a	0 a	24.71 a	1.3 a	2.4 a	0.0	0.0	0.0	0.0 a	0.3 a	5.4 a
Juniper woodland	15	30 a	245 a	343 a	3916 a	1 a	24.13 a	0.5 a	0.0	0.2 a	0.1 a	0.0 a	0.0 a	0.2 a	5.0 a
Pinyon-juniper woodland	64	13 a	153 a	252 a	3198 a	1 a	19.10 a	1.0 a	1.9 a	0.1 a	0.1 a	0.2 a	0.0 a	0.3 a	9.0 a
Douglas fir	12	15 a	238 a	342 a	4114 a	2 a	24.34 a	2.4 a	0.0	0.1 a	0.0	0.2 a	0.0 a	0.3 a	10.3 a
Ponderosa pine	4	12 a	215 a	223 a	1905 a	1 a	12.30 a	6.7 a	0.0	0.1 a	0.0	0.3 a	0.1 a	0.0	12.6 a
White fir	3	8 a	152 a	161 a	3293 a	2 a	18.74 a	4.7 a	0.0	0.1 a	0.0 a	0.2 a	0.1 a	0.5 a	11.4 a
Engelmann spruce	4	9 a	94 a	138 a	1814 a	13 a	13.07 a	7.0 a	2.9 a	0.0	0.0	0.0	0.0	0.0	11.9 a
Engelmann spruce-subalpine fir	1	4 a	258 a	145 a	1417 a	4 a	8.92 a	58.7 a							14.7 a
Subalpine fir	6	9 a	114 a	153 a	1288 a	3 a	8.23 a	7.4 a	0.0	0.1 a	0.0 a	0.3 a	0.1 a	0.3 a	5.2 a
Lodgepole pine	2	31 a	95 a	129 a	927 a	36 a	6.37 a	23.2 a	0.0	0.5 a	0.0	0.8 a	0.0 a	0.5 a	3.4 a
Aspen	14	17 a	291 a	249 a	2339 a	1 a	14.75 a	5.7 a	2.9 a	0.1 a	0.2 a	0.2 a	0.1 a	0.3 a	6.6 a
Deciduous oak woodland	14	12 a	291 a	271 a	3449 a	1 a	20.62 a	4.7 a	0.0	0.1 a	0.1 a	0.3 a	0.1 a	0.4 a	7.0 a
Cercocarpus woodland	1	9 a	129 a	177 a	1760 a	2 a	10.62 a	26.7 a							16.3 a

www.ingramcontent.com/pod-product-compliance
Lightning Source LLC
Chambersburg PA
CBHW082013290526
45787CB00016B/2412

* 9 7 8 1 5 0 7 6 5 6 8 0 8 *